MOTIVATING STRATEGIES
FOR PERFORMANCE AND PRODUCTIVITY

Recent Titles from Quorum Books

Joint Venture Partner Selection: Strategies for Developed Countries
J. Michael Geringer

Sustainable Corporate Growth: A Model and Management Planning Tool
John J. Clark, Thomas C. Chiang, and Gerard T. Olson

Competitive Freedom Versus National Security Regulation
Manley Rutherford Irwin

Labor Law and Business Change: Theoretical and Transactional Perspectives
Samuel Estreicher and Daniel G. Collins, eds.

The Constitutional Right to a Speedy and Fair Criminal Trial
Warren Freedman

Entrepreneurial Systems for the 1990s: Their Creation, Structure,
and Management
John E. Tropman and Gersh Morningstar

From Organizational Decline to Organizational Renewal: The Phoenix Syndrome
Mary E. Guy

Modern Analytical Auditing: Practical Guidance for Auditors and Accountants
Thomas E. McKee

Multiple Use Job Descriptions: A Guide to Analysis, Preparation, and
Applications for Human Resources Managers
Philip C. Grant

Cost-Effective Marketing Research: A Guide for Marketing Managers
Eric J. Soares

Corporate Philosophies and Mission Statements: A Survey and Guide for
Corporate Communicators and Management
Thomas A. Falsey

Strategic Executive Decisions: An Analysis of the Difference Between Theory
and Practice
Michael J. Stahl

MOTIVATING STRATEGIES for PERFORMANCE and PRODUCTIVITY

A Guide to Human Resource Development

Paul J. Champagne
and
R. Bruce McAfee

Q

QUORUM BOOKS
NEW YORK • WESTPORT, CONNECTICUT • LONDON

Library of Congress Cataloging-in-Publication Data

Champagne, Paul J.
    Motivating strategies for performance and productivity : a guide
to human resource development / Paul J. Champagne and R. Bruce
McAfee.
        p.   cm.
    Includes index.
    ISBN 0–89930–312–9 (lib. bdg. : alk. paper)
    1. Employee motivation.   2. Performance.   3. Labor productivity.
4. Psychology, Industrial.   I. McAfee, R. Bruce.   II. Title.
HF5549.5.M63C43   1989
658.3'14—dc19   88-18261

British Library Cataloguing in Publication Data is available.

Library of Congress Catalog Card Number: 88–18261
ISBN: 0–89930–312–9

First published in 1989 by Quorum Books

Greenwood Press, Inc.
88 Post Road West, Westport, Connecticut   06881

Printed in the United States of America

The paper used in this book complies with the
Permanent Paper Standard issued by the National
Information Standards Organization (Z39.48-1984).

10 9 8 7 6 5 4

To our mothers

Mary I. Champagne
and
Virginia W. McAfee

Contents

Exhibits

Preface

The purpose of this book is to provide managers with a wide range of techniques for achieving excellence by enhancing employee performance and productivity. In every chapter we discuss the relevant theories in order to provide a framework. However, the emphasis in all chapters is on the actions organizations are taking to implement these theories and improve productivity. In addition, we point out which techniques a manager can use even if the company does not intend to invest in a formal program.

Throughout this book we have used the terms *manager* and *supervisor* interchangeably. Even though some firms make a very clear distinction between the two, we maintain that there is a great deal of overlap between them. If for no other reason, the need for variety dictates that both terms be used throughout the book.

This book is intended for managers in many different kinds of organizations, including hospitals, schools, the government, and not-for-profit institutions. We have tried to reflect this broad orientation in both the presentation of material and in the various company examples cited.

We are grateful for the assistance provided by the editorial and production staffs at Quorum Books. We would also especially like to thank Patricia McClenney for her diligent effort in typing and preparing the several drafts plus the final manuscript.

MOTIVATING STRATEGIES
FOR PERFORMANCE AND PRODUCTIVITY

1

Introduction to Employee Motivation and Productivity

It is virtually impossible to find a reasonably well-informed business person today who is not aware of the productivity problem in American industry. For the last ten years, productivity has clearly been the most widely discussed topic in business publications, management seminars, industry conferences, and executive offices.[1]

Management ineffectiveness is by far the single greatest cause of declining productivity in the United States.... In company after company, managers are ignoring major opportunities for productivity improvement.[2]

This book focuses on an issue that is important to every manager: improving employee productivity. This issue is critical because, unlike some other managerial responsibilities, it cannot be ignored, swept under the rug, or delayed until next week. First, maintaining a highly productive work force is every manager's job, and all managers are evaluated in terms of how successfully they accomplish this objective. Second, every action a manager takes affects the productivity of subordinates in one way or another. Each time a manager gives instructions, provides feedback on job performance, or asks an employee questions, it affects someone's job performance in some way. Even saying or not saying "Good morning" may affect productivity. In general, whenever a manager interacts with an employee, that individual's performance is affected. One could argue that even noninteraction affects job behavior. Imagine what would happen to employee productivity if a manager went into the office for several days in a row, shut the door, and never looked out to see what anyone was doing.

DETERMINANTS OF PRODUCTIVITY

With the advent of computers the terms *input* and *output* have become very familiar. Output is what one gets out of a system, a task, or an employee. Input consists of those things one needs to put into the system, task, or employee before output will occur. The productivity of employees is a question of output. Consider the following:

Killing two birds with one stone is better than killing one bird with one stone, and

Killing four birds with one stone is better than killing three birds with one stone, but

Killing four birds with two stones is no better than killing two birds with one stone.

As this example suggests, "productivity" can be viewed in two different ways. It can be thought of in terms of the total outcome produced, unrelated to the inputs needed. (Killing four birds is better than killing two birds.) In addition, it can be viewed in terms of efficiency, that is, by judging the output of an employee against the inputs necessary to obtain that output. In this regard, killing two birds with one stone is better than killing one bird with one stone. The important point is this: An effective manager is one who maximizes productivity in terms of efficiency, not just overall output.

Over the years, theorists have observed that employee productivity is a function of both one's ability and motivation to perform. Based on personal experience, we know that some people can do very well on a job without exerting much effort. Others may not perform well even though they are highly motivated to do so and seem to work very hard. The explanation is that how one performs a task is not strictly a function of the person's desire to do well. Ability is also an important factor. Many theorists have suggested the following equation to express the relationship of ability and motivation to performance:

Ability × Motivation = Job Performance

Note that both motivation and ability can potentially be zero. Because the equation calls for a multiplicative combination of the two factors, if either one is zero, the job will not be accomplished.

Ability

"Working smarter, not harder" is a meaningful slogan at Intel Corporation, a Santa Clara, California, manufacturer of tiny microprocessors. Based on this concept the company was able to:

— reduce from 364 to 250 the number of steps it takes to hire a new employee

— cut by 29,700 a month the number of xerox copies made in the accounts payable department in Santa Clara

— start putting expense accounts through in days rather than weeks

The procedure used to make these improvements is quite straightforward. The company takes each administrative procedure, examines it carefully, lays it out in meticulous detail, removes unnecessary work, and puts it back together in an efficient, more rational manner.[3]

Advanced technology is another factor that can affect abilities. As high-speed computers have become more widely accepted, jobs that used to take hundreds of hours are now being done in minutes. Technological innovations have, of course, taken other forms as well. For example, the automotive industry is using more and more robots in many of their plants. At one Chrysler plant, a long steel accordionlike arm reaches out from a rotating turret, halts, dips, and swings its swiveling metallic wrist into position next to a car-body skeleton. Clamping its steel fingers on the roof line, it makes a machine-perfect spot weld. This is but one of 67 robots used in 1983 by this single plant. By 1990, General Motors is expected to have over 14,000 robots.[4] While the automotive industry uses about half of the robots currently in operation, many other industries are following its lead.

The use of teleconferencing is another technological innovation which allows employees to produce more. Companies including Allstate Insurance Company, Citibank, and Atlantic Richfield are using it to significantly reduce employee travel costs. Aetna Life and Casualty uses it to connect some of its branch offices. Aetna has installed conference rooms with cameras and color television screens in various branches, which permit employees to converse and also to view each other. Elaborate two-way sound systems allow employees to interact easily, and separate screens let staff members view each other's charts, graphs, and other visual materials.

Ability clearly has an important effect on job performance. The amount of training, education, and work experience employees have, the equipment they are given, and the simplicity of the task itself all affect ability. In addition, the employees' innate mental and physical capabilities also affect their ability to perform. Remember, no amount of motivation can make up for low ability. If an employee is unable to perform a job, no incentive or punishment will change matters.

Motivation

Employees can increase productivity by working smarter, but they can also do it by working harder. They can work longer hours, more intensely, or a greater percentage of the work day. Potentially, they can work more nearly to their capacity.

Earlier we said that no amount of motivation can make up for a lack of ability. Now we should add that the opposite is also true. Keep in mind the old adage—You can lead a horse to water, but you can't make it drink!

Working harder was the topic of a nationwide Gallup poll conducted in the early 1970s covering 1520 adults, 18 years and older, all of whom were employed. One of the poll's purposes was to determine the average U.S. worker's motivation level. The poll asked: "In your own case, could you accomplish more each day if you tried?" Fifty percent said "yes," 47 percent responded "no," and 3 percent had "no opinion." These figures suggest that half of the work force believed that they could be more productive if they were more highly motivated.

The Gallup organization also conducted a poll in both Japan and Canada similar to the one described above. It found that 37 percent of the Japanese workers and 48 percent of the Canadian workers said they could accomplish more each day if they tried (compared to 50 percent in the United States). These figures suggest that while lack of motivation may be an important problem in other countries, it is worth serious consideration in the United States.

A more recent survey (1983) conducted by the Public Agency Foundation polled 850 U.S. workers and found, among other things, that:

— Only 23 percent of workers said they were performing to full capacity, and 44 percent said they did not put extensive effort into their work beyond what was required.

— Most workers respect employers, but said employers had little knowledge of how to motivate employees.

— Only 22 percent said there was a direct relationship between how hard they worked and how much they were paid; 73 percent said their job effort had declined as a result.

— Only 13 percent said they believed they would be the primary beneficiaries if they worked harder. Most believed that the gains went to employers.[5]

Taken as a whole these studies indicate that many workers are not making as large a contribution to their organizations as they might if they really desired to work harder. Furthermore, they largely blame management for their lack of motivation.

In the late 1890s, Frederick Taylor conducted a classic study in pig iron handling at the Bethlehem Steel Company. The company had five blast furnaces and a seventy-five-man gang who manually handled the pig iron. A railroad siding ran into a field next to the factory and pig iron was stacked in piles alongside. Planks were located against the side of the railroad cards and the worker's task was to pick up the pig iron on a shovel, walk up the inclined plank, and drop the pig iron into the rail cars. Taylor determined that each worker loaded an average of 12½ tons a day.

Believing that productivity could be increased substantially, Taylor carefully analyzed the workers' motions and steps and studied the proper distribution of work and rest. Based on this analysis, he determined a more appropriate methodology for performing each aspect of the job. He then carefully selected employees and gave them detailed instructions on how to perform the job using the new method. He required that employees follow the instructions precisely. As an incentive, all workers were told that they would receive a substantial pay increase provided they followed instructions. As a result, worker productivity increased from 12½ tons to 47 tons per worker per day.[6]

Note the process Taylor used. Not only did he improve employee ability but also their motivation. The moral of the story is that if managers really want improved productivity, a double-barrel approach may be required.

BASIC PRINCIPLES OF MOTIVATION

In this book we will focus on various techniques managers can use to enhance employee productivity. However, all of these are predicated on several assumptions about motivation.

What Motivates One Person May Not Motivate Another

One basic principle of motivation is that everyone is different, and what motivates one person may not motivate another. An unmarried employee may not get excited over a new dental insurance plan while someone with a large family may find this a very attractive benefit. Or, a young worker may have little desire for an improved pension plan whereas a senior worker who is close to retirement probably does.

One practical implication of this principle is that a manager must understand the differing needs and motives of workers and use a motivation approach appropriate to each. No one approach will be equally effective for all.

In addition, managers need not search for some super strategy that will somehow solve all employee problems. There never has been such a strategy and it is unlikely that one can ever be developed.

What Motivates a Person May Change over Time

A second basic principle is that people's preferences change over time and what motivates a given person today may not have the same effect in the future. Many studies have been conducted on what people want from work. The findings have consistently shown that age, sex, education, and a host of other factors affect one's expectations.

The practical implication here is that managers must be sensitive to the changing needs of subordinates and adapt their motivation approach accordingly. What was an effective strategy at one time may not work now.

People Are Always Motivated, but Not Necessarily Toward Organization Goals

Typically, people have many values and needs that motivate them toward various goals. To the extent that the organizational goals satisfy their needs subordinates will be motivated to accomplish them. If accomplishing the organization's goals does not allow for workers' need satisfaction, they may not be so motivated. Keep in mind that subordinates in this latter situation are still as motivated as those in the first. They are simply seeking alternative goals.

The practical implication, then, is that the best performance can only be obtained if there is a fit between employee needs and organizational goals. In order to increase employee productivity, one must attempt to align the two.

A PLANNED PROGRAM FOR IMPROVING PERFORMANCE

Clearly there are a variety of techniques and strategies managers can use to enhance employee performance. In this book ten specific strategies will be discussed in detail. These include behavior modification, punishment and discipline, monetary rewards for high performance, treating employees fairly, setting goals, redesigning jobs, satisfying individual needs, team development, reducing employee stress, and enhancing employee participation. While this list is far from exhaustive, it does cover the more currently popular programs. Unfortunately, some firms have tried one or more of these strategies and the results have not always been positive. We would contend, however, that the problem is often not that the idea is bad but that the implementation is poor and managers fail to lay the groundwork for a successful program. The point then is that if managers want to implement successful performance improvement strategies they should operate in a systematic fashion. As Exhibit 1–1 shows, they need to gather data to diagnose specific problems, create desire by making employees aware of the situation and heading off resistance, implement the improvement program, and evaluate its effect. Each of these actions depends on the one prior to it and positive outcomes are much more likely when managers proceed logically.

Exhibit 1–1
Elements of a Performance Improvement Program

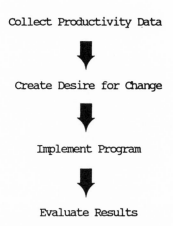

Collect Productivity Data

Create Desire for Change

Implement Program

Evaluate Results

Gathering Data on Employee Productivity and Diagnosing Specific Problems

Before a firm can begin implementing any productivity improvement program, it must analyze its work force's productivity and the specific problems employees are facing. This is where data collection and diagnosis enter into the picture. Gathering data about productivity is important in that it provides a better understanding of the situation. But gathering valid and reliable information is often not a simple process and before the actual data gathering can commence several important questions need to be addressed. First, someone must decide who will be included. Which departments, units, or individual employees will be analyzed? Second, what data-gathering method(s) will be used? Third, when will all this be done? If, for example, a questionnaire is to be administered, should it be given to everyone at the same time? Will employees be asked to fill it out at their convenience or before a lunch break? Should it be given a half or three-quarters of an hour before quitting time? Fourth, where should a questionnaire or interview be done? At the employee's work site, in someone's office, or in a neutral location? Fifth, why is a particular data-gathering technique being used and what is the purpose of the information?

Consider, for example, the process used at Tenneco's Walker plans.[7] Following an initial visit, four company consultants needed a full week to finalize their plans for data gathering. This included scheduling interviews, fine-tuning interview strategies, and logistical preparations. The plant also needed time to plan and prepare so that the interviews would not disrupt normal production schedules any more than necessary.

There are a variety of data-gathering techniques one might use. However, the methods used most frequently are interviews, questionnaires, observation, and secondary data.[8]

The interview is a widely used data-gathering technique. It has the advantage of being direct, personal, and flexible. It allows one to gather subjective data on values and attitudes because it is possible to probe and ask people to clarify statements. The disadvantages include the time plus the additional training that interviewers may require. Also, recording what transpires is a difficult and time-consuming task. Finally, maintaining the individual's anonymity may be an issue, and if employees fear reprisals for what they say, they will be hesitant to express their true opinions.

Questionnaires are self-administered and can be given to many people at the same time. Once they are completed, answers can be scored and tabulated according to the department or work area. By profiling a department's responses, management can see how much improvement is needed and where.

A third important source of productivity-related data is direct observation of the employees' behaviors and interactions. An observer may choose to sit in on meetings, roam through the plant, or visit work sites. The primary advantage is that the observer is seeing what people actually do rather than depending on reports. Sometimes what employees think they do and what actually goes on are not the same. However, observation, like interviewing, is time-consuming and requires skill and knowledge. In addition, the observer is perceiving the interaction, and personal biases may influence what is seen and recorded.

A fourth method is to use secondary data. Every organization, even a small firm, collects enormous amounts of data as part of routine operations, including reports, absenteeism and turnover rates, output measures, overtime records, grievances, minutes of meetings, interoffice memos, and so on. All these can be helpful. The primary advantage of secondary data is that it can be gathered without directly interfering with people's work, and with a relatively low investment of time and money. However, the data may not be in a usable format and comparisons from one department to another can be difficult. An additional problem involves the interpretation of the data.

Once the productivity data has been collected, it is typically analyzed, and specific problems are diagnosed. If the interpretation is not sound the real problem(s) cannot be addressed. For example, a few years ago, a New England paper mill hired a consultant to help analyze its problems.[9] The consultant found that productivity was down, morale was low, and conflicts were apparent between individuals and units. In light of this information, team building was selected as an appropriate improvement strategy. There was, however, little real change in plant operations after implementation. One day a visiting engineer listened to the main mill machinery and commented, "It sounds like the major drive shaft is out of line." Following this lead, the drive shaft was examined, found to be faulty, and replaced. Productivity immediately jumped, morale improved, and conflicts decreased. Top management then asked the embarrassing question, "Why did we do all that team building when what was needed was a new drive shaft?"

In this case, the consultant did not accurately diagnose the mill's problems. The parties failed to specify the exact issues requiring solution, to identify the underlying causal factors, and to establish a rationale for selecting an appropriate intervention strategy.

Several common mistakes are made during diagnosis.[10] One of these occurs when everyone becomes so wrapped up in the diagnosis that they lose sight of the real goal, which is to improve productivity. So many problems may be identified that employees becomes overwhelmed with information and are likely to be disgusted and frustrated. They begin to think that since the problems are so out of control, they need not bother to try solving them.

Another typical mistake results from attending only to the short-term crisis that the organization sees as immediate and important. Because of time pressures, the problems may be quickly diagnosed. This often leads to an emphasis on the more visible problems, while important but less conspicuous concerns are missed.

A third common problem involves focusing on the symptoms rather than on the underlying problems. In the incident involving the New England paper mill, management was unduly influenced by the attitudinal data and assumed that this was the cause of the productivity decline. In fact, the poor morale and increased conflict were only symptoms of the technological deficiency.

Making Employees Aware of the Need for Improvement and Heading Off Resistance

No productivity improvement program can be implemented unless employees are willing to change their behavior. In some instances, managers and employees clearly see that the organization is not operating effectively or that even though things are proceeding well enough the current situation could be improved. At other times, however, the level of awareness is quite low and management's first problem is to raise everyone's consciousness.

Take, for example, the productivity awareness program at Manufacturers Hanover Trust.[11] In an effort to implement a corporatewide productivity program the Operations Division developed a series of subcommittees, one of which was the Awareness Subcommittee. The primary purpose of this group was to create an awareness about productivity and productivity improvement programs. During a series of discussions the panel began to realize that its task was not simple or straightforward. Not only did employees need to be educated about productivity, but also management needed to understand the extent to which the program was relating to the felt needs of individual workers. To answer its questions and understand people's perceptions of work, the subcommittee decided to conduct a survey. Based on an analysis of the results, it was determined that the success of the productivity improvement program was much more likely if three goals could be achieved: improved communication between all levels, greater recognition of staff efforts, and improved teamwork. A number of awareness programs were then designed to address these issues, including awareness presentations, productivity posters, slogans, contests, and various awards. In other words, management was able to heighten awareness by working with employees and seeking their input. Rather than assuming that they (management) knew all the problems and answers, they brought employees into the process as active participants.

Why Employees Resist Change

Performance improvement efforts often encounter resistance. Even though good managers are aware of this fact, they frequently do not take time to determine who might resist and why. Since employee resistance can sabotage a program before it ever gets started, such problems need to be addressed early.

Everyone reacts differently to change—some people will passively resist while others will aggressively try to undermine the effort. In order to predict what form resistance might take, consider some of the common reasons for resisting change as shown in Exhibit 1–2.[12]

Inertia

In order to overcome their fear of the unknown, people try to maintain the status quo, even when the current situation is unsatisfactory. Doing things in the accustomed manner is usually easier than trying something new, unless, of course, present circumstances are totally unpalatable. One common problem is the individual who never quite gets around to something. When pressed, the response is likely to be, "Okay, I'm all tied up right now, let me see what I can do next week."

Fear of the Unknown

Regardless of how bad the existing situation may be, everyone at least knows what the problems are and has probably learned to adjust. Any deviation from known procedures involves risk, and while the proposed change offers potential improvements nothing is guaranteed. Employees may be unwilling to trade something they know for new procedures about which they are uncertain. The old adage about a bird in the hand being worth two in the bush clearly applies here.

Exhibit 1–2
Causes of Resistance to Change

```
Inertia

Fear of the unknown

Insecurity and fear           Resistance
   of failure

Obsolescence

Ideological objections
```

Insecurity and Fear of Failure

Individuals who must accept the new idea may see no need for any new programs or resist because they are afraid of failure. In this case it might be necessary to implement the strategy on a trial basis and also reassure people that success is possible. In addition, this approach will give those involved a chance to get more facts about the program in a nonthreatening way.

Obsolescence

Some changes in work methods or procedures may cause people to fear that their skills or knowledge will become obsolete. Those who have invested years of experience in building up a high level of skill and knowledge for a specific activity might resist new proposals if they doubt their ability to become proficient in the new system. If there is any chance that the program will result in the loss of jobs or even status in the organization, it is very unlikely that they will go along with the idea.

Ideological Questions

People may resist a new program because it threatens or questions their basic values and attitudes. For example, a manager who truly believes that participative management is a lot of foolishness will not be enthusiastic about allowing employees to participate.

Overcoming Resistance to Change

While there are no hard and fast rules, most practitioners would agree that there are ways of making a new program more salable and palatable.[13] One recommendation is to convincingly explain the need for improvement to all those who might be affected, using straightforward, clear language that avoids jargon and buzz words. For example, in the case of Walker Manufacturing Co. mentioned earlier, one of the first steps in the productivity improvement program was a meeting between the project team, the plant manager at each site, and the plant manager's boss. The purpose was to clarify expectations, evaluate whether or not conditions seemed suitable to proceed, and complete the planning that required the plant manager's input. The main objective was to inform all parties about the program and demonstrate the need for it.

A second recommendation is to use participation whenever it is appropriate by consulting with employees and inviting their opinions and suggestions. This increases commitment by giving people a sense of ownership. Sun Petroleum Products Company, a subsidiary of Sun Company, Inc., was able to ease the transition process by encouraging resisters to air their complaints and to influence acceptable solutions. In addition, everyone was kept informed of progress through a specifically designed newsletter. By demonstrating the importance of identifying and acting on areas of concern, top management was able to convince employees that they were at least being heard.

Third, a manager may be able to overcome resistance by trying to design the program so that it is introduced in stages. Sometimes people can be convinced of an idea if they are allowed to work their way into it gradually. The magnitude of some proposals frightens people and arouses objections.

Fourth, employee resistance may decrease if managers clearly point out what is in it for them. What do they have to gain by going along? If the program offers the promise for more compensation, job security, better working conditions, and so on, employees will be more likely to support it.

Implementing Specific Productivity Improvement Programs

Once a firm or manager has collected preliminary productivity-related data, developed an approach for creating employee awareness of the need for improved performance, and determined how potential employee resistance can be overcome, it is necessary to determine which productivity improvement program to implement.

Almost any program can be of value in certain situations and, in fact, there are often several that will do the job equally well. Several important criteria can be used in selecting a strategy.[14]

Time

One important consideration is how soon a new program must be implemented. Some strategies such as behavior modification and discipline can be implemented fairly rapidly. Others such as job redesign or team building may take several months or years. There is, however, a fine line between haste and waste.

Financial Resources

A second consideration is the financial issue. The ideal program might be to have a top-flight external consultant work closely with the management team over the next year and a half. But this could easily cost many thousands of dollars and the budget may not allow for such an expenditure. If the budget is restrictive, it may be better not to start a program at all rather than to try something that is too limited in scope.

Employee Support

Employee support for a program is another factor to be addressed. Unless all parties support the action and believe it to be a viable idea, it is likely to fail. Of course, sometimes people simply misperceive the program and see it as a threat when in fact none exists. This is may be due to the callousness of top management in introducing the idea, lack of skill and preparation on the part of the department manager, or poor communication all around. Still, even though giving people sufficient information may help overcome resistance, it does not guarantee enthusiastic support. The important point is that employee reactions to a program need to be taken into account before a final decision is made. Employees may willingly accept one program but totally reject another.

Evaluating the Results of a Program

Evaluating the effects of a productivity improvement program is frequently the most important step. In some cases, however, top management says, "Okay, let's start the damn thing and worry about measuring it later." This attitude may be reasonable in some instances but ultimately someone is bound to ask for proof that the program is working. How long can a manager keep claiming something is effective unless it begins to filter through, in an identifiable way, to the bottom line of the earnings statement?[15]

As John Bilangi, vice president of the American Hospital Supply Corporation, points out, measurement is important for at least two reasons.[16] One is that it is a technique for getting people involved in determining their productive impact on the business. They get involved in this decision process when they establish measurement criteria for their own jobs. Second, measurement is important because all of the processes involved in making people more productive cost money.

Some businesses are reluctant to invest in processes with long-term paybacks unless they are pretty sure the benefit will really materialize. One of the ways to evaluate payback is to establish some measurement criteria that can be tracked before and after implementation. This makes it easier to sell division management committees on the investment required to create an effective program.[17]

PLAN OF THE BOOK

As noted earlier, this book examines ten different strategies for enhancing employee motivation (see Exhibit 1–3). A brief description of each is presented below:

Using behavior modification. One way to improve an employee's job performance is to reward desired behavior but not undesired behavior. When, how, and how frequently an employee should be rewarded is an integral part of this approach.

Using punishment and discipline. This approach to improving employee productivity stresses the importance of having and using effective disciplinary procedures. How and when to discipline an employee so as to actually improve job performance while avoiding undesirable side effects is the real issue in this chapter.

Rewarding high performance. A manager who uses this approach provides bonuses and other monetary rewards based on the quality and quantity of the employees' work. The higher the subordinate's productivity, the greater the reward.

Treating employees fairly. This strategy for improving employee productivity recommends that managers treat their employees fairly or convince employees they are now in fact receiving fair treatment. What is meant by treating people fairly and how employees determine if they are being treated fairly are important components of this strategy.

Setting goals. This strategy argues that setting difficult and measurable goals for employees or allowing employees to set goals for themselves can result in higher employee productivity.

Redesigning jobs. The recommendation here is that jobs be designed or structured in such a way that they provide employees with feelings of accomplishment, achievement, and responsibility.

Meeting the unique needs of employees. One of the oldest and best known productivity-enhancing strategies is to determine what an employee's needs are and to make need-satisfiers available. This approach requires an understanding of basic human needs and the ways people differ in the strength of their needs.

Building effective work teams. Since most employees work in groups, their productivity is influenced by their ability to work as a team. Managers can use informal, day-to-day techniques as well as more formal procedures to create teamwork.

Reducing employee stress. Stress is an inevitable fact of life and in measured doses it can have a positive effect on employee productivity. Rather than trying to eliminate stress, it should be managed wisely in order to

Exhibit 1–3
Strategies for Improving Employee Productivity

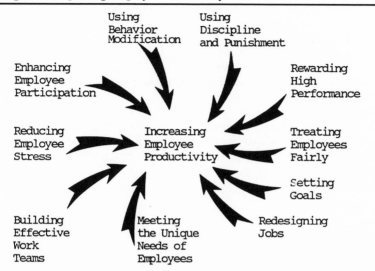

avoid the problems it can cause and at the same time improve organizational effectiveness.

Enhancing employee participation. Managers who use this strategy look for ways to allow employees greater involvement in the decision-making process. Seeking employee input on a variety of issues and problems potentially enhances one's sense of ownership and leads to greater commitment and employee satisfaction.

NOTES

1. C. P. McNamara, "Productivity Is Management's Problem," *Business Horizons*, March–April 1983, pp. 55–59.

2. A. S. Judson, "The Awkward Truth about Productivity," *Harvard Business Review*, September–October 1982, pp. 93–97.

3. J. Main, "How to Battle Your Own Bureaucracy," *Fortune*, June 29, 1981, pp. 54–58.

4. J. Teresko, "Robots Come of Age," *Industry Week*, January 25, 1982, pp. 35–42.

5. W. Serrin, "Management Erodes Work Ethic, Workers Say," *Virginia Pilot-Ledger Star*, September 5, 1983.

6. F. W. Taylor, *The Principles of Scientific Management* (New York: W. W. Norton and Co., 1911).

7. "Productivity Improvement at Tenneco, Inc.," in J. W. Kendrick, ed., *Improving Company Productivity* (Baltimore, Md.: Johns Hopkins University Press, 1984).

8. D. F. Harvey and D. R. Brown, *An Experiential Approach to Organization Development* (Englewood Cliffs, N.J.: Prentice-Hall, 1988).

9. G. Dyer, "Selecting an Intervention for Organizational Change," *Training and Development Journal*, April 1981, pp. 62–68.

10. Harvey and Brown, *Experiential Approach.*

11. R. J. Lambert, "Productivity Awareness at Manufacturers Hanover Trust," *National Productivity Review*, Summer 1983, pp. 298–306.

12. J. Stanislav and B. C. Stanislav, "Dealing with Resistance to Change," *Business Horizons*, July–August 1983, pp. 74–78.

13. Ibid.

14. Dyer, "Selecting an Intervention."

15. M. Mooney, "Productivity Improvement at American Hospital Supply Corporation," *National Productivity Review*, Summer 1983, pp. 307–13.

16. Ibid.

17. Ibid.

2

Using Behavior Modification

A person who smiles and displays a friendly attitude toward others is likely to stimulate them to react in a friendly manner. Gruff and insolent behavior usually brings negative reactions.[1]

All organisms, including humans, are greatly influenced by the consequences produced by their own behavior.[2]

When a given act is followed closely by a reinforcer (reward), the [person] tends to increase the frequency of that act under the same or similar conditions.[3]

In 1981 the employees at Diamond International faced an uncertain future.[4] The firm, which manufactures paper egg cartons, was encountering stiff competition from several firms producing styrofoam containers. In an effort to improve its fortunes the firm devised a system of productivity incentives called the 100 Club. Under this program, employees were allocated points for above-average performance. Any employee who worked a full year without an industrial accident was awarded twenty points, 100 percent attendance was worth twenty-five points, and so on. Every year, on the program's anniversary date, the points would be added up, and a record sent to the individual's home. Upon reaching 100 points, the worker received a nylon jacket emblazoned with the company logo, and a patch signifying membership in the 100 Club.

After two years the plant's productivity was up 16.5 percent and quality-related errors were down 40 percent. Workers' grievances had decreased 72 percent and lost time due to industrial accidents was reduced 43.7 percent. Beyond these improvements, the relationship between labor and management was improved and the atmosphere at the plant had shifted from one of suspicion to one of cooperation.

What this situation illustrates is that appropriate rewards do indeed have a powerful effect on employee behavior. Managers constantly affect the behavior of others by using the reinforcers at their disposal. In the workplace, managers intuitively use reinforcement all the time, yet their efforts often produce limited results because the methods are applied improperly, inconsistently, or inefficiently. All too often employees are given rewards that are not clearly related to the behavior the manager wishes to promote, and even when they are, there can be long delays between the occurrence of the desired behavior and the manager's response. Special privileges, activities, and other rewards are often based on length of service rather than on an individual's performance. In many cases employees are inadvertently rewarded for wrong or inappropriate behavior. In short, managers may be trying to motivate employees, but they do the opposite by failing to understand what reinforcement is all about.[5]

This chapter will examine how reinforcement can be used to improve employee behavior on the job. We will discuss the rationale for using reinforcement, consider how a firm would actually implement what is called organizational behavior modification, examine several applications, and look briefly at some of the major criticisms.

RATIONALE FOR USING REINFORCEMENT

In presenting the rationale for using reinforcement our purpose is to provide the reader with sufficient detail to understand the concepts and place them in context. We do not maintain that managers need to become accomplished theoreticians. But neither do we advocate that they act like robots, simply following a set of prescribed steps and procedures.

The Law of Effect

The actions associated with reinforcement all rest in part on Edward Thorndike's Law of Effect.[6] Briefly stated, Thorndike believed that "when a modifiable connection between a situation and a response is made and is accompanied or followed by a satisfying state of affairs, that connection's strength is increased; when made and accompanied by an annoying state of affairs, its strength is decreased." In other words, if a person's behavior is followed by a pleasant response (a reward), it is much more likely that the same or a similar behavior will be repeated in the future, provided the circumstances are essentially the same. But if the response is somehow punishing, the probability of the behavior being repeated is decreased. The Law of Effect rests on two major assumptions: first, that people seek pleasure and want to avoid pain; second, that there is indeed a reasonably predictable relationship between what a person does and the consequences that follow the behavior.

Operant Conditioning

Building upon the work of Thorndike, B. F. Skinner developed the notion of operant conditioning, the basic premise of which is that behavior is a function of its consequences.[7] Skinner believes that there are two different kinds of learning, each involving a separate kind of behavior. One type, respondent or reflexive behavior, is based on the notion of stimulus-response. Every time a given stimulus is presented to the individual, a particular response occurs automatically.

A second and more prevalent type is what Skinner terms operant behavior. As distinguished from respondent behavior, the primary characteristic of operant behavior is that it operates on the environment. The individual either does or does not behave in a certain way because of the feedback (reinforcement) received in another similar situation at an earlier time. There is nothing reflexive about this process, and, in fact, no particular stimulus will consistently bring forth or elicit an operant response. From this point of view, even if we assume that a person is hungry to the point of starvation, the sight of food alone will not necessarily cause the individual to reach for it. The particular response will depend on a variety of factors.

Suppose for a moment that you are this hungry person and you happen to be walking by a restaurant. Behind a plate glass window a variety of foods are on display. Would you automatically put your fist through the window to get the food? Obviously, you would be risking serious personal injury and you could certainly be arrested for such an act. Besides, if you had some money you could go inside and buy what you wanted. On the other hand, if you were literally starving and had no money, or it was late at night on a deserted street, you might break the window. But still you might find a stone or a stick rather than using your fist. The point is that operant behavior is much more complex than simple stimulus-response connections.

According to Skinner, learning takes place as individuals experience the consequences of their own actions. Positive consequences increase the probability that the person will repeat the behavior and make it a part of his or her regular conduct. If, on the other hand, individuals experience negative consequences, the behavior is less likely to occur. The way to either maintain or change behavior is to control and systematically manipulate its consequences.[8]

Skinner contends that the time lapse between the person's behavior and the feedback is also significant. For best results, positive or negative consequences should follow as soon as possible after the occurrence of the behavior. That way, the individual can relate the feedback to the behavior and the connection between them will be much stronger.

IMPLEMENTING BEHAVIOR MODIFICATION

When reinforcement concepts are applied to work, the term *Organizational Behavior Modification* (OB Mod) is normally used. The primary assumption of OB Mod is that if we can manipulate the consequences, we stand a good chance of affecting someone's behavior. The application involves four specific steps as shown in Exhibit 2–1.

Pinpointing Behavior

Pinpointing requires that a manager identify specific performance-related behavioral events. When we pinpoint a behavior, we define it in such a way that anyone listening to a description could, in effect, see the behavior, count it, and describe the situation in which the behavior occurred.[9] Remember that since attitudes and "inner" states cannot be directly observed, there is no way to provide consequences that are directly linked to them. Therefore, they cannot be used in pinpointing.

For example, consider the way in which a manager might describe a worker, first without pinpointing:[10]

I would say that Joe is just a disruptive worker. He sulks a lot and when he's not behaving aggressively, I often see him daydreaming. He seems to lack motivation and is pretty stubborn. Personally, I think that his lack of drive and general hostility may be due to a problem at home, but I don't have any specifics.

Notice the labels applied to Joe. He sulks, daydreams, is stubborn, lacks drive, is hostile, and has a problem at home. Many of these are inner states and at the moment the manager has no idea how to deal with this employee. If Joe were given this information about himself, he would not know specifically what he should do to improve his performance.

Now, consider how the same manager would describe Joe, using a pinpointing approach:

Well, whenever Joe is given an instruction, he immediately responds by telling you why it can't be done that way. He verbally threatens other workers, and there have been one or two actual fights. He leaves his own job and walks over to other areas to tell jokes and generally distracts other workers. Sometimes he just sits in a corner, or can be found looking out the window for several minutes at a time, while ignoring his own responsibilities.

He can't seem to tell the left-handed flanges from the right-handed ones, no matter how often we tell him. Sometimes he will begin a task and then seem to forget what he's doing, and start doing something entirely different.

He has arrived at work late eight times in the last month, and has returned late by over five minutes from six lunch breaks and six coffee breaks. I have spoken to him about this, but he refuses to acknowledge that he's late, and says he needs more time anyway.

Exhibit 2–1
The Steps in Organizational Behavior Modification

1. Pinpoint the behavior of employees.

2. Count and chart the pinpointed behavior.

3. Change the behavior by altering the consequences.

4. Evaluate the improvement in the employee's behavior.

Source: P. J. Brown and J. Presbie, Behavior Modification in Business, Industry, and Government (New Paltz, N.Y.: Behavior Improvement Associates, 1971).

Look closely at the differences between these two statements. In the latter instance, the manager is addressing much more specific behavioral problems. Rather than criticizing the employee's attitude, he is talking about problems that can be observed, measured, tied to job performance, and solved.

Counting and Charting Behavior

The second step is for the manager to measure the pinpointed behavior. This is often done through frequency counts, which are then graphed over time to provide a typology of the behavior. The measurement and the graph serve several important functions. They indicate the severity of the problems; they let the employees know exactly where they stand in relationship to company standards; and they provide a baseline against which future behavior can be judged.[11]

The recording of employee behavior is certainly not a new idea. Nearly every organization measures performance in some fashion. What is different is that the objective counts of behavior are done systematically using event counting or time sampling.[12]

Event counting is simply a direct count of each time a particular pinpointed behavior occurs. For example, a manager can count the number of times an employee is praised or criticized by customers, the number of parts each person produces in a day or week, or the number of unauthorized absences from a work area. In each case, every event is counted.

Time sampling involves making a series of checks throughout the day on certain pinpointed behaviors. For example, rather than counting the total number of times workers properly use safety guards on manufacturing equipment, a supervisor could take a count at several randomly determined times every day for a week in order to determine the average number of safety guards being used. For individual behaviors, time sampling is often useful when it is not practical to observe someone constantly for a period of time. Suppose a worker has a reputation for smoking in a nonsmoking area. The supervisor could place the area under constant surveillance. A less costly approach, however, would be for the supervisor to check at different times and note on a small card whether or not the person was engaged in a prohibited activity. Once behavior has been counted, the preparation of a simple frequency chart offers managers and employees a useful visual presentation of the behavior being counted.

Changing Behavior

If behavior is a function of its consequences, then it follows that any manager who wants to change an employee's behavior must rearrange and structure the outcomes that follow the person's actions. This third step is sometimes called "consequating" because the manager attempts to arrange the consequences that reinforce and improve behavior.[13]

Types of Consequences

Any behavior can result in one of four different consequences: positive reinforcement, negative reinforcement, extinction, and punishment. The first two will increase or stimulate behavior, while punishment and extinction decrease or stop it.

Positive reinforcement. A positive reinforcer is any pleasant event that strengthens the behavior it follows and makes the behavior more likely in the future.[14] If an employee is praised for completing a particular project on time and, as a result, the employee completes other projects on schedule in the future, the praise would be an example of a positive reinforcement. Remember, however, that it is the employee's definition of the situation that counts here. Just because the manager thinks that the praise will be rewarding does not make it a positive reinforcer. The concept *positive reinforcer* applies only if it does in fact strengthen and subsequently improve the employee's behavior. In addition, what serves as a positive reinforcer for one individual may not work the same way for another.

Negative reinforcement. A negative reinforcer also strengthens behavior when it is contingent upon a response. The individual exhibits a desired behavior in order to avoid something unpleasant. Suppose that workers get busy every time the supervisor walks through the area so as to avoid being "chewed out." In this instance, negative reinforcement is at work. The individuals wish to escape some aversive outcome (being chewed out), and their work behavior improves. Thus the effect of negative reinforcement is often called avoidance learning.[15]

Punishment. Punishment is typically defined as the presentation of an aversive (unpleasant) event or the removal of a positive event following a response that decreases the frequency of that response.[16] In other words, punishment involves two basic actions: (1) taking direct punitive action against an employee or (2) withholding a reward. In both, the manager is attempting to reduce or eliminate a certain behavior.

While punishment tends to decrease behavior, it is a very complex device. There are often undesirable side effects and it is quite easy to arouse very strong emotions that may result in sabotage, work slowdowns, and so on. Because it is so controversial, we have devoted an entire chapter to this topic. As a general rule, managers trained in behavior modification procedures will try to apply positive reinforcement whenever possible. Punishment is used with care and typically in conjunction with positive reinforcement.

Extinction. Briefly stated, extinction occurs when an individual is engaged in some behavior and receives no feedback in the form of reinforcement or punishment.[17] When there is no feedback, chances are that the behavior will decrease and eventually stop. For example, an employee who is constantly wisecracking or making asides during a meeting may be getting reinforcement from the smiles, laughter, or even the frowns of others in the group. Suppose, however, that they really find this behavior distracting but nobody wants to make a scene by directly reprimanding the individual. In this case they could act as if nothing happened every time that the person made a comment. Completely ignoring the individual should cause the comments to diminish or stop.

Like punishment, extinction is easier said than done. In the first place, it is very difficult to totally ignore someone. Second, people do not give up a behavior easily. It may take quite a while before the extinction takes effect. Third, extinction may be misread by the individual as well as by others in the environment to mean that the manager does not care. As a result, ignoring the behavior has the effect of increasing, rather than eliminating, the inappropriate behavior. Fourth, extinction may give an individual a sense of what not to do but does not provide any clear idea of what behavior is appropriate. To be effective, it is recommended that extinction always be paired with positive reinforcement.

Using Shaping to Improve Behavior

Shaping is a process in which positive reinforcement is used to improve behavior. With this technique, behavior is gradually changed by systematically reinforcing successive approximations of the desired pinpointed behavior.[18] The employee is rewarded for progress toward the goals, not perfect performance. Consider the example of an employee who has chronically been ten minutes late for work. Using shaping, the manager would wait until the employee's behavior improves and then reward it. If he or she arrives only eight minutes late, the manager would reward the improvement. Reinforcements would continue to be given each time the behavior improves (e.g., five minutes late, three minutes late, one minute late). Whenever the employee's behavior remains constant or gets worse, no positive reinforcement is given.

Under most circumstances, the reinforcer used in shaping is social reinforcement or praise. Even though there are other types of reinforcement that could be used, praise can often be very effective in changing behavior. It is something that any manager can use and it requires no formal program or approval by top management. In addition, it costs nothing. The problem, however, is that all too often praise is applied in a totally unsystematic way and as a result has no real effect on behavior. How then should praise be used?

One of the most frequent recommendations is that praise be contingent on behavior. In other words, the manager should be able to observe and measure what employees are doing using pinpointing. In addition, praise should be given shortly after the desired behavior has occurred.

In order for praise to be effective, it must also be specific. With regard to specificity, research has shown that such praise communicates more clearly to the employee what the manager thinks is appropriate behavior.[19] For example, compare these two statements:

The amount of effort you've shown is really excellent.

I just wanted you to know that I think you did an excellent job coordinating the negotiations on the Smith and Wesson contract.

The second statement is much more specific and to the point. Notice also that it deals with an identifiable behavior rather than with an attitude or a personality trait.

It is also suggested that praise be delivered in a sincere way and be perceived as such by the employee. Sincerity can be increased by paying attention to body language (posture, eye contact) and to the tone of one's voice. A manager could, for example, say, "I appreciate your work on that report," in a monotone voice that expresses no enthusiasm, emotion, or real conviction. On the other hand, if these qualities were present, the feedback would seem more positive. Even though any form of praise is usually better than none at all, the way in which this reinforcer is administered is extremely important.

Using Reinforcement Schedules to Maintain Behavior

Once the employee achieves the desired level of performance, some provision must be made for maintaining the new behavior. If the reinforcement is terminated, the individual is likely to revert to prior behaviors. In most cases, the manager will find it necessary to continue reinforcing the new level for some time. As Exhibit 2–2 shows, several different reinforcement schedules can be used to maintain the behavior. These can be divided into two major types—continuous and intermittent.

Exhibit 2–2
Reinforcement Schedules

Continuous reinforcement	Reinforcement each time behavior improves
Intermittent reinforcement	Reinforcement according to predetermined ratio or at various times
Fixed ratio	Reinforcement given after fixed number of responses
Variable ratio	Reinforcement based on an average number of responses
Fixed interval	Reinforcement spaced over uniform time intervals
Variable interval	Reinforcement distributed over unpredictable time intervals

Continuous reinforcement means that individuals receive reinforcement (positive or negative) each and every time their behavior improves or changes in the desired direction. With intermittent reinforcement, not every desired behavior is reinforced. Instead, behavior is reinforced according to a predetermined ratio or at various times. This type of reinforcement can be subdivided into four categories.[20]

Under fixed ratio (FR) schedules, reinforcement is given after some fixed or specified number of responses. Once an employee has reached the point of no errors in typing memos, the supervisor might praise the person only for every third memo typed perfectly. Another example would be to award employees a paid day off for every thirty working days they complete without being absent.

Variable ratio (VR) schedules provide reinforcement based on an average number of responses. The person whose behavior is being reinforced is not able to predict which response will be followed by reinforcement. Salespeople working on a commission basis are really being reinforced on a variable ratio schedule.

Fixed interval (FI) schedules allow for the spacing of reinforcement at uniform time intervals. The critical variable is time, which is held constant. Most pay schedules that provide for the delivery of reinforcement at the end of one week, two weeks, or a month are on a fixed interval schedule. If the organization uses a performance appraisal system in which the supervisor meets with employees once or twice a year on a predictable basis, a fixed interval schedule is also in effect.

Variable interval (VI) schedules distribute reinforcements on the basis of time, but the exact scheduling of reinforcement is not predictable. Managers may tell subordinates that they will be around to observe their work and that what they see will significantly affect their recommendations for merit pay increases. In this situation, they are using a VI reinforcement schedule because the employees do not know exactly when their managers will show up.

All intermittent schedules suffer from one serious problem. As noted earlier, reinforcement always has its greatest effect on behavior when delivered immediately after the behavior occurs. Any delay between the employee's performance and the delivery of reinforcement will lessen the impact. Consider the following example. Suppose your assistant has worked hard on reorganizing the filing system. It has taken several days, and once or twice the person has even had to work overtime to accomplish this task. You decide that lunch at a nice restaurant is in order. If you really want this to have the maximum effect, you should offer to buy lunch either that day or the next. Assuming the assistant is aware of the fact that the free meal is really to show your appreciation for the extra effort, the lunch will very likely be reinforcing. If, however, you wait a week or two before going to lunch, the impact on the assistant's behavior will probably be much weaker. In effect, a week or so of extinction will have taken place before reinforcement. You could, of course, reduce the effect of extinction by praising the work immediately and promising the free lunch soon. This will make the delay much less critical.[21]

Evaluating Behavior Improvement

Once an OB Mod program has been implemented, managers need to develop an evaluation procedure in order to determine whether performance is really improving. In most cases, this involves the continuation of the counting and recording initiated earlier in the process. One of the added effects of this evaluation is that it provides a built-in reinforcement for both manager and employees. Everyone can experience direct reinforcement from observing the line on a graph go up or down.[22]

If a sales agent typically makes ten calls on clients a day, one would record a ten for the baseline figure and then the number of customer contacts made on each subsequent day. If the program is working as expected, the volume of calls should increase to some number above ten and then continue to rise at a more or less steady rate until some reasonable maximum is reached. The manager could graph the number of calls for ready reference, but it is often better to have the sales agents keep their own records and make daily entries on a graph so that progress is readily apparent to everyone.

ORGANIZATIONAL BEHAVIOR MODIFICATION
APPLIED TO COMPANIES

Even though there has been considerable controversy about the use of behavior modification when applied to organizations, many firms have used it successfully when dealing with problems of quantity and quality of work, absenteeism, turnover, tardiness, and safety.[23] In the following section, we will examine several organizations that have implemented OB Mod programs.

Each of the programs discussed illustrates the potential for OB Mod. In two of the cases, the primary form of reinforcement was praise. The other shows how even small contingent monetary rewards can be used. In addition, other organizations have successfully used tokens and even free time contingencies. The point is that there are a variety of alternatives, and under the right circumstances operant principles can be used to teach new behavior and to strengthen and reinforce existing responses in many situations.

Emery Air Freight

Perhaps the most well-known industrial application of a reinforcement-based strategy occurred at Emery Air Freight.[24] Emery's approach involved designing a program that would let employees know how well they were meeting specific goals, and reward improvement with praise and recognition.

As a first step, Emery conducted a performance audit in order to determine the status of employee behavior before any systematic behavior change plans were implemented. Based on the audit, the firm set standards or goals for each job in various departments. It then required that all workers measure their own performance in relation to this goal as they progressed.

The second step involved providing feedback designed to let employees know how they were performing according to those standards. At the end of each day, the performance report was given to the supervisor. In some departments, charts showing both company goals and employee performance were conspicuously placed on the wall.

The third procedure was to administer positive reinforcement to employees for anything they were presently doing on the job that was desirable or for any improvement in their job performance. At no time was the supervisor to criticize or threaten the employee. To illustrate, the Emery Air Freight studies cite the case of John, a cargo handler whose attendance was unsatisfactory. The supervisor used positive reinforcement and feedback to improve his attendance. He would reward John and at the same time would give him a reminder of the company goal. For example:

First Day: John, you came to work nineteen times out of twenty-two last month. When you are here we make more flights. Try to shoot for twenty-one or twenty-two days.

Second Day: Appreciate your coming to work today, John. Keep that up and you'll be here twenty-one or twenty-two days out of twenty-two.

Third Day: You've been here three days in a row now. Look at the percentage of flights we've made in the last three days. Keep shooting for twenty-one or twenty-two days.

Fifth Day: You've been here all week. Thank you, John. Only seventeen days to go for a perfect record this month.

In order to help managers determine which rewards should be used as reinforcers, Emery developed two elaborate instruction workbooks prepared in house and geared to the specific situation of the company. One of these, entitled "Positive Reinforcement," enumerated more than 150 different types of rewards a manager could use. They included interacting with employees, approving of employee requests, reducing or eliminating employee constraints, giving employees recognition, and inviting individuals to participate in discussions. In addition, as Exhibit 2–3 shows, managers were told to follow eight basic rules when administering positive reinforcement.

How successful has Emery Air Freight's approach been? When the company first implemented behavior modification, they concentrated on two departments: customer service and containerized shipping. Before behavior modification was introduced in the customer service department, company standards were met only 30 to 40 percent of the time. The program increased this figure to 90 to 95 percent, and even after four years performance remained at this high level. In the containerized shipping operation, the results were similar. Container usage rose from 40 percent to 95 percent and stayed there.

From a financial viewpoint, behavior modification was a success. During one three-year period Emery saved over three million dollars. At the same time, the costs of implementing the program averaged only $5150 per year.

Friendliness in a Fast Food Franchise

In another situation, a fast food restaurant designed a behavioral program to improve customer service by developing the friendliness of front-line personnel.[25] Even though this study was done in a small firm, it is particularly interesting in that it demonstrates that even a highly abstract trait such as friendliness can be behaviorally defined, observed, recorded in a reliable way, and improved. It also points out some of the problems encountered in measuring and improving customer service in a retail setting.

Exhibit 2–3
Rules for Using Positive Reinforcement

1. Find and reward any good performance, however slight, setting goals for what is not done rather than calling attention to what is bad.

2. Shape behavior gradually toward the goal.

3. Use the many nonfinancial rewards available to you.

4. To establish a desired behavior, use a continuous schedule of reinforcement.

5. A high frequency of reinforcement is needed to get performance started toward a desired goal.

6. Once improvement is ongoing, fewer reinforcements are needed.

7. Generally, one to two reinforcements per week after the initial improvement stage (which may require one or more per day, at least three per week) will sustain performance.

8. The schedule of reinforcement should be determined by fluctuations in performance.

Source: R. B. McAfee and P. J. Champagne, *Organizational Behavior: A Manager's View* (St. Paul, Minn.: West Publishing Co., 1987), p. 164. Reprinted by permission.

In the study two behaviors were identified to describe a friendly employee: (1) smiling at and (2) talking with customers. Preliminary on-site observations revealed that there was substantial agreement on whether talking with customers had occurred, but observers often disagreed when recording smiling. In order to establish a common ground for observation, smiling was defined as having the corners of one's mouth turned up with one's teeth showing.

Establishing a baseline was accomplished by having trained, noncompany observers assess the level of employee friendliness. An observer, acting as a customer, sat in the dining area and observed employees for fifteen minutes while completing his or her meal. The observer noted whether the desired behaviors occurred in the presence of a customer at two different areas within the restaurant, the cash register and the dining area. Observations were conducted five to seven times each week for a period of thirteen weeks.

During the baseline period a behavioral analysis was conducted to determine what might be hindering employees from being more friendly. The formal training all employees received included suggestions about greeting customers, smiling sincerely, giving a warm goodbye, and so on. It appeared, however, that despite the training, the quality of customer service suffered because of a lack of on-the-job consequences. The manager herself was a good model of friendliness, but most of her time was spent in the back dealing with food preparation. Rarely was she able to observe and praise employees for acting in a friendly manner.

To improve friendliness in the cash register area, the company singled out smiling due mainly to the relatively low baseline level (42.1 percent) of this behavior. The store manager explained to employees the importance of increasing friendliness. Employees practiced smiling in front of a mirror and with each other. Then it was suggested that each employee smile at least four times with every customer—when greeting the person, taking the order, asking about a dessert special, and giving the customer change. In addition, the self-recording checklist shown in Exhibit 2–4 was posted by the timeclock. Here, employees estimated how often they had smiled when interacting with customers. Another consequence was provided by the manager in the form of praise and recognition. She tried to comment at least once a day to each employee seen smiling. The manager also filled out a checklist at the end of the day.

In the dining area, three different approaches were introduced to improve friendliness. The first involved teaching employees who might be working there to initiate conversations with customers. These ranged from asking about the food to discussions about general topics such as the weather. The second intervention used was an informal contingency contract. Employees earned a five-minute break each hour for talking with at least five customers. Finally, the third approach had employees walk up to customers in the dining area with a tent-shaped sign in hand. The sign described food items available in the restaurant, and employees were encouraged to use this as a topic of conversation.

The results of the company's efforts in the cash register area showed that smiling increased substantially. Front-line personnel were found to smile 67.37 percent of the time compared to 41.2 percent during the baseline. On the other hand, the results for talking and smiling in the dining area were mixed. The company found that employees did not initiate general discussions with customers more frequently, probably due to the fact that in the dining area potentially reinforcing consequences were delayed or infrequent. Customers often would not speak in return and the manager was less likely to provide positive feedback since she found it difficult to accurately determine whether or not the employee had initiated a conversation. However, in the second intervention, when employees earned a five-minute break by talking with five customers, talking increased from 19 percent during the baseline to 35.1 percent. Finally, the third intervention also proved unsuccessful. The use of tent-shaped signs was not implemented as planned. Over half the time the manager was out of town in

Exhibit 2-4
Employee Self-Recording Checklist for Estimating the Frequency of
Smiling in the Cash Register Area

Name_____   Week of_____

Please fill out during the end of the
day when you have a free moment. Try
not to leave work until you have
answered the following questions.
Using the key on the right, note how
often each of the items (noted below)
occurred. For any day that you did not
work, note "NW." Be honest. This is
meant as an aid and will not be counted
against you.

A Every time
B Most of the time
C Some of the time
D None of the time

	W	T	F	S	S	M	T
1. SMILE when you greeted a customer?							
2. SMILE when customer placed order?							
3. SMILE when you asked about the dessert special?							
4. SMILE when you gave customer change?							
5. Customers smiled back at you at the register?							

Source: J. Komaki, M. Blood, and D. Holder, "Employee Self-recording Checklist for
Estimating the Frequency of Smiling in the Cash Register Area," *Journal of Organizational Behavior Management* 2, no. 3 (Summer 1980), p. 157. Reprinted
by permission.

preparation for a new job assignment and therefore was not available to
provide recognition.

Customer service presents special problems because it often involves
customer-employee interactions that are not readily observable except to
the parties involved, making it hard for on-site personnel to reinforce employees in a timely way. In the above case, for example, it was particularly
difficult for the manager to assess the level of service being provided in the
dining area. There were no permanent products and the interventions
were fleeting at best. Still, the study demonstrates the potential for behavior modification in a setting far removed from the plant or office.

Improving Safety in a Paper Mill

This field study was conducted at a large midwestern paper mill and involved all of the 1400-plus employees.[26] The employees were divided into

twenty-eight safety teams with about fifty individuals assigned to each group. Team assignments were determined by the plant's safety action committee; they tried to ensure that each team had approximately the same exposure to job hazards as any other team. All teams were identified by the common name of a tree growing in the vicinity of the plant. An ID button showing the team's name and the individual's name was worn by each employee.

In order to improve employee safety, the company experimented with three types of contingent monetary rewards: (1) mill awards, (2) team awards, and (3) individual awards. During the three-year study, the mill and team awards totaled $310,000. These two awards were earned and administered as follows:

If the members of a given safety team worked for a full month without sustaining a lost time accident, then each member of the team received one silver dollar (1984) or tokens worth about one dollar convertible into gifts (1985) or tokens redeemable for gift certificates or raffle tickets for major prizes such as boats or cameras (1986).

If the members of a given safety team worked for two consecutive months without sustaining a lost time accident, then each team member received two silver dollars (1984) or tokens (1985 and 1986).

In the third month, the progression continued for an award of three silver dollars (1984) or tokens (1985 and 1986). Additionally, if the entire mill (all safety teams) worked for three consecutive months without sustaining a lost time accident, then all team rewards for that month were doubled (i.e., in the above example three more silver dollars or tokens were given). Finally, the company provided free coffee and doughnuts for a twenty-four-hour period to celebrate.

Individual awards were based on a worker's direct awareness of the company's safety program and his or her safety habits. Each month members of the plant's safety inspection committee toured the entire mill site and observed safety-related items such as housekeeping and safe or unsafe acts. In addition, the team randomly selected individuals in different departments and asked them to quote the safety slogan of the month. If they knew it, they were awarded two silver dollars (1984) or tokens worth about $2.00 (1985 and 1986) on the spot. The individual was then checked for wearing appropriate safety articles such as safety shoes, safety glasses, hearing protection, hard hat, or any other applicable protective gear. Once again, employees were given a silver dollar (or token) for each of these safety actions, assuming they were wearing their safety team ID button. In total approximately 150 employees were inspected each month, and $8600 worth of Susan B. Anthony silver dollars were distributed during the first year (10/1/83–9/30/84), $20,000 worth of tokens were distributed during the second year (10/1/84–9/30/85), and approximately $22,000 worth of tokens were given during the third year (10/1/85–9/30/86).

The use of financial rewards constituted only one part of the company's safety improvement program. Several steps were also taken to provide employees with information regarding safety. To keep employees up to date on a daily basis, a safety status board was set up alongside the entrance to the mill. It contained information regarding any lost time accidents at the mill including the person's name, accident description, and department. It also showed how well each safety team was doing. In addition, twenty-four safety poster boards were set up in various departments showing the details of lost time accidents, doctor cases, serious potential incidents, inspection reports, and safety successes. A safety bulletin newsletter was also sent out two or three times per month to clarify policies or rules of the safety programs and other safety information. Finally, each day the company issued a corporate bulletin showing the number of working hours without a lost time accident, along with other company news.

One further aspect of the company's safety program also warrants discussion. For several years prior to this study, the company had a safety suggestion program whereby employees could submit suggestions about ways to improve plant safety. At the start of this study the company hired a safety advisor to follow up on these suggestions and to see that they were implemented. The advisor also encouraged employees to submit new suggestions. During the three-year study period, 230 safety suggestions were submitted and 190 were implemented. As a minor incentive, the company offered a free dinner for two with a maximum value of $25 to the employee who submitted the best suggestion each month.

The results of the company's use of contingent monetary awards and safety-related feedback are shown in Exhibit 2–5. Lost time accidents (i.e., when an individual could not report to work due to an injury suffered on the job) declined dramatically from thirty-one to thirteen incidents during the study period. Light duty cases, which occurred when an employee was reassigned to a different, less physically demanding job due to an injury, decreased from thirty-four to twenty-two incidents. Finally, accidents that required a doctor's treatment rather than first aid also declined sharply from 252 to 138 cases.

Other Company Examples

These cases represent only a few of the many companies that have successfully used OB Mod in recent years. Organizations such as Weyerhauser, Michigan Bell, General Electric, PPG Industries, Standard Oil of Ohio, and B. F. Goodrich have also been actively involved with OB Mod.

In the three cases discussed, the primary form of reinforcement was praise or money. But these are not the only options available. Positive reinforcement can also take the form of prizes and even free time contingencies have been used successfully.

For example, Valley Fair, a major midwestern amusement park, uses a

Exhibit 2–5
Results of Safety Program

	10/1–82– 9/30/83	10/1/83– 9/30/84	10/1/84– 9/30/85	10/1/85 9/30/86
Lost time accidents	31	8	14	13
Light duty cases	34	23	17	22
Doctor cases	252	131	108	38

system based on a point concept. Customers are asked to fill out evaluation cards for the various attendants with whom they come into contact. Favorable responses allow employees to accumulate points. Once a given level of points has been reached, individuals are able to use them to purchase gifts and prizes such as small household appliances.

In an effort to reduce absenteeism among production workers, a manufacturing firm[27] devised a system that allowed employees who came to work on time each day to draw a card from a deck. At the end of each week, those who were present all five days had a five-card stud poker hand. The company paid the high hand twenty dollars. During the four months of this experiment, absenteeism decreased at an average rate of 18 percent.

Connecticut General Insurance Company[28] uses positive reinforcement in the form of release time. Employees receive one extra day off for each ten weeks' perfect attendance. As a result, chronic absenteeism and tardiness have been drastically reduced, and employees are very happy with the system.

CRITICISMS OF OB MOD PROGRAMS

In recent years, critics of Organizational Behavior Modification have become increasingly vocal.[29] Some have contended that these programs are manipulative. In using the shaping technique, for example, people are rewarded for making progress toward a goal while undesired behaviors are ignored. Since the manager is deliberately trying to change the employee's behavior and does not tell the employee what is being done, is this not being manipulative and therefore unethical? Behaviorists have countered that every action a manager takes affects employee behavior in some way. Even taking no action at all has effects. Since there is no way to avoid affecting the subordinate's behavior, it is better to operate systematically. In addition, they argue that making employees aware of the consequences provides them with an opportunity to make explicit choices between well-defined alternatives.

OB Mod has also been criticized for being mechanical, dictatorial, and, above all, dehumanizing. Yet, proponents maintain that behavior modification simply recognizes that people's behavior is subject to rational control.

A third common criticism is that positive reinforcement is just another way of describing bribery. If every time somebody improves their performance you give them a reward, such as money or praise, is that not bribery? Shouldn't people learn to perform effectively just for the enjoyment work itself brings rather than for what they can get out of it? Behaviorists believe that behavior modification is not bribery any more than any other motivational strategy and, if it works, use it.

The important point here is that before an organization or a manager implements a program the controversy surrounding OB Mod must be addressed. Every firm must judge for itself the legitimacy of the arguments, both pro and con, and then determine whether or not it makes sense to continue.

SUMMARY

In the workplace, managers intuitively use reinforcement all the time. Yet their efforts often produce limited results because the methods are applied improperly, inconsistently, or inefficiently. All too often, employees are given rewards that are not directly related to specific behaviors, and even when the link is clear, long delays between behaviors and consequences can upset the process. A manager starts out trying to motivate employees but ends up doing just the opposite because of a failure to really understand reinforcement.

When reinforcement concepts are applied to work, the term *Organizational Behavior Modification* (OB Mod) is normally used. The underlying assumption of OB Mod is that if we can manipulate the consequences we stand a good chance of affecting someone's behavior.

The application of OB Mod involves four specific steps. The first is called pinpointing and requires identification of performance-related behavioral events. When we pinpoint a behavior we define it in such a way that anyone listening to a description could, in effect, see the behavior, count it, and describe the situation in which the behavior occurred. Step 2 is the measurement of the pinpointed behavior using simple frequency counts. These counts can be graphed over time to provide a typology of the behavior. The measurement process indicates the severity of the problem, lets employees know exactly where they stand in relation to company standards, and provides a baseline against which future behavior can be judged. Step 3 involves changing the behavior by arranging consequences or reinforcers. Any behavior can result in four different consequences: positive reinforcement, negative reinforcement, extinction, and punishment. The actual process that one often uses in implementing positive reinforcement is called shaping. Here, behavior is gradually changed by systematically reinforcing successive approximations of the desired pin-pointed behavior. Once the individual achieves the appropriate level of performance, various reinforcement schedules can be applied in order to maintain the behavior. The schedules can either be continuous or inter-mittent. The latter can be further subdivided into fixed ratio, variable ratio, fixed interval, and variable interval. Ultimately, any OB Mod pro-gram requires that managers evaluate performance in order to determine whether or not it has really improved. In most cases, this involves a contin-uation of the counting and recording initiated earlier.

Even though there is considerable controversy about behavior modifi-cation as applied in organizations, many firms have used it successfully when dealing with problems such as quantity and quality of work, absen-teeism, turnover, tardiness, and safety. The experiences of several organi-zations, including Emery Air Freight, a fast food franchise, and a midwestern paper mill, have been discussed in some detail. In these three instances, the primary forms of reinforcement were praise and money. Other firms, however, have used prizes or free time contingencies.

Finally, the chapter has looked briefly at several of the more common criticisms of OB Mod. These include the charge that programs are ma-nipulative and unethical, dehumanizing, or just another way of describ-ing bribery. Every firm must judge for itself the legitimacy of the arguments, both pro and con, and then determine whether or not OB Mod should be implemented.

NOTES

1. F. Carpenter, *The Skinner Primer* (New York: Free Press, 1974), p. 12.

2. Ibid., p. 5.

3. Ibid., p. 17.

4. "Hot 100," *Time*, July 4, 1983, p. 6.

5. C. Hamner and E. R. Hamner, "Behavior Modification on the Bottom Line," *Organizational Dynamics* 4 (Spring 1976), pp. 3–21.

6. W. E. Hill, *Learning: A Survey of Psychological Interpretations* (Scranton, Pa.: Chandler Publishing Co., 1971).

7. Ibid.

8. S. B. Parry and R. Reich, "An Uneasy Look at Behavior Modeling," *Training and Development Journal*, March 1984, pp. 57–62.

9. P. L. Brown and R. J. Presbie, *Behavior Modification in Business, Industry and Government* (New Paltz, N.Y.: Behavior Improvement Associates, 1978). See also F. Luthans and M. Martinko, "Organizational Behavior Modification: A Way to Bridge the Gap Between Academic Research and Real World Application," *Journal of Organizational Behavior Management* 3, no. 3 (1982), pp. 33–58.

10. Brown and Presbie, *Behavior Modification*.

11. Luthans and Martinko, "Organizational Behavior Modification."

12. Brown and Presbie, *Behavior Modification*.

13. Ibid.

14. F. Luthans and R. Kreitner, *Organizational Behavior Modification* (Glenview, Ill.: Scott, Foresman and Co., 1985).

15. F. Luthans, *Organizational Behavior* (New York: McGraw-Hill, 1985). See also J. L. Gray and F. A. Starke, *Organizational Behavior* (Columbus, Ohio: Charles E. Merrill, 1984).

16. E. Kazadin, *Behavior Modification in Applied Settings* (Homewood, Ill.: Dorsey Press, 1975).

17. Luthans and Kreitner, *Organizational Behavior Modification*.

18. L. M. Miller, *Behavior Management* (New York: John Wiley & Sons, 1978).

19. Ibid.

20. Ibid. See also S. Robbins, *Organizational Behavior* (Englewood Cliffs, N.J.: Prentice-Hall, 1983).

21. Miller, *Behavior Management*.

22. Brown and Presbie, *Behavior Modification*.

23. K. O'Hara, C. M. Johnson, and T. A. Beehr, "Organizational Behavior Management in the Private Sector: A Review of Empirical Research and Recommendations for Further Investigation," *Academy of Management Review* 10, no. 4 (1985), pp. 848–64.

24. R. B. McAfee and W. W. Poffenberger, *Productivity Strategies* (Englewood Cliffs, N.J.: Prentice-Hall, 1982).

25. J. Komaki, M. Blood, and D. Holder, "Fostering Friendliness in a Fast Food Franchise," *Journal of Organizational Behavior Management* 2, no. 3 (Summer 1980), pp. 751–64.

26. R. B. McAfee, "The Effects of Contingent Monetary Rewards and Feedback on Employee Safety," unpublished research paper, 1986.

27. E. Pedalino and V. U. Gamboa, "Behavior Modification and Absenteeism: Intervention in One Industrial Setting," *Journal of Applied Psychology* 59 (1974), pp. 694–98.

28. Hamner and Hamner, "Behavior Modification."

29. McAfee and Poffenberger, *Productivity Strategies*.

3

Using Punishment and Discipline

> If a fellow is just a slacker, the foreman should straighten the man out for the sake of everybody. . . . You don't like to do your best while the other guy goofs off, loafs—it burns you.[1]

> Almost every experienced supervisor has been faced with the necessity of dealing with a marginal employee at some time during his or her career. A supervisor's failure to identify and deal with marginal employees may result in not only lowered performance on the part of these employees but also diminished motivation and effectiveness of the entire work group.[2]

> Positive discipline involves the creation of attitudes and of an organizational climate that encourages employees to willingly conform to established rules and regulations—the positive approach is rehabilitative and emphasizes self-control rather than punishment.[3]

An analysis of performance difficulties among 48,000 Union Carbide employees indicated that a new disciplinary system was necessary. As a result, the company scrapped its progressive discipline system and replaced it with a new one called "Positive Discipline." This system stresses coaching and counseling and involves three formal levels of disciplinary action—an oral reminder, a written reminder, and a one-day paid decision-making leave.

Data generated from employee attitude surveys conducted before and after Positive Discipline was implemented showed improvement in several key areas. Employee perceptions of the quality of their relationship with their immediate or near-immediate supervisors improved; general morale increased, the quality of communication improved. In addition, the company found that absenteeism declined an average of 5.5 percent in five plants as a result of the new system. In one plant alone, grievances declined from thirty-six during the year prior to implementation to eight for the following year, saving the company $11,000 in grievance processing.[4]

Discipline and punishment is another approach organizations often use to change employee behavior and increase productivity. Indeed, every organization and manager uses penalties or the threat of penalties in some form. These penalties can range from "chewing out" employees, cross glances, finger pointing, and rebukes to suspensions and termination. They can be oral or spelled out in writing.

Punishment is rather controversial. Debates often surface about whether to discipline an employee and what the penalty should be. Unlike the use of rewards, penalties are often associated with problems, disagreements, and tensions. In this chapter, we will examine the arguments for and against the use of punishment, and consider how punishment should be administered in order to improve behavior. Finally, both the organization's and the manager's roles in the disciplinary process will be discussed.

PUNISHMENT: SHOULD A MANAGER USE IT?

"Punishment" is typically thought of an aversive event that follows an employee's behavior and decreases the frequency of that behavior. For example, an employee who is tardy (behavior) might be given a written reprimand (punishment). Assuming that the employee dislikes reprimands, the frequency of tardiness should decrease. A second form of punishment occurs when a manager withdraws something valued by the employee as a result of that person's behavior. For example, a manager may withhold a raise because the employee was excessively tardy.

In comparison, "discipline" has three basic meanings: (1) training that molds, strengthens, improves, or corrects; (2) control gained by enforced obedience; and (3) punishment for violations of rules, standards, and direct orders.[5] In other words, discipline has both a training and education aspect plus an enforcement and punishment side. The former is preventive and concentrates on gaining voluntary support for necessary rules and regulations while the latter is corrective and aims at eliminating the unwanted behavior in the future.

Given these definitions, should managers and organizations use punishment and take corrective disciplinary action against employees? Many people have argued that punishment should be avoided as a means of influencing behavior. They contend that discipline can cause anxiety in the person disciplined and, for that matter, in the person delivering the discipline. The former's anxiety can result in hostility toward the person administering the discipline (the supervisor), which in turn can lead to attempts to "get even" later (e.g., sabotage or restricting output). In addition, the hostility may cause employees to use their creative abilities to figure out ways to break the rules without incurring discipline.

The fear associated with discipline/punishment may lead the employee to avoid the manager, making it more difficult for the manager to monitor that person's job performance and possibly improve it. Fear of being punished may also encourage employees to hide any errors they make. Factory workers might put a small damaged tool into their lunch box or throw it into the trash rather than report the damage to management. Expensive monitoring and surveillance may be necessary in such cases.

Critics also contend that the fear of punishment can cause rigidity in behavior. Employees may become hesitant to do anything without first obtaining the supervisor's approval. In some cases this may be beneficial to an organization, but it can also result in reduced initiative and creativity among employees.

Finally, some critics argue that punishment never really eliminates undesirable behavior but only temporarily suppresses it. These behaviors will recur once the threat of punishment is removed or will reappear in different situations, perhaps in a somewhat modified form.

While critics cite many arguments against the use of punishment, others have countered that it has some important advantages. Unlike some other motivational strategies, the use of penalties has the potential for changing an employee's behavior quickly. When employees engage in totally unacceptable behaviors such as violating important safety rules, damaging company property, or fighting, quick behavioral change is often necessary. Disciplinary action may be the only potentially effective strategy in these situations.[6]

In addition to being relatively quick, penalties are often inexpensive. It costs little or nothing to give an employee an oral or written warning. Even suspensions are usually quite inexpensive, since employees are typically not paid for the period. It is important to add that setting up a disciplinary system and communicating it to all employees does involve some initial expense. However, even this one-time cost is usually not very high.[7]

Advocates of the use of punishment argue that it is a natural part of our life.[8] We learn not to run on ice, drive too fast around curves, or wear light clothing in the winter, all because nature punishes us. Furthermore, nature changes our behavior without any long-term emotional damage or neuroses. Advocates of punishment conclude that punishment is a natural occurrence and need not result in adverse consequences for either the employee or the organization.

Finally, some suggest that punishment is the only feasible strategy one can use to change behaviors that are themselves rewarding. For example, if an employee goes to sleep on the night shift, sleeping is its own reinforcer. To change the behavior, some consequence must be used to offset the reward sleeping provides. Advocates contend that punishment is the only feasible and equitable consequence in these situations.

It is important that managers be aware of the potential disadvantages of using punishment. By the same token, punishment or the threat of it, seems to be the only feasible, equitable, or economically justifiable approach a manager can use in some situations. The critical question is not whether punishment should be used, but when and how it should be implemented.

HOW SHOULD PUNISHMENT BE ADMINISTERED?

The "hot stove" rules of discipline are one of the most useful analogies we have encountered.[9] A stove is one of the most cherished and useful possessions of any family. It is a source of hot apple pie, turkey at Thanksgiving, and chocolate cake. Its heat helps remove the chill on a frosty November morning. There is one simple rule: "Don't touch." The stove is a powerful teacher because it takes only one touch to teach us that when it is hot it can hurt us. It causes us to change our behavior immediately and permanently. The stove is a consistent teacher, too. It will deliver its lesson to anybody at any time. It does not discriminate.

The stove accomplishes all of this without causing any damaging emotional reactions. We do not even harbor any resentment or hatred toward the stove even though it punished us. Why is it that the stove can change our behavior so effectively and yet not create any resentment, anger, or hostility? Contained in the answer to this question are the principles of an effective disciplinary policy and of the effective use of penalties.

Punish Immediately

The effectiveness of punishment is enhanced when the manager punishes an employee as soon as possible after the undesired behavior occurs. If employees are to change their behavior they must clearly associate the disciplinary stimulus with the inappropriate behavior. The longer the time between the unacceptable behavior and its consequences, the less likely the employee will associate the two.[10]

There is another important reason why discipline should be immediate. Since employees typically work in groups, the behavior of one employee is observed by many others. If one person engages in an inappropriate behavior (e.g., fails to wear safety glasses, smokes in unauthorized places, arrives at work late), and the manager appears to be taking no action, other employees may conclude that the behavior is acceptable or that the organization is not consistently enforcing its rules. In addition, the other employees may respond by "testing the limits" of the rules.

Another risk associated with the use of delayed discipline is that rule violators may continue their inappropriate behavior leading to dysfunctional consequences for the organization, the employee, or both.

For example, construction workers who work without hard hats once and are not disciplined immediately may continue to do so and ultimately suffer an injury. Or, an employee who is not disciplined immediately for stealing company property may continue to steal until some action is taken.

Penalize Consistently

It is recommended that managers administer penalties consistently. In other words, the penalty given today for a specific offense should be the same as the one given tomorrow, next week, next month, or next year (assuming the rules have not changed). In addition, all employees should be disciplined equally. Prejudice, bias, and favoritism should not enter into the process.

One issue that frequently surfaces is whether or not extenuating circumstances should be taken into account. For example, suppose two workers are both seen without hard hats in a restricted area, and one has thirty years' seniority, a spotless record, and is considered one of the best employees in the company. The second worker is new and is viewed as marginal at best. If the company has a policy that workers who fail to wear hard hats in designated areas will be suspended for three days, should both employees receive equal penalties? Should the superior worker be given special consideration because of the work record, and so on?

One could argue that if an organization considers any extenuating circumstances when administering penalties, it contradicts the idea of consistency. On the other hand, one might say that if an organization always considers these factors when disciplining employees and does so uniformly at all times and for all people, it would not necessarily be violating the consistency principle. Given a set of extenuating circumstances, the organization could then be potentially consistent.

At least one study has suggested that managers should be consistent in yet another way: they should administer those penalties prescribed by the organization's disciplinary policy. In that study the researcher analyzed the personnel records of 150 employees: fifty employees had been penalized according to the policy and the penalty remained a permanent part of their record; fifty had been penalized but in a manner not consistent with the normal progression and/or subsequently had the penalty removed from their record; and fifty had broken the organizational rule regarding absenteeism but had not received any penalty. The investigator found that absenteeism over the subsequent twenty-month period was lowest for the group of employees who had been penalized in accordance with company policy.[11]

Penalize Actions, Not Personality

Punishment is more effective if it is dispensed in an impersonal manner where the focus is on the act and not on the employee.[12] This does not mean that it must be done in writing, nor does it imply that a manager should attempt to emulate a robot and not express any personal feelings when disciplining the employee. What "impersonal" means is that a manager should discipline workers in private whenever possible and focus on the employee's behavior and the consequences of that behavior, rather than on his or her personality. When an employee engages in an inappropriate action, a manager may be tempted to get angry and say something like, "You are a complete idiot for doing that!" or "You are totally irresponsible." While such statements may seem warranted at that moment, generalizations about someone's entire personality can cause that person to become angry and defensive, a condition that is not conducive to either rational understanding or effecting behavioral change. Discussions of a specific behavior are considerably less threatening and are more likely to provide a clear picture of the supervisor's expectations. Two examples will illustrate.

Poor: What is the matter with you? Don't you know that those reports have to be done correctly the first time?

Better: When you don't complete your sales reports accurately, shipments of your orders are delayed. This costs us money, and it costs you money.

Poor: You are totally irresponsible. It's absurd that you are late so often. Shape up!

Better: I see that you're late again. When this happens it really delays others from completing their work and slows customer service.

Provide a Rationale

Punishment is more effective if managers provide a clear, unambiguous reason for it, tell what the employee can do to avoid further penalties, and explain what the consequence will be if the employee continues to behave inappropriately.[13] Administering discipline immediately, consistently, and impersonally all have some informational value, but the information they provide is often not clear.

Some large organizations now require managers to provide this information in writing. These organizations often stress the importance of making sure employees know the consequences of further deviant behavior.

Establish Supportive Relationships

Should a manager administering punishment have a relatively close and warm relationship with the employee being punished, or should the relationship be cold and distant? Based on the available evidence it is clear that penalties are most effective when delivered within the context of a warm and friendly relationship between the supervisor and subordinate.[14] The reason is that subordinates are more apt to accept a penalty and change their behavior if the supervisor has helped them develop their skills and abilities and has often rewarded and been supportive of them.

In some organizations, managers and employees have developed tremendous animosity over the years. Ideally, managers in these situations would attempt to gradually improve the relationships. In the interim, however, they still need to administer penalties in a less than ideal atmosphere and prepare themselves for one or more negative side effects of discipline.

THE ORGANIZATION'S ROLE IN THE DISCIPLINARY PROCESS

The organization's primary role in the disciplinary process involves establishing rules, communicating them to employees, and developing a penalty system for enforcing them. Normally, rules are developed by the human resource function in cooperation with operating managers and top management. However, in some organizations, lower-level employees may be consulted and encouraged to participate in the process. While rules often focus on a wide variety of employee behavior, the most frequent ones cover insubordination, dishonesty and stealing, substance abuse, absenteeism and tardiness, assault and fighting, gambling, damaging and misusing company property, sleeping and loafing, and safety. An example of one organization's work rules is shown in Exhibit 3–1. Keep in mind that while some rules are common to most organizations, many companies have ones that are unique.

Establishing rules is one thing, but equally important is communicating them to employees. Typically this is achieved via orientation sessions, employee handbooks, posted lists, or union contracts. Managers also communicate rules through their own words and actions.[15] For example, when a company states that employees are to wear hard hats at the construction site but managers fail to do so, employees may conclude that the company is not serious about the rule. If the written company rule states, "No gambling is permitted on company property," but the manager looks the other way when employees gamble during their lunch hour, the employees may conclude that the rule does not apply.

Arbitrators have made two recommendations that are particularly important. First, they suggest that all rules should be communicated to employees before enforcing them. Many organizations require employees to sign a form stating that they have read the company's rules, understand

Exhibit 3-1
Example of Work Rules from a Large Hotel

1. When entering or leaving the hotel, please use the employee's entrance.
2. Do not frequent the hotel on your day off or remain when not on duty.
3. Please report promptly and when finished with your work, leave immediately. Promptness is very important. If you know you are late, you must notify your department head as to the reason.
4. If you are unable to report for work, notify your supervisor or department head as far in advance as possible. Do not just tell a co-worker. Repeated tardiness or absenteeism will result in termination.
5. It is the company's right to examine all packages carried into or out of the hotel. Please leave all packages home. A pass may be obtained by your department head when absolutely necessary.
6. You must report any injury sustained while on duty, no matter how small. Notify your supervisor immediately.
7. Personal matters (pay, personal business, etc.) or hotel business should not be discussed in guest areas. Any arguments or loud discussions about your work in public areas or where guests might hear are not tolerated. Violations may result in termination.
8. No lost and found articles may be retained. Turn them in immediately to your department head.
9. Employees must confine their presence to their work station. It is not permissible to roam the hotel. Always use the service elevators.
10. Working time is for work.
11. The hotel is your place of business; do not use it as a mailing address. Do not receive personal phone calls unless it is an emergency. Use the pay phones for outgoing personal calls.
12. Do not use public facilities unless authorized by management.
13. Uniforms must be kept clean and neat at all times. Treat them as you would your own suits and dresses.
14. Smoking, eating, etc., are prohibited in any guest or public area.

Give special attention to the following rules. Failure to comply can be cause for termination.

1. Possessing or using illegal drugs, narcotics, or alcoholic beverages while on hotel property or reporting for work under the influence of the same.
2. Taking hotel, guest, or co-worker property.
3. Willfully defacing hotel, guest, or co-worker property.

Exhibit 3–1 *(continued)*

4. Inciting or participating in illegal gambling, fighting;
   using profane or abusive language or participating in
   malicious gossip.
5. Falsifying employment or time records.
6. Sleeping while on duty.
7. Carrying weapons, explosives, or the like.
8. Unauthorized personal use of hotel equipment or material.
9. Improper attire on duty.
10. Violating or neglecting any safety rules.
11. Failure to notify the company immediately of any accident
    occurring on hotel property.

Certain rules and regulations may change. We will keep you
informed.

Source: R. B. McAfee and P. J. Champagne, *Organizational Behavior: A Manager's View* (St. Paul, Minn.: West Publishing Co., 1987), p. 191. Reprinted by permission.

them, and will abide by them. Second, they suggest that if managers have been inconsistent in rule enforcement, they must forewarn employees that henceforth rules will be enforced.

In addition to establishing and communicating its disciplinary system, an organization also has the responsibility for developing an enforcement system. The most common is the progressive penalty system. Two other approaches have also been suggested: the "discipline without punishment approach" and the "affirmative discipline approach."

The Progressive Penalty System

The progressive penalty system is based on the premise that employee behavior can be changed through a system of ever-increasing degrees of punishment. The system consists of a series of steps, one or more of which can be eliminated or added. However, most organizations have between three and five steps. Exhibit 3–2 presents an example of a progressive penalty system used by a large construction organization. Typically, if employees violate a rule, they are warned verbally and told that if the infraction occurs again within a specific period, they will receive a more severe penalty. If employees then commit the same or similar violation, they are given a written warning, a copy of which is placed in their personnel file. They are often asked to sign the written warning, which serves as proof that they have been warned. Employees are told that if their misconduct is repeated, they will be disciplined again, but more severely. If employees again transgress, they are suspended without pay and are warned that one more infraction will result in discharge. Finally, after one more rule infraction, employees are terminated.

Exhibit 3-2
Example of a Progressive Disciplinary System from a Large Construction Company

1. PURPOSE--The purpose of this disciplinary policy is to set forth principles and guidelines designed to achieve fair and consistent treatment of employees in disciplinary matters. In all but serious offenses, the organization will follow a progressive disciplinary policy designed to correct behavior or attitudes which are not acceptable in a work environment.

2. TYPES OF OFFENSES--Offenses by employees are of two general classes:

   A. SERIOUS OFFENSES--Serious offenses are offenses which justify a termination or suspension without prior verbal or written warnings or other attempts to correct the conduct of the employee involved. Serious offenses are of the type set forth in paragraph 3 below.

   B. LESS SERIOUS OFFENSES--Less serious offenses are offenses which do not call for termination of an employee for the first offense but for milder forms of discipline aimed at correcting the improper conduct of employees. Less serious offenses are of the type set forth in paragraph four below.

3. SERIOUS OFFENSES--The following offenses are of the type which are considered serious offenses which justify termination for the first offense. The following are for purposes of illustration and are not considered to be all-inclusive; theft or mishandling of monies, deliberate falsification of records, refusal to follow a direct order, use of drugs or intoxicants on company property, immoral conduct, assault, dishonesty, insubordination, and gross negligence.

4. LESS SERIOUS OFFENSES--The following offenses are of the type which are considered less serious offenses. In disciplining employees for less serious offenses, progressive disciplinary procedures set forth in paragraph 5 are to be followed. The following are for purposes of illustration and are not to be considered all-inclusive: absenteeism, leaving the work site without permission, failure to be physically present at work site, failure to notify the supervisor of an absence, tardiness, horseplay, and failure to turn in required reports on time.

5. PROGRESSIVE DISCIPLINARY PROCEDURE--In disciplining an employee for less serious offenses, the following sequence will take place: a) First offense, Verbal warning; b) Second offense, Written warning; c) Third offense, Suspension; d) Fourth offense, Termination.
   No two cases are ever alike and the progressive disciplinary path will vary from case to case. The steps set forth above are a suggested norm.

6. REVIEW PROCEDURE--Any employee who wishes to contest disciplinary action must comply with the following procedure: STEP ONE--The employee first must discuss the matter with the immediate supervisor.

Exhibit 3-2 *(continued)*

STEP TWO--If the matter is not resolved under Step One, the employee may file a written grievance with the immediate supervisor within five (5) working days of the date of the event or the occurrence giving rise to the grievance. Such written grievance shall be on forms provided by the supervisor and shall describe the facts surrounding the grievance and set forth the relief desired. The supervisor shall answer the grievance in writing.

STEP THREE--If the matter is not resolved under Step Two, the employee may, within three (3) working days after receipt of the supervisor's written answer, request that the matter be appealed to the President. The decision of the President will be final and binding on all concerned.

Source: R. B. McAfee and P. J. Champagne, *Organizational Behavior: A Manager's View* (St. Paul, Minn.: West Publishing Co., 1987), p. 193. Reprinted by permission.

Many organizations that use the progressive penalty system such as the one in Exhibit 3-2 differentiate between serious or major offenses and less serious or minor offenses. Serious offenses, such as theft, gross insubordination, assault, fighting, and dishonesty, usually result in termination or suspension on the first offense, thereby skipping the first two steps (oral and written warning). Minor offenses, such as tardiness, horseplay, and leaving the work site without permission usually result in an oral warning on the first transgression. No steps are skipped when further violations occur.

Discipline without Punishment

An alternative to the traditional progressive penalty system is "discipline without punishment." First used at a Douglas fir plywood mill, its most unique feature is the attempt not to use "punishment." The procedure itself consists of sequential steps that managers follow when an employee breaks a rule:

Step 1: The manager offers the worker a casual and friendly reminder on the job that a work rule has been broken.

Step 2: Upon a second rule violation, the manager again corrects the violation, usually on the job and, in addition, calls the employee into the office for a friendly discussion. During the discussion the manager explains the need for the rule and makes sure the worker understands the explanation.

Step 3: In the event of another violation, step 2 is repeated with a few modifications. The manager's boss is also present during the discussion. The employee is told that if the work or work rule is distasteful perhaps he or she should seek another job. The employee is told that vocational counseling is available through the personnel office. The conversation is confirmed in a letter sent to the employee's home.

Step 4: Following the next rule violation within six to eight weeks of step 3, the manager and his or her boss meet again with the employee. The employee is directed to go home for the rest of the day and consider seriously whether to abide by the company rules. The employee is paid for the time at home and is told that another violation will lead to termination.

Step 5: If a further incident occurs within six to eight weeks, the employee is terminated.

If several incidents occur within a short time, the company may skip steps 2 and 3. If criminal behavior or fighting occurs within the plant, the employee is terminated immediately.

How successful has this approach been? After the plan had been in operation for two years, its originator reported that it was very successful. The plan had the full support of the supervisory staff. Eighty-seven letters were sent to a total of sixty-two employees during the two-year period. These letters resulted in eleven voluntary terminations (no discharges), while the remaining fifty-one employees improved their job behavior to a satisfactory level.[16]

Several other companies have successfully used a similar system, including Union Carbide, whose plan was described at the beginning of the chapter. Fraser Mills (British Columbia) Division of Crown-Zellerbach (Canada) implemented the plan, as has a plant of Goodyear Tire and Rubber Company located in Sun Prairie, Wisconsin. G. C. Rawley, Personnel Manager of the Goodyear plant states that

The counseling approach (as opposed to the reprimand approach) permits the employee to maintain his dignity and enables him and his supervisor to maintain a proper working relationship. This in itself increases the odds that the employee will be willing to correct his behavior. The counseling approach is less distasteful to the supervisor than the reprimand approach, so he is more apt to administer discipline in a timely and consistent manner than to put it off.[17]

General Electric's Meter Business Department in Somerworth, New Hampshire, implemented a similar plan in 1981. During the first year 3565 informal counseling sessions were conducted by supervisors (step 1), ninety formal oral reminders were issued (step 2), eleven employees were sent home on a decision-making leave (step 4), and only one was terminated (step 5). During the second year, 3295 counseling sessions were followed by only sixty-five reminders. Seven employees progressed to a decision-making leave and none of these were terminated. In other words, the company found that approximately 98 percent of the employees improved their performance after the initial informal counseling session. They considered the program an "extremely positive experience."[18]

One of the issues that could be raised here is the extent to which this approach really eliminates punishment as a means of changing behavior. How do the parties, particularly the subordinates, view the process? Being reminded of or counseled for an offense in the manager's office, perhaps with the manager's boss present, is hardly a cause for rejoicing. Neither is being sent home on a decision-making leave or being told to consider other employment opportunities.

Affirmative Discipline

A second alternative to the progressive penalty system is the "affirmative discipline" approach. Its underlying philosophy is that traditional penalty systems suffer from an illogical premise, that is, if an organization treats workers progressively worse, they will get progressively better. Further, it argues that the traditional approach is based on the faulty idea that employees must "pay for the crime" but that once they have paid, they are then released from any further responsibilities. In contrast, the affirmative discipline approach holds that when employees are hired, they should be asked to make a commitment or promise to follow company rules. Later, if they break a rule, they are asked to reaffirm this commitment as consideration for continued employment.[19] In effect, this approach asks employees to make a moral or personal promise to abide by rules.

Exhibit 3–3 briefly shows the steps or "events" recommended by the affirmative discipline approach. Perhaps the most unusual feature of this approach is the recommendation it makes in the fifth and sixth steps. It suggests that employees be asked to sign an agreement that any further rule infractions are to be construed as a lack of desire to work for the organization and as a sign that the employee voluntarily resigns. Then, if and when a rule violation occurs, the company accepts the resignation and closes the employee's file by showing that the employee voluntarily quit.

THE MANAGER'S ROLE IN THE
DISCIPLINARY PROCESS

While organizations have the responsibility for developing, administering, and communicating rules and the penalty system, managers are responsible for detecting violations and administering appropriate discipline. How the manager handles these responsibilities is critical to the success of an organization's disciplinary system. One of the easiest ways of conceptualizing the manager's functions is to think of it as the five-step process shown in Exhibit 3–4.

Exhibit 3–3
Steps in the Affirmative Discipline Approach

1. Initial Hire—Employee is given company rules and signs a statement of assent and commitment to follow them.

2. Completion of Probation—Employee is asked to sign a second statement of assent and commitment to abide by company rules.

3. First Decisional Conference—When an employee violates a minor rule, the supervisor asks the employee if he or she understands the rule and the commitment made earlier to follow it. The employee is asked to reaffirm his or her commitment to follow the rule in the future. The details of the conference are confirmed to the employee in writing.

4. Second Decisional Conference—If the employee violates any of the firm's minor rules a second time within a specified period of time, the employee is again counseled as in Step 3. In addition the employee is required to reaffirm his or her commitment to follow rules on a special reaffirmation statement.

5. Final Decisional Conference—If the employee violates a minor rule for the third time, the supervisor asks, "Do you want to continue your employment with the company?" If the employee says, "yes," he or she is asked to sign a statement which states that he or she did violate the rule, that he or she wishes to remain employed, and that he or she promises to follow the rules in the future. In addition, the employee agrees that if he or she violates a rule again, the company should consider the action as a voluntary termination.

6. Voluntary Resignation—If the employee violates yet another rule, the company notifies him or her that in accordance with the previous agreement, the employee has voluntarily quit by virtue of the violative act. The employee's record is closed as a voluntary resignation.

Source: J. R. Redeker, *Discipline: Policies and Procedures* (Washington, D.C.: Bureau of National Affairs, 1983). Reprinted by permission.

Determining If a Rule Violation Occurred

At first glance, it would seem quite easy to determine whether an employee has broken a company rule. One need only compare the employee's behavior with the company's rules. If, for example, there is "No Smoking in the Elevator" and the manager sees an employee doing this, clearly a violation has occurred. Unfortunately, most cases are not this clear-cut. Suppose that a manager sees employees resting against the desk with their eyes closed. Are they breaking the company's "No Sleeping on the Job" rule?

Exhibit 3–4
The Supervisor's Role in the Disciplinary Process

```
1. Determine if a rule violation occurred
2. Determine if sufficient proof of a rule violation exists
3. Determine appropriate corrective action
4. Take corrective action
5. Document action taken and inform others
```

Source: R. B. McAfee and P. J. Champagne, *Organizational Behavior: A Manager's View* (St. Paul, Minn.: West Publishing Co., 1987), p. 197. Reprinted by permission.

Maybe they are meditating, engaged in deep thought, or praying. In addition, an employee may have fallen asleep because of medication prescribed by a doctor. If this is the case, did a rule violation really occur?

The point is that it is not always easy to compare rules with actual behavior. One step a manager can take is to completely understand the company rules. Another is to rely on witnesses for information. For example, if a fight occurs that the manager does not see, the manager could conduct an investigation into the facts of the case. This often entails interviewing witnesses and obtaining statements and other supporting documentation. The accused workers could also be questioned and allowed to give their interpretation of the events.

Determining If Sufficient Proof of Rule Infraction Exists

It is one thing to perceive that a rule violation has occurred; it is quite another to prove it. A manager may feel confident that an employee has broken a rule but may not have sufficient proof. In disciplinary situations, the employee is considered innocent until proven guilty and the burden of proof rests on the manager.

How much proof does one need? There is no clear answer to this question. Some arbitrators suggest that the severity and nature of the offense are important considerations. There is a difference between stealing or immoral conduct and being five minutes late to work. In addition, the likely penalty is also important, and the proof a manager needs is directly proportional to the penalty. Finally, managers may want to consider whether the disciplinary action will be appealed and what standards are likely to be used by the ultimate "judges" (e.g., other managers, personnel specialists, Equal Employment Opportunity Commission officials, company lawyers).

Determining Appropriate Corrective Action

Assuming there is sufficient proof of a rule violation, the next step is to decide on the appropriate disciplinary action. In most large organizations, the penalty is spelled out in the employee handbook, union contract, or other document, and the manager is expected to follow this. The complicating factor is that the prescribed penalty may be inconsistent with prior practice. When this occurs, the manager might check with someone higher up about the appropriate course of action.

In some organizations, particularly small ones, managers have considerable leeway in determining the appropriate penalty or action, and they tend to follow past precedents. But suppose none exist; what should a manager do? Some firms suggest that the manager determine the penalty by considering some or all of the following:

1. The seriousness of the offense
2. The employee's work record
3. The employee's past disciplinary record
4. The employee's length of service
5. Any mitigating or aggravating circumstances
6. What other organizations do

The manager needs to select a penalty that is just sufficient to change the employee's behavior in the desired direction. Sometimes a minimal penalty, such as a verbal rebuke, may be all that is necessary. At other times, a suspension or other severe penalty may be required. Remember, penalties should not be used to "get even" with an employee, to "set an example," or to "show the employee who is the boss."[20]

Taking Disciplinary Action

Just as organizations typically prescribe penalties, they also spell out the steps a manager should take when administering discipline. These will vary depending on each company's disciplinary philosophy, the system used, and the type of penalty to be given (e.g., oral warning, written warning, suspension, or discharge).

In spite of the fact that most companies have prescribed procedures, managers usually have considerable freedom in carrying out the steps. A wise manager would probably follow the recommendations suggested by the "hot stove" rules described earlier: (1) punish immediately; (2) be consistent in administering punishment; (3) penalize actions, not personality; (4) provide rationale for the punishment; and (5) establish close relationships with employees.

Documenting Disciplinary Action Taken

The final issue is to document the action taken and inform others in the organization. Any time a firm takes disciplinary action, it must consider the possibility of an Equal Employment Opportunity complaint. For example, a midwestern manufacturing company found itself in federal district court defending itself in a suit brought by a fifty-six-year-old formerly employed lab technician who claimed he had been discharged because of age. The company asserted that the employee had never been a particularly satisfactory worker, that his attitude and attendance record had been far from acceptable, and that he had received oral warnings from his superiors on several occasions. Finally, in the wake of a slow-down in business, the firm decided to terminate his employment.

The lab technician, however, claimed that his work had been acceptable, that his attitude was not negative, and that his superior had never indicated any dissatisfaction with his performance. In addition, the employee argued that he had received regular pay increases (the company claimed these had been cost of living and not merit). Thus, he maintained that his record could not have been bad enough to warrant dismissal.

The court, after hearing other arguments, ruled in favor of the employee and ordered the company to reinstate him to his former job and pay back wages and court costs. The reason for the ruling was simply that the company had not offered to the court's satisfaction written documentation that the employee's performance was indeed substandard. The records of the department claiming poor attendance by the employee were incomplete and erratically kept. Further, there was nothing in the files to confirm that the employee had been told of management's dissatisfaction with his work.[21]

The question raised by this example is how much documentation is enough. One useful rule of thumb is to assume that another manager at a similar level in the firm should be able to come to the same conclusions or at least see clearly why the decision was made.[22] This is not to say that every detail of an individual's work needs to be recorded. Rather, the manager should keep accurate records of those elements that significantly contribute to or hamper the work effort. In addition, this information, both positive and negative, should be communicated to the employee either orally or in writing.[23]

When documenting performance, vague statements such as, "Harry did a poor job on his last assignment," should be avoided. Instead, there should be specific items that show why his performance was poor and what he might have done to improve it.

SUMMARY

This chapter has examined the use of punishment and discipline as ways of increasing employee effectiveness. Over the years, a controversy has developed about their use. Some have argued that punishment should be avoided because it causes dysfunctional consequences for both the employee and the supervisor. Advocates have countered that punishment is the only feasible and financially justifiable approach a manager can use in some situations. The important question for the manager is not whether punishment should be used but when and how it should be implemented.

The "hot stove" rules make several recommendations about how punishment should be administered. They suggest that action should be taken as soon as possible after an undesired behavior occurs and that the manager should focus on what the employee did rather than personality. Penalties should also be administered consistently over time, and prejudice, bias, and favoritism should not enter into the process. In addition, punishment may be more effective if managers provide a clearly understood rationale, tell the employee what can be done to avoid future penalties, and explain the consequences that will follow if the behavior does not improve. Finally, penalties are more effective if delivered in the context of a warm and friendly relationship between the superior and subordinate.

If a company is to have a successful disciplinary and penalty system, both the organization and the manager have important roles to play. In practice, companies assume the responsibility of establishing rules, communicating them to employees, and developing a penalty system for enforcing them. By far the most common disciplinary system used by organizations is the progressive penalty system. This approach typically involves four progressively punitive steps designed to change the employee's behavior: oral reprimand or warning, written warning, suspension, and discharge. An organization can also use a system called "discipline without punishment" which attempts to minimize the use of punishment and takes a counseling approach. In addition, companies can use "affirmative discipline." This, too, attempts to reduce the use of punishment but also stresses the importance of gaining employee commitment by requiring employees to sign an agreement in which they promise to follow the rules.

The manager's role in the disciplinary process is distinct from that of the organization, yet the two do overlap and support each other. Managers have the responsibility for implementing the organization's disciplinary system. This requires that they do several things: they must compare their organization's rules with employee behavior to determine if a rule has been broken; they must determine if they have sufficient proof that the employee did indeed break the rule; they must decide what corrective action should be taken and then take it; and they must document whatever action is taken. To the extent that all managers perform these steps effectively, the disciplinary system will be effective and there is a very good chance that employee behavior on the job can be significantly improved.

NOTES

1. L. Sayles and G. Strauss, *Managing Human Resources* (Englewood Cliffs, N.J.: Prentice-Hall, 1977), p. 115.

2. C. A. O'Reilly, III and B. A. Weitz, "Managing Marginal Employees: The Use of Warnings and Dismissals," in R. M. Steers and L. W. Porter, eds., *Motivation and Work Behavior* (New York: McGraw-Hill, 1987), p. 446.

3. L. V. Imundo, *Employee Discipline: How to Do It Right* (Belmont, Calif.: Wadsworth Publishing Co., 1985), p. 13.

4. W. R. Hutchison, "Positive Discipline," in the *Proceedings of 1986 Annual National Conference*, Council on Employee Rights and Responsibilities, pp. 205–8.

5. D. Caruth, B. Middlebrook, and T. A. Pressley, "This Matter of Discipline," *Supervisory Management*, April 1983, pp. 24–31.

6. R. B. McAfee and W. Poffenberger, *Productivity Strategies: Enhancing Employee Job Performance* (Englewood Cliffs, N.J.: Prentice-Hall, 1982).

7. Ibid.

8. A. Bandura, *Principles of Behavior Modification* (New York: Holt, Rinehart and Winston, 1969).

9. D. McGregor, "Hot Stove Rules of Discipline," in G. Strauss and L. Sayles, eds., *Personnel: The Human Problems of Management* (Englewood Cliffs, N.J.: Prentice-Hall, 1967).

10. R. D. Arvey and J. M. Ivancevich, "Punishment in Organizations: A Review, Propositions, and Research Suggestions," *Academy of Management Review* 5, no. 1 (1980), pp. 123–32.

11. A. L. Gary, "Industrial Absenteeism: An Evaluation of Three Methods of Treatment," *Personnel Journal*, May 1971, pp. 352–53.

12. Arvey and Ivancevich, "Punishment in Organizations."

13. Ibid.

14. Ibid.

15. R. B. McAfee and B. R. Ricks, "Communicating Employee Rights and Responsibilities: The Influence of Role Modeling," in Chimezie A. B. Osigweh, ed., *Communicating Employee Responsibilities and Rights: A Modern Management Mandate* (Westport, Conn.: Quorum Books, Greenwood Press, 1986).

16. J. Huberman, "From the Thoughtful Businessman," *Harvard Business Review* 43 (1965), pp. 182–86. See also J. Huberman, "Discipline without Punishment," *Harvard Business Review* 42 (1965), pp. 62–68.

17. J. Huberman, "Discipline without Punishment Lives," *Harvard Business Review* 53 (1975), pp. 6–8.

18. A. W. Bryant, "Replacing Punitive Discipline with a Positive Approach," *Personnel Administrator*, February 1984, pp. 79–87.

19. J. R. Redeker, *Discipline: Policies and Procedures* (Washington, D.C.: Bureau of National Affairs, 1983), chap. 3.

20. McAfee and Poffenberger, *Productivity Strategies*.

21. S. Stanton, "The Discharged Employee and the EEO Laws," *Personnel Journal*, March 1976, pp. 128–33.

22. M. Smith, "Documenting Employee Performance," *Supervisory Management*, September 1979, pp. 30–37.

23. Ibid.

4

Rewarding High Performance

> Numerous examples exist of reward systems that are fouled up in that behaviors which are rewarded are those which the rewarder is trying to discourage, while the behavior he desires is not being rewarded at all.[1]

> If employees believe that a given behavior will result in a desired outcome (a pay increase), they will be motivated to work harder.[2]

> Failure to tie pay to performance in many companies would mean that pay is not motivating job performance. In order for pay to motivate performance, it must appear to be related to performance; and employees are not likely to believe that pay is related to performance if it actually is not.[3]

Sterling Optical Company, a retail optical company based in Woodbury, New York, has developed an incentive program for its two thousand employees located in more than two hundred locations.[4] The program consists of two parts. First, employees receive awards when the branch attains its sales targets. These awards are designed to encourage employees to help the branch achieve its sales goals for each quarter and the year. In addition, the company distributes cash awards to each employee for the branch's sales of specific products determined each quarter. The second part of Sterling's incentive program is to give employees awards for outstanding service to the branch and to patients. Approximately forty employees receive these awards annually. For each district there is an employee of the quarter, doctor of the quarter, and support employee of the quarter, as well as a manager of the quarter for each region. Savings bonds, certificates, and plaques are given as awards. The program reportedly costs Sterling $600,000 in cash awards each year and $9000 in trophies, plaques, certificates, and printed materials.[5]

In this example we see how one organization has attempted to increase employee productivity by providing a variety of extrinsic rewards in exchange for high performance. Employees whose job performance was relatively high received greater rewards than those whose productivity was low.

This chapter will examine how various rewards can be used to motivate employees. We begin by identifying the rationale behind rewarding exemplary job performance. Then we will describe examples of organizations which have used this approach. Throughout the chapter we will point out potential problems with the use of this strategy and guidelines for using it effectively.

WHY REWARDS SHOULD BE BASED ON JOB PERFORMANCE

Managers are often told that they should reward employees based on their job performance and that high performers deserve larger rewards than poor performers. But why? The answer to this question rests in a body of research known as "expectancy theory," which contends that employees make conscious decisions about how hard they will work. If employees believe they can maximize desirable rewards by working hard, they will do so. When working slowly has the greatest payoff, people will do just that. The desirability of the rewards is also an important part of the theory. Expectancy theory assumes that because employees have different needs and values, what motivates one person may not have the same effect on another. Thus, each person uniquely determines to what extent each reward (or punishment) is desirable. Still, if rewards can be clearly tied to performance, people's behavior should improve.

More specifically, expectancy theory argues that an employee's productivity ultimately depends on the answers to three questions (see Exhibit 4–1):

1. If I try to reach high (or low) productivity levels, will I succeed? (Can I do it?)
2. If I succeed (or fail) what will the rewards and penalties be? (What will I get?)
3. How much do I want the rewards and wish to avoid the penalties I could receive? (How much do I want what I could get?)

Can I Do It?

Consider the following situation. If someone offered to pay you $1.00 to kick a ninety-five-yard field goal, would you try to do it? Or if someone offered to give you $10 for running a three-minute mile, would you attempt it? Would it matter if the amount was raised to $1000 or even $1,000,000? The point is that if you know you cannot reach a goal regardless of how

Exhibit 4–1
Major Components in the Expectancy Model

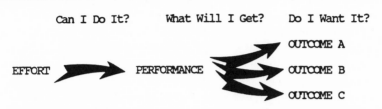

Can I Do It?   What Will I Get?   Do I Want It?

EFFORT ➤ PERFORMANCE ➤ OUTCOME A / OUTCOME B / OUTCOME C

Source: R. B. McAfee and P. J. Champagne, *Organizational Behavior: A Manager's View* (St. Paul, Minn.: West Publishing Co., 1987), p. 121. Reprinted by permission.

hard you try, you will not even try. This is true regardless of how large or desirable an incentive is offered.

Most employees know or believe that there are certain goals they cannot reach. They also realize that some goals are attainable if they put forth the effort. You know, for example, that unless you break a leg, running a twenty-minute mile is reasonable. You probably also believe that you should be able to kick a five-yard field goal if the goal posts were sufficiently lower. Therefore, if you are reasonably certain of success, it is much more likely that you will expend the necessary effort.

However, people do not always know whether they can succeed at a task. Could you, for example, kick a ten-yard field goal assuming the goal posts remained at their proper height? Could you run an eight-minute mile? Most people are not certain about whether or not they could succeed.

Expectancy theory argues that people intuitively calculate the probability of success or failure for accomplishing various goals and that this is one of the three major factors affecting their motivation. These probabilities range from 0 (no chance to achieve the goal) to 1 (certain of goal accomplishment).

If we say that the higher the assumed probability of success, the greater the person's effort, what does this mean? Two conclusions seem warranted:

1. If employees truly cannot accomplish a goal regardless of how hard they try, do not ask them to do it. Doing so will only lead to frustration for everyone.

2. Employee failure may result from a lack of self-confidence. Some individuals may think they cannot achieve a goal even though they have never tried to do it. Alternatively, people may underestimate their ability to perform well. By offering encouragement, information, suggestions, and, above all, support, managers may be able to increase employees' own beliefs that they can accomplish a task. Additional training and peer support may also be helpful.

What Will I Get?

Once the first question has been answered, the next question is, "What will I get in the way of rewards and penalties if I do succeed?" Expectancy theory argues that when people choose between alternative courses of action, there is always this notion of, "What's in it for me?"

There are several important aspects to this question. First, it involves a probability of receiving various outcomes given successful performance. Again, the range is from 1 (a given outcome will definitely occur) to 0 (a given outcome will definitely not occur). Also, be aware that the term *outcome* refers to both intrinsic and extrinsic rewards. Intrinsic outcomes are those inherent in task performance itself. Examples are feelings of competence, personal satisfaction, and achievement. Extrinsic outcomes are external to the work itself. Examples include pay, promotion, and praise. Expectancy theory contends that employees implicitly review and determine the probabilities associated with the various rewards and punishments they are likely to receive by performing a task, and then act in a way that will maximize the most desirable outcomes.

What, then, is the major implication in terms of employee productivity? Essentially, rewards should be linked directly to job performance, and high and low performance should result in different outcomes. In addition, rewards and penalties should be pointed out so that employees are aware of all possible outcomes. Finally, the probabilities of receiving these outcomes given different levels of performance should be clarified.

How Much Do I Want It?

If a person believes that a given level of performance is possible and rewards will be forthcoming, the final question is, "Do I want the outcomes?" In other words, what is the strength of an individual's desire for a particular outcome? This is typically referred to as "valence." An outcome is positively valent when it is preferred and negatively valent when it is not. The range is from +1 to −1. If a person has ambivalent feelings, the valence will be 0 and these outcomes will have little or no effect on motivation. When valence is +1 the person finds the outcomes very desirable and will probably work toward them. A valence of −1 means that the person will probably seek other outcomes.

Expectancy theory makes no prediction about what valences are associated with given outcomes. Stated differently, the theory does not say what an employee will find rewarding or punishing or to what extent someone will pursue certain outcomes. Instead, it argues that everyone makes an individual determination.

Briefly stated, the implication is that managers should offer valued rewards in return for high performance. In other words, if at all possible, tailor reward and penalty systems to fit the employee.

Combining the Factors

The theory argues that ultimately an individual's motivation is a function of the model's three components. It is determined by the effort-performance expectancy multiplied by the products of the performance-outcomes expectancies and the valences of the outcomes. The algebraic products of the expectancies and valences are computed for all the outcomes that an employee perceives to be linked to a given performance level.

Since the components of the model are multiplied, if any one of them is zero, the final product is also zero. Motivation, therefore, will not exist if people believe that they cannot perform well regardless of how hard they try, they do not think that performing well will be adequately rewarded, or they do not want the rewards being offered. Conversely, effective job performance is most likely if the employees know they can accomplish a task, perceive that rewards are linked to task accomplishment, and the rewards are desirable.

ORGANIZATIONAL APPLICATIONS OF REWARD FOR PERFORMANCE

Basing rewards on job performance is a strategy that many organizations have tried, and since money is one of the major rewards firms offer, much attention has been given to pay-for-performance programs. But money is not the only reward. Managers might also consider a variety of merchandise/recognition incentives. The following sections will discuss some of the different ways in which companies use rewards and incentives.

Merit Raises

As a basis for rewarding employees, merit is a widely accepted managerial practice. Merit pay is defined as any compensation system that bases an individual's wage or salary on measured performance. One way to ascertain whether an organization really uses merit is to examine the differences in the raises various employees receive. In a true merit pay system there will be radically different pay boosts from one person to another. For example, suppose that a company gave 5 percent for outstanding performance, 4 percent for average, and 3 percent raises if performance was marginal. Could you expect someone to do what was necessary to be outstanding if the expected outcome was only a 2 percent higher raise than marginal? The important point is that genuine merit raises must give significantly higher rewards to those who perform at very high levels versus average or marginal ones.

Despite the fact that merit is a logical idea, there are several problems associated with its use. A major concern is that it must be possible to measure each employee's output. If pay increases are based primarily on subjective judgments, the whole process can break down. From an expectancy point of view, if the outcomes and performance criteria are not clear, the effect on motivation will not be positive. Also, merit pay may result in employees competing with one another rather than working together and unfortunately, this is often detrimental to organizational effectiveness. Finally, merit pay systems may be more costly than conventional ones and may encounter employee and union resistance.

If a merit pay system is to be successful, organizations must have accurate performance appraisal systems, agreed-upon performance criteria, and an atmosphere that engenders openness and trust. They must also be willing and able to revise their pay and appraisal systems regularly. If these criteria are not met, the plan will have problems.

Relative to merit pay, how should raises be disbursed? The typical approach is to distribute the raise over fifty-two weeks. This, however, tends to dilute its effect. Another possibility is to give the money in one lump sum. This approach has been used by a number of organizations in order to improve motivational effect. For example, a Texas company in the oil well service industry uses a lump-sum approach for its field engineers. Two large New England insurance companies, one having four thousand employees, gave lump sums to deserving salaried employees above the supervisory level. And a large manufacturer of rubber products offered an up-front merit increase program to all salaried employees except officers.[6]

Given that few firms use a lump-sum approach, it is difficult to draw definitive conclusions about its effect. However, in the case of the Texas oil company, it decreased turnover among the field engineers and the productivity of engineers did seem to improve. In any event, the company liked the system so much that they extended it to all nonbonus personnel in the supervisory and executive ranks, and ultimately to all clerical employees. From an expectancy point of view, the new system increased the valence (attractiveness) of the merit raise.

Bonuses

A second performance-based system is the bonus, that is, a sum of money paid in addition to base salary.[7] Many firms use bonus systems especially for executives and even though their use varies by industry, anywhere from 22 to 66 percent of the firms in different industry groups use some type of bonus system. In most cases the dollar amounts range anywhere from 27 to 45 percent of salary, depending upon the individual's position. There are, however, some executives who receive bonuses that are equal to, if not greater than, their salary.

Bonuses are typically based on a combination of three criteria: (1) overall company performance; (2) department or unit performance; and (3) individual performance. The rationale is that if people believe that they can earn more they should work harder.

Should a company attempt to use a cash bonus plan? The answer seems to depend on a number of factors, particularly the following:[8]

1. Whether the amount paid can be closely related to the individual's level of performance, and performance is clearly measurable.
2. Whether the amount paid after taxes represents a clearly noticeable rise above base salary.
3. Whether the amount paid can be reduced dramatically whenever an individual experiences a real and continuing decrease in performance effectiveness.
4. Whether the amount paid can be closely related to the level of company performance.
5. Whether it is possible to base the amount paid on an easily understandable system of allocation.
6. Whether employees trust management and accept the bonus plan.

Individual and Group Financial Incentive Programs

Another common application of the pay-for-performance strategy involves the use of individual and group incentive systems. In the former, financial rewards are based strictly on individual employee behavior, while the latter uses the job performance of the total work group.

Individual Incentive Programs

Many individual financial incentive systems can be used, but the best known is piece- rate, a system that ties an employee's pay directly to output. Oyster shuckers, for example, are often paid based on the number of gallons of oysters shucked per day. Garment workers may be compensated according to the number of ties or shirts they produce each week.

Even though piece-rate systems were originally developed for production workers they can also be applied to clerical employees. One example is the wage-incentive system used extensively since the early 1960s by the Aetna Life and Casualty Company. Since that time, the company has placed more and more employees on wage-incentive so that today most of its clerical staff participates. The system is based on five basic elements:

1. Establish work standards.
2. Record the number of tasks for each job.
3. Determine the amount of time allowed for a given week's work (standard minutes).
4. Record the number of minutes each employee spends on measured work (measured minutes).
5. Evaluate each employee's efficiency by dividing standard minutes by measured minutes. For example, if a job should take 2000 minutes and the employee actually spends 2130 minutes to do that work, the efficiency would be 2000/2130 = 94 percent.

Under wage-incentive, every job is evaluated using time and motion techniques in order to determine reasonable efficiency standards. Throughout the workday, tasks are timed and records are kept. When an employee produces at a rate greater than or equal to 70 percent of the time standard, a bonus is added to the base salary. The greater the productivity, the higher the bonus.

Closely related to piece-rate systems are commissions. Indeed they are often thought of as piece-rate applied to sales. The pay of car salespeople, for example, is almost always based on the number of cars they sell. In fact, almost anyone who sells "big ticket" items (e.g., televisions, appliances, encyclopedias, furniture) works on a commission basis. Stockbrokers and other financial advisors are usually paid this way as well.

Are these plans successful? Firms that use them would say yes. But unfortunately, it is always difficult to establish clear cause-and-effect relationships. However, it does appear that the plans will succeed if employees really desire the rewards offered by the plan. In addition, as Exhibit 4–2 points out, there are other factors that may help the plan to succeed.

Group Incentive Plans

A fourth type of financial incentive system which managers might consider is awards to groups rather than single employees. Variations between plans often reflect differences in what constitutes the "group." With some, such as a group piece-rate plant, the "group" constitutes an employee's immediate work unit. Other systems consider the "group" to be either the entire plant or possibly the whole organization.

Scanlon plans. By far the best-known group incentive is the Scanlon Plan, developed during the mid-1930s by Joe Scanlon, a union leader in the steel industry. The plan consists of a pay incentive system combined with an employee suggestion plan.

Scanlon realized that if his management philosophy was to be implemented, some structural changes were needed in organizations. He pointed out that most wage systems fail to reward individuals for cooperative behavior, and as a result do not produce a convergence between the

Exhibit 4–2
Recommendations for Making an Individual Financial Incentive System a Success

1. Explain the plan to everyone before it is installed. If problems can be talked out before the plan takes effect, employees are much more likely to accept it.
2. Be sure that employees understand the relationship between behavior and earnings. In other words, explain exactly what each employee must do in order to earn the bonus.
3. Be sure the program is understandable so that employees can easily calculate their wages. If people don't understand the plan, they are less likely to trust it.
4. The differential in pay between guaranteed and incentive rates should be large enough to make extra effort worthwhile. In this regard, one researcher has suggested that if a system is to have "incentive pull." i.e., to actually motivate an employee to increase his or her job performance, it should enable the employee to potentially earn 30–35 percent over his or her base pay. Thus, if employees have a guaranteed minimum of $5.00 per hour, then potentially they should be able to earn between $6.50 and $6.75 per hour. Keep in mind, of course, that the 35 percent rule applies only in situations that guarantee workers a minimum amount per hour.
5. Never interfere with an existing bonus standard unless some error in calculation has been made or the job is significantly redesigned. Be sure the standard has been fairly set.
6. Insist on production being up to the designated quality. Employees should not be paid for poor work.
7. If employees are not meeting the standard, check immediately to see why. Every employee should be able to make some bonus. Maybe additional training is needed.
8. Once installed, keep the incentive plan rigidly maintained. Be sure that conditions of work, materials, and methods remain as constant as possible.
9. Be sure employees understand what is expected of them and what they can expect from management. A changing or weak policy toward bonus payments can easily destroy employee confidence.

Source: R. B. McAfee and P. J. Champagne, *Organizational Behavior: A Manager's View* (St. Paul, Minn.: West Publishing Co., 1987), p. 127. Reprinted by permission.

goals of employees and the organization. His solution was a bonus program applied companywide. The basis of this plan is typically the relationship between labor costs and sales revenue. The ratio is determined on the basis of the firm's accounting history, or from companies within the industry. It then becomes the standard of the company. When the ratio of costs to sales decreases, the difference is savings, most of which are divided up among the workers based on their salaries.

Scanlon also believed that most organizations ignored the potentially valuable opinions and ideas of people at the lower levels of the hierarchy.

To correct this situation he suggested the use of a suggestion system involving an elaborate committee structure. Production committees composed of the supervisor plus elected workers would be formed in each working unit to process, refine, and review employee suggestions. A single screening committee composed of top executives plus elected worker representatives would deal with suggestions beyond the scope of the production committees such as those involving significant expenditures or changes in methods across two or three departments.

The Scanlon Plan has been used by many firms throughout the United States since it was initiated at the LaPointe Tool Company in 1947. Atwood Machine Company, a maker of automotive hardware located in Rockford, Illinois, has used the plan, as has the Pfaudler Company, a division of Sybron Corporation, located in Rochester, New York. In addition, Parker Pen Company has used it in its manufacturing division located in Janesville, Wisconsin.

At Rocky Mountain Data Systems, the "Productivity Sharing" program provides an interesting example of a Scanlon Plan in action. The company provides diagnostic information to the dental profession based on computerized analysis of X-rays. The pay for performance plan used here is based on the following formula:

1. Initially, the period from July 1973 to July 1974 was established as the base year.
2. Two figures were calculated—total gross receipts and total salary figures.
3. Gross receipts were divided by the salaries paid to obtain a productivity index.
4. Each month, sales are divided by salaries paid to determine the productivity rate for the month. If the month's productivity is greater than the productivity index, the company pays a bonus that month to each employee equal to one-half of the increase. Hence, the productivity gain is shared between management and labor. For example, if the productivity index improved 20 percent, employees receive a separate check at the end of the month for 10 percent of their salary.

After using the plan for five years, the company reported that both sales and profits were up and employees' pay had gone up substantially. In addition, employee attitudes had improved and turnover dropped to 5 percent per year (a 70 percent decline). On the negative side, the company reported that some communication breakdowns occurred regarding the plan and that problems developed because some managers wanted to keep costs down by not hiring new employees. Finally, wages for certain employees were considerably above market rates, causing some dissension among managers about the appropriateness of the bonus formula.[9] The problems, however, were not severe enough to dissuade management from continuing.

Lincoln Electric Company. The Lincoln Electric Company, a motor and arc welding equipment manufacturer, located in Euclid, Ohio, has developed a unique incentive plan that combines the advantages of an individual and a group plan. The total bonus money paid out is determined by the company's profitability, but the amount each employee receives is based on individual performance ratings. (In most cases, the bonus effectively doubles a worker's base pay.) The plan attempts to relate individual performance more closely to individual pay, while at the same time encouraging employees to work together in a cooperative spirit to increase the total bonus pool.

A second element of the plan is guaranteed employment providing security against layoff for all workers. Every full-time employee who has worked two or more years for the company is guaranteed employment for at least 75 percent of the standard forty-hour week. In fact, the company has not had a layoff in the past thirty years although in 1982 it did shorten the employees' workweek.

In 1985, the company paid its fifty-second consecutive yearly bonus to employees; 2405 workers received $41,800,785 in bonuses, an average of $17,381 per employee. One employee commented, "I have bought three houses with my annual bonus checks. I may use this year's check as a down payment for another one."[10]

Nucor Corporation. Another organization that rewards group productivity is the Nucor Corporation located in Charlotte, North Carolina. Its approach is unusual in that it consists of four different incentive plans, each covering a different segment of the work force from top executives to production and clerical employees.[11]

One of the plans involves approximately 2500 production workers divided into bonus groups. Each shift on every production line forms a separate bonus group with bonuses based roughly on 90 percent of the time it takes to make a steel joist. For example, if during one week employees make joists in 60 percent less time than the standard time, they receive a 60 percent bonus. The bonuses are added to their regular pay the next week. Employees who are absent for one day forfeit their bonus for the week. Anyone who is more than a half-hour late loses the bonus for that day.

A second incentive system applies to department heads. These bonuses are based on division or corporate return on assets. Success is determined by comparing the profits of the division to expenses under its direct control. The amount of the bonus can run as high as 51 percent of the individual's salary.

A third program applies to employees who are not department heads or production workers. This group includes accountants, engineers, secretaries, and receptionists. For these employees, bonuses are based, once again, on the division's return on assets or the corporation's return on assets and they average about 30 percent of salary.

The fourth incentive plan applies to senior officers. It is determined by company earnings and accounts for more than half their total compensation. Base salaries for this group are set at 70 percent of what an individual in a comparable position with another company would receive. When the company's profits are low, officers receive only their base salaries; if the firm does well, salaries will be higher than comparable firms.

Evaluation of Group Incentive Plans

How successful are group incentive plans? The evidence shows that in the right situations they can be a powerful motivator. Still, not every organization's experience has been as positive as the cases cited here. For example, in one study of twenty-three companies which used or had a Scanlon Plan, the investigators found that twelve had abandoned the program.[12] The average duration for these unsuccessful plans was six years. When successful and unsuccessful plans were compared, several significant differences were found:

1. Successful plans were characterized by high amounts of employee participation; unsuccessful plans were not.
2. Successful plans were strongly related to favorable managerial attitudes; unsuccessful plans were characterized by unfavorable managerial attitudes toward the plan.
3. Success was highly related to the number of years a company had used the plan. The longer a firm had a plan, the more likely it was to be successful.
4. Success was more likely when a company's chief executive officer was visible and actively supported the plan.

These findings indicate that if a company wants to successfully implement a group incentive plan employee participation must be high, managers must support it, the firm's chief executive officer must back it and be active in it, and the organization must be patient during implementation.

Keep in mind, however, that even when a group plan does not have an immediately measurable effect on productivity, there may still be valid reasons to use one. For example, a company may use group incentive plans to instill in employees a sense of partnership with management that may ultimately improve relationships between the two groups. In addition, some firms establish these plans to improve cooperation and/or reduce conflict among the workers themselves. Finally, other organizations may retain incentive systems because they allow management greater flexibility in compensating employees. With some plans, the amount paid to employees will vary as company profits and productivity change. Having this flexibility represents a significant advantage to companies since it permits them to avoid becoming locked into high wage costs during recessionary periods. Therefore, group incentive plans serve many purposes for an organization in addition to promoting higher productivity.

Merchandise/Recognition Incentives

While money is the most frequent incentive, merchandise and recognition rewards can also be used to motivate employees. In a 1986 survey done by *Personnel Journal* almost nine out of ten subscribers had some type of recognition or awards program, costing an average of $33,000 per year. The survey revealed that plaques and certificates were by far the most frequent incentives (almost two-thirds of the respondent firms used them). Also common were merchandise (41 percent), jewelry (more than 50 percent), cash (15 percent), and travel (11 percent).[13]

First Knox National Bank in Mount Vernon, Ohio has developed an employee recognition award program based on employee achievement. The Outstanding Teller Service Award is given to an employee at each branch based on five criteria: teller choice (33 points), customer satisfaction based on selection cards included in customers' bank statements (34 points), balancing record (11 points), number of transactions (11 points), and supervisor rating (11 points). Each award recipient receives a Mark Cross pen and one share of bank stock.[14]

The American Hospital Association, a Chicago-based firm, has also developed a recognition program called the Service Leader Award program. Each month an employee receives the award based on five criteria:

1. Performs work beyond expectations.
2. Responds positively and creatively to difficult requests.
3. Exhibits thorough, helpful, consistent, and quick responses to members and staff.
4. Generates unsolicited positive feedback from members and staff outside the staff member's division.
5. Contributes ideas that result in members and staff receiving better service.

Award recipients are given a certificate and engraved plaque at the monthly manager's meeting together with a check for $100. A service leader of the year award is selected from the twelve monthly service leaders and that individual receives another engraved plaque plus a $100 check.[15]

Toyota Motor Sales, U.S. Parts and Service Division, provides another example of how noncash incentives can be used to motivate employees.[16] In 1982, the company decided to increase the sale of Toyota parts. In order to accomplish this, it developed a four-segment year-long promotion involving dealers, service and parts managers, plus tie-in promotions for consumers. Participants were offered trips for two to Hawaii based on points gained from: (1) increasing customer paid transactions; (2) improving customer relations; and (3) running at least one tie-in co-op advertisement each month.

Toyota divided dealerships into two groups depending upon whether annual parts and service sales exceeded or were below $800,000. Trips were awarded to the top fifty dealerships in each division. In addition to these prizes, Toyota gave recognition awards to fifty dealers who had the most profitable parts and service facilities. The recipients were flown to Palm Springs, California, to receive the awards and also to become members of the President's Service and Parts Advisory Board, chaired by the U.S. Toyota president.

Do these programs really enhance employee motivation and productivity? Toyota reported that sales of parts and services improved substantially (sales during the last three months of the program were more than double those of the same period one year earlier). Customer relations also improved as evidenced by the fact that over one hundred thousand customers registered their car keys in a special program designed to help customers get back lost keys.

The Toyota program offered trips and recognition rewards, but merchandise awards are also common. For example, companies have used stamps, coupons, or tokens that can be converted into gifts. Often these programs focus on some specific goal such as improving safety, attendance, suggestions, or production quality control. A typical program using stamps in an effort to reduce absenteeism is shown in Exhibit 4–3. Normally, stamps are awarded only for perfect attendance during the month. If employees are absent, they revert back to the scale of awards for the first month.

Advocates argue that merchandise plans have many benefits over cash awards. Frequently cited are the facts that: (1) they reach other family members (spouse and children), thus increasing their valence and motivational impact; (2) unlike cash, which is spent and forgotten, merchandise can last for years; (3) merchandise has an economic benefit since a $100 gift may cost the company only $60; and (4) merchandise provides a permanent reminder of the program, its objectives, and source (the company).

SUMMARY

In this chapter we have examined the use of rewards to motivate employees and enhance job performance. We have discussed expectancy theory which suggests that motivation is dependent upon one's answers to three questions: (1) Can I achieve a given job performance level or goal if I try?; (2) If I do succeed, what rewards am I likely to receive?; and (3) How

Exhibit 4–3
Monthly Awards Schedule Using Stamps

1st month	300 stamps	7th month	900 stamps
2nd month	300 stamps	8th month	900 stamps
3rd month	300 stamps	9th month	900 stamps
4th month	600 stamps	10th month	1200 stamps
5th month	600 stamps	11th month	1200 stamps
6th month	600 stamps	12th month	1200 stamps

Source: R. B. McAfee and P. J. Champagne, *Organizational Behavior: A Manager's View* (St. Paul, Minn.: West Publishing Co., 1987), p. 132. Reprinted by permission.

much do I want the rewards? The application of the theory has been addressed in terms of merit raises, bonuses, individual and group incentive systems, and merchandise/recognition programs.

Clearly, the most frequent performance-based reward is money. Everyone needs money and most people value it to some degree. Indeed, it is important for managers to remember that money serves at least two primary functions. First, it can be viewed as a medium of exchange, that is, work is traded for income which is then spent for personal consumption. Second, money is also a medium of evaluation. The financial payoff for working is an important way of stating the value of a person's work. If one earns more than another, his or her productive effort may be perceived to be more valuable. For many people a substantial bonus or raise is an appropriate way to recognize a job well done.

In recent years, some behavioral scientists have attempted to convince top executives that pay is not all that important to employees and that by itself money can have no positive impact on their behavior. It has become part of the folklore of the workplace to assert that wages and salaries are not useful incentives for work. Studies are cited to show that workers at all levels of organizations rank earnings well down the list when asked what is most important about their jobs. Does this mean, then, that incentive systems based on financial rewards cannot affect work behavior? The answer is a clear negative. Indeed, appropriate pay incentive systems can affect the decision to come to work (participation) and engage in productive activity once there (performance). In many instances, top management fails to consider the important role of pay when attempting to improve organizational effectiveness and employee productivity.

In U.S. society "money does make the world go around." Most workers want economic advancement and security for themselves as well as for their families, and taking a job is typically a means to this end. As long as we continue to measure most forms of human activity in monetary terms, income will remain a primary device for satisfying human needs and wants and the proper design of incentive systems will offer a continuing challenge to organizations.

Finally, it is important to remember that at times extrinsic rewards cannot and should not be used to motivate job performance. Many production and clerical jobs can be measured quite easily, but what if there are no objective measures of performance? Even when it is possible to measure some important on-the-job behaviors, linking them to rewards can create a number of new problems. The measurable aspects may receive all the employee's attention, while other less measurable behaviors are neglected. Clearly, in this situation, it may be better not to motivate using extrinsic rewards.

NOTES

1. S. Kerr, "On the Folly of Rewarding A, While Hoping for B," *Academy of Management Journal* 18 (1975), pp. 769–83.

2. R. A. Printz and D. A. Waldman, "The Merit of Merit Pay," *Personnel Administrator*, January 1985, pp. 84–90.

3. E. E. Lawler, *Pay and Organizational Effectiveness* (New York: McGraw-Hill, 1971).

4. "A Case for Rewarding Recognition," *Personnel Journal*, December 1986, pp. 66–73.

5. Ibid.

6. D. M. Gluckman, "Lump-Sum Merit Increases," *Compensation Review* 15, no. 1 (1983), pp. 66–72.

7. M. J. Wallace and C. H. Fay, *Compensation Theory and Practice* (Boston: Kent Publishing Co., 1983).

8. T. H. Patten, Jr., *Employee Compensation and Incentive Plans* (New York: Free Press, 1977).

9. R. J. Schulhof, "Five Years with a Scanlon Plan," *Personnel Administrator*, June 1979, pp. 55ff.

10. Lincoln Electric Company News Release, December 6, 1985.

11. J. Savage, "Incentive Programs at Nucor Corporation," *Personnel Administrator*, August 1981, pp. 33ff.

12. J. K. White, "The Scanlon Plan: Causes and Correlates of Success," *Academy of Management Journal* 22, no. 2 (1979), pp. 292–312.

13. "A Case for Rewarding Recognition."

14. Ibid.

15. Ibid.

16. "Toyota Sells Parts with Perks," *Sales and Marketing Management*, September 1982, pp. 106–10.

5

Treating Employees Fairly

> Employee complaints exist whenever there is employment. Ignoring these problems won't solve them and may create additional problems —particularly with morale, motivation, and productivity.[1]

> Employee complaints are a part of every supervisor's job, and handling them correctly and fairly is vital to maintaining good morale.[2]

> A manager may establish a policy or procedure with the best intentions of producing a situation of fairness. The mistake in this approach is the presumption that what is obviously fair to the manager will also be seen as fair by the employees involved.[3]

The management of a major automobile manufacturing organization has set a policy regarding the sizes of its executives' offices and related matters. The policy states that all executives of equal rank in the company will have offices of equal size. The higher the rank of the executive, the larger the office will be. Thus, when employees are promoted in the company, they receive a larger office. In addition to the size of the executive's office, the size of the secretary's office increases as the boss's rank in the company increases. Finally, the furnishings in each office are standardized for both the executive and the secretary. The higher one's rank in the organization, the more furnishings of increasing size, luxury, and quality one receives. To facilitate this process, an extensive book of specifications exists, complete with sample swatches of the appropriate carpeting, draperies, upholstery, nameplate dimensions, type and wall placement of paintings, and so on.

In the above example, we see a situation in which a large company has developed an elaborate system for allocating offices and furnishings. But why? Are they making far too much of a simple matter?

The company has the policy for a very good reason: it wants employees to feel that they are being treated fairly. The firm recognizes that there is a strong relationship between employee productivity and equity perceptions. If employees feel unfairly treated, they may reduce their productivity or take actions detrimental to the firm.

In this chapter, we will examine actions organizations and managers can take to promote a perception of equity. One of these is to develop fair policies and practices. Another is to openly communicate policies to employees. The third is to develop effective procedures and systems for resolving employee complaints and problems. Before considering these actions however, we want to address two questions: (1) How do employees determine if they are being treated fairly? (2) Why should managers treat employees fairly? The answers to these questions constitute what is referred to as "equity theory."

DETERMINATION OF EQUITY

Equity theory[4] says that in order to determine whether or not we are being treated in a fair and equitable way, we compare ourselves to others, especially those who occupy similar positions in the firm.

What information do we use in making these comparisons? According to the theory, all the information can be divided into four categories:

1. Your outcomes—all the outcomes such as pay, job status, and feeling of responsibility you receive for performing your job.
2. Your inputs—all that you contribute and bring to the job, such as your time, physical and mental effort, and education.
3. Comparison person's outcomes—all the outcomes such as pay, job status, and feeling of responsibility that a comparison person receives for performing his or her job.
4. Comparison person's inputs—all that a comparison person brings to and contributes to his or her job, such as time, physical effort, and education.

Equity theory states that we consider our own outcome/input ratio in relation to the outcome/input ratio of some comparison other. Based on this we determine whether or not we are being treated fairly. Thus, if the ratio of person A's outcomes to inputs is not equal to the corresponding ratio of the comparison person, A probably will feel unfairly treated. When the equations balance, the theory suggests that we will be satisfied and all should be well. However, when inequities are perceived, tension is created and at a certain point we do something to relieve it.

Assume that you and one of your co-workers both make widgets. You produce one hundred widgets a day, but your co-worker, who is extremely industrious and efficient, produces two hundred widgets a day. You are

Exhibit 5–1
"Fair" Ratios of Outcome to Input

	You	Co-worker
Outcomes	$50	$100
Inputs	100 widgets	200 widgets

paid fifty dollars per day. If your co-worker receives twice the pay you do, would you consider this unfair? Probably not, since your production is only half that of your co-worker. Other factors being equal (like quality of widgets, amount of scrap produced, and so on), the ratio of your outcomes to inputs is equal to the ratio of your co-worker's (Exhibit 5–1).

Now, assume that instead of producing only one hundred widgets per day you also produce two hundred. However, you still receive only fifty dollars pay. How would you feel then? Assuming that other factors are equal, you would probably feel unfairly treated since you are receiving only one-half the pay and the ratio of outcomes to inputs would not equal that of your co-worker. Exhibit 5–2 presents this situation. Compare Exhibit 5–1 with Exhibit 5–2. How could you adjust your outcomes or inputs?

WHY TREAT EMPLOYEES FAIRLY?

If employees are not treated fairly, they will very likely take actions to reduce the inequity. There are a variety of options available to them. They may, for example, reduce their inputs. This often takes the form of directly restricting work output. If a large number of employees begin cutting back, the effect could be severe. Equity theory suggests that people can be expected to decrease their production levels until inequity, as they perceive it, is eliminated. In our earlier example, in which you were asked to imagine that you were producing two hundred widgets and receiving only fifty dollars for this effort, while a co-worker also produced two hundred widgets and was paid one hundred dollars, you would probably curtail your production. In fact, you might cut back your production to one hundred widgets in order to achieve equity since 50/100 is equal to 100/200.

A second means for achieving equity is to attempt to increase your outcomes. You could ask for a raise, or make the job more rewarding by accepting only those assignments you really enjoy. Some have speculated that white-collar and blue-collar crime are strategies for regaining equity since it serves to increase outcomes.

A third possibility is to decrease the outcomes of a comparison other until the ratio of that person's outcomes to inputs equals yours. This can be done in various ways, but the net effect is to "make life miserable" for

Exhibit 5–2
"Unfair" Ratios of Outcome to Input

	You	Co-worker
Outcomes	$50	$100
Inputs	200 widgets	200 widgets

the comparison other. Sabotaging another's work or attacking a rate buster are two more vivid examples.

Finally, equity can be achieved by increasing the other's inputs. An example would be not helping the other person with problem situations thus requiring him or her to do it alone. This action is not necessarily all bad since the productivity of the comparison other may increase.

In addition to these four reactions, an individual could employ a combination of approaches, or as a last resort, simply withdraw from the situation entirely, that is, quit the job and seek employment elsewhere. Finally, up to a certain point, a person could just rationalize the inputs or outcomes and, in effect, "live with" the inequity.

In general, studies support the major predictions that equity theory makes.[5] Many have found that equity ratio discrepancies are a source of perceived unfairness. Most also find that inequity is a source of tension and that the greater the inequity, the greater the drive to reduce it.

PREVENTING INEQUITY

How can managers and organizations prevent employees from feeling unfairly treated? Rather than waiting for problems to occur, many organizations develop policies and procedures designed to promote perceptions of fairness, a primary example of which was our opening example. These policies cover a wide variety of topics including promotions, wages and salaries, performance appraisals, and work rules.

Consider examples from two different companies. One photographic products company has the policy covering employee vacations shown in Exhibit 5–3. In contrast a large automotive plant in "deer hunting country" has a totally different vacation policy as shown in Exhibit 5–4. The important point is that while policies may help prevent perceptions of unfairness, there is no one policy which is universally deemed as fair and which all organizations should adopt. What constitutes "fairness" always depends on the particular situation.

Another preventive maintenance approach is to keep open the lines of communication between managers and employees through surveys, meetings, memos, or whatever. General Electric, for example, maintains

Exhibit 5–3
Vacation Policy of a Photographic Products Company

When there is a conflict of vacation time between two or more
employees, the employee with the longest seniority shall have
preference. Any employee, however, who makes his request after
May 15, will not be given seniority recognition and vacation
times will be alloted on a first come first served basis.

Vacation time cannot be carried over from year to year. Unused
vacation will be paid for at the end of the year. The company
may, however, require the employee to take his unused vacation in
lieu of pay.

An employee who takes his vacation during the period from
November 1 through April 30 will receive one extra vacation day
with pay for each vacation week taken. The employee has the
option to take the day off with pay or work the extra day with
extra pay if the company requests it.

employee opinion survey staffs, which are on call to line managers at various plants and locations.[6] One plant in New York found from a survey that employees had difficulty finding space to eat lunch. As a result the lunch period was staggered so that only one-fourth of the employees were out at one time. As a result, subsequent surveys showed a real improvement in employee morale.[7]

At a foundry in New Jersey, employees said on a survey that it was exceedingly difficult to find space in the company parking lot. The firm paved the lot and each worker was assigned a space based on seniority. Once again, the result was improved employee morale.[8]

While surveys can be helpful in opening up lines of communication, teaching managers to improve their listening skills can also improve communication. When executives at a major technology company in the Midwest were asked what part listening played in their work, one admitted that he spent about 80 percent of his time "either listening to someone or being listened to." One of his colleagues considered the things that had gone wrong in the firm during recent years and realized that "many of the snafus have been the result of someone not hearing something or hearing it in a distorted way." A third executive observed that even though his company emphasized communication, it had "inadvertently overlooked listening." "Listening," he continued, "is one of the weakest links in our whole communication network, yet it is also one of the most important."[9]

Problems such as these can be overcome by teaching managers to become active listeners rather than just "passive receivers." The best example of how to do this comes from those whose job it is to be good listeners—professional psychologists and psychiatrists. Not only do they

Exhibit 5-4
Vacation Policy of an Automotive Manufacturing Plant

1. Employees may make application to their supervisor, during the regular vacation application period, for vacation time off during the approaching deer hunting season.

2. Applicants with unused vacation time remaining available to them shall be granted time off during the deer hunting season, as herein provided, up to the amount of vacation time to which they are still entitled, but not to exceed one (1) full week.

3. The parties recognize the principle that all applicants cannot always be allowed time off during the early part of the season; accordingly, the following shall apply: (a) where 25% or less of the total employees in a classification apply for time off during the early part of the season, all applicants will be allowed such time off. (b) where the total applicants in a classification exceed 25% but are less than 50% of the total employees in a classification, the excess over 25% shall be granted time off during the second week of the season. (c) In the event 50% or more of the employees in a classification apply for time off during the early part of the season, the applicants will be divided into two (2) groups, one group being granted the time off during the first week of the season and the other group being granted the requested time off during the second week.

4. The order of preference for the above time off shall be based on date-of-entry seniority in their respective classification.

give their full attention to the speaker, they also know how to use questions to obtain deeper, clearer responses. But even without the benefits of professional training there are a few straightforward things that anyone can do to improve listening skills.

An effective listener encourages others to speak and divulge important information by asking "open-ended" questions. Instead of saying, "Have you heard about the new merit system that's been proposed?" a better approach would be to ask, "How do you feel about the new merit system that's been proposed?" The first question may generate a yes or no answer, which then requires another question. On the other hand, asking how the person "feels" makes it more difficult to answer in a word or two and offers the possibility of finding out how someone really perceives the situation. Unfortunately, many managers use the more restrictive approach exclusively and, as a result, never receive important information.[10] Still, there are times when a closed question can be helpful and a mixed approach might be useful.

Consider the following:

Supervisor: Mary, have you heard about the new grievance procedure the company is considering?

Employee: Yes, but I don't know all the details.

Supervisor: Well, what are your thoughts based on what you do know?

Employee: Well, it sounds like we are supposed to bring our problems to you, and if a mutual agreement can't be reached we could request that the department head look into it.

Supervisor: How do you feel about that?

As you can see, the supervisor is using different types of questions to encourage Mary to say how she really feels about the new procedure. The boss is letting the employee know that her opinions are valuable.

Another technique that improves listening is to restate what the other person has just said. A manager using restatement needs to rephrase the feeling component of the message. Examples of phrases that can be used to restate what someone has said are: "You feel you were fortunate in . . ." or, "You were pretty upset by the fact that. . . ." Reflecting what the speaker has said by restating it allows you to convey several messages:

1. It tells the sender that you have been listening carefully.
2. You are conveying a concern for the person's opinion.
3. You are not making any judgment about the person's feelings.
4. You are approving of sharing such feelings and would seem to permit sharing other feelings as well.

In addition, restatement often has another positive effect on the listener. It takes intensive effort to really hear what another person is saying and to isolate the feelings. By doing this the manager is better able to isolate and respond to the real message.

Another device is to summarize the main points of the message. Again, this increases retention and helps the listener improve overall understanding. In addition, it can help establish a basis for further discussion of problems. Examples of summarizing statements are: "If I understand you correctly, you seem to be saying . . ." or, "As I understand it, you would like to see the following changes made. . . ." Summarizing differs from restatement in that the purpose of the latter is to get employees to express their true feelings while the former is designed to validate the accuracy of the information.

Finally, a good listener is not afraid of silence. In fact, this can be used to either get or keep an employee talking, as in the following example:

Employee: I've really come to dislike this job. I find myself dreading coming to work in the morning. (*Pause*)

Manager: (*Silence*)

Employee: It's just that so much of it is routine. Each day we do the same thing.

Unfortunately, too many supervisors jump in as soon as the employee pauses. In so doing, they may upset the entire flow of the conversation. Having learned that their role is to tell employees what to do, it is often difficult to be quiet and listen. Being aware of this problem is important, but one action step any listener can take is to consciously monitor the conversation to determine who does most of the talking. When it becomes apparent that the employee is not getting a chance to speak, one should make a conscious effort to substitute silence for talk.

An example of a company that has made a serious commitment to improve the listening skills of its managers is the Sperry Corporation.[11] They have developed an ongoing program consisting of a seven-hour seminar that uses audio and video cassettes plus role playing. It covers some introductory concepts of listening as a learnable communication skill and then gets into skill enhancement exercises. Each division of the company has tailored the program to fit its own environment. In Sperry New Holland, they discuss agricultural equipment in their role plays. At Sperry Univac they use computer-related situations. In addition, the program varies depending upon the educational delivery system available at each site.

Since Sperry Univac has permanent educational facilities, they use a highly centralized and rather formal approach to this training. Other divisions tend to be more decentralized and to use a variety of other delivery mechanisms, ranging from outside instructors to self-instruction programs. But no matter how they do it, training exposes people to the idea that listening involves understanding, evaluating, interpreting, and ultimately responding to what one hears.

ORGANIZATIONAL SYSTEMS FOR RESOLVING INEQUITY PROBLEMS

In spite of all the actions taken to prevent perceptions of inequity, some employees will inevitably feel unfairly treated. When this occurs, the perceptions must be addressed and the problems resolved. There are several different devices that firms use.

Open Door Policies

Perhaps the most common approach for resolving employee complaints is to establish an "open door policy." An example of one organization's policy is given in Exhibit 5–5. It suggests that all complaints of inequity be resolved by the immediate superior. If it is not handled here, the employee can discuss the complaint with any other member of management.

Exhibit 5–5
Example of an "Open Door" Policy

In an organization of this size, questions and employee problems that cannot be resolved by referring to a handbook are bound to arise. That is why we, over the years, have developed an open door policy under which you can expect immediate, fair, considerate treatment of your problems.

Your supervisor holds her/his present position not only because he/she is proficient in your department's operation but because he/she has demonstrated her/his ability to deal with people. We have found that a frank talk with the supervisor is usually the easiest way to handle specific problems. This is true because your supervisor is responsible for seeing that you get treated fairly and he/she is generally in the best position to help you.

A talk with your supervisor will normally be the only step necessary to get a problem straightened out. However, after talking to your supervisor, you should not hesitate to take your problem to any other member of management.

Source: R. B. McAfee and P. J. Champagne, *Organizational Behavior: A Manager's View* (St. Paul, Minn.: West Publishing Co., 1987), p. 137. Reprinted by permission.

Implicit in the open door approach is the belief that the immediate superior is in the best position to resolve complaints and should be the first one the employee sees. While this is often true, at times it is not. For example, the superior may be the source of the employee's problem in the first place, and the person may feel reluctant to complain. Then, too, the boss may be too busy with other work or may just dislike dealing with employee complaints. Secretaries and other "gatekeepers" often mind the "open door" and make it difficult to use it. If this happens employees' complaints will not be handled and a more formal procedure may be necessary.

Formal Complaint Systems

As opposed to the "open door," formal complaint systems spell out the precise steps employees should take when they feel unfairly treated. Bank of America in California has such a procedure called "Let's Talk It Over." It potentially involves six steps, beginning with the employee taking the complaint to the immediate superior. If there is no resolution at this stage the individual has the option of appealing to the district administrator or department head. If an agreement is still not reached, the employee can then discuss the problem with one of the bank's employee assistance officers. At this point, any unresolved complaint must be put into writing and submitted to the district administrator or department head (step 4), the regional senior vice president or statewide department head (step 5), and/or a committee of three executives (step 6).[12]

The Bank of America has also instituted an "Open Line" in which employees can address complaints to the program coordinator. The complaint is retyped and sent to the appropriate bank officer for a reply within ten working days. Responses are mailed to the writer's home, or an interview is arranged to discuss the problem. New Jersey Bell, New England Bell, and a large division of General Electric have set up similar systems that rely primarily on telephone inquiries.[13]

Ombudsmen have also been used in an effort to solve employee complaints. The term *ombudsman* is a Norwegian word meaning administration man, the king's representative. Historically, an ombudsman was an individual appointed by the king as the people's representative. In recent years a number of large companies including the Xerox Company, General Electric, Western Electric, and Boeing Aircraft have used this approach.

Ombudsmen typically report to a senior officer of the company and serve as an important outlet for employee dissatisfaction. While serving as ombudsman for General Electric Aircraft Group, Fredrica Dunn investigated three hundred cases in her first year.[14] She suggests that the mere existence of an ombudsman encourages managers to be sure they can justify their actions. She also points out that to be effective, ombudsmen should not "please people whose idea of justice is having their own way, even when it is objectively wrong."

Pitney Bowes has a council of thirteen employee representatives elected for two-year terms, which meets monthly to resolve complaints related to companywide issues and policies affecting job performance. The representatives have full-time council responsibilities and are paid at the wage rate for their regular job. The company also holds what it calls "job-holder" meetings at some of its larger plants. Top executives attend these meetings and listen as employees express their complaints and concerns.[15]

The Polaroid Corporation has established an employee committee to hear complaints of unfair treatment. Its members are elected from the company at large for staggered three-year terms. While the committee decisions are advisory and not binding, they are rarely overturned by management. Employees are free to submit their complaints to an outside arbitrator if they cannot support the committee's decision.[16]

In sum, organizations have developed a variety of methods for resolving employee feelings of unfair treatment. The examples cited above suggest that many companies believe that employee feelings of inequity can be harmful to the organization's productivity and employee job satisfaction, and that a formal process should be established for resolving their complaints.

RESOLVING INEQUITY PROBLEMS AT THE MANAGERIAL LEVEL

In addition to formal, companywide programs, individual managers can also attempt to resolve complaints of unfair treatment on the job. The first step is to actually determine what problems employees are encountering. This can be accomplished effectively if the manager assumes the role of an active listener, that is, tunes in to what the employee says, asks questions to establish clarity, restates, and summarizes in order to determine if he/she truly understands the situation. The goal here is for the manager to see things from the employee's point of view.

But suppose that the employee really does not have a grievance, but simply wants to "blow off steam"? One way to figure this out is to ask the employee something like, "What would you like me to do for you?" or "What do you want from me?" Such questions, however, should be raised only after the employee has completely presented his or her grievance. Sometimes the individual has specific requests, but often he or she does not really want the manager to take any specific action to resolve the "complaint." This is a clear indication that the individual simply wanted to vent his or her frustrations.

Unfortunately some managers do not want to be bothered with "complainers" who just want to blow off steam. They feel it is a waste of their time and, besides, what the employee really needs is to grow up. What these managers fail to realize, however, is that letting someone "spout off" helps to establish strong relationships between themselves and their employees. By acting as a sounding board they gain respect and trust and become more effective leaders.

If an employee truly has a complaint, as opposed to just venting his or her frustrations with life, then the manager needs to respond to it. Of course, one could just ignore the problem and side-step the issue, but this is typically counterproductive.

In many cases, employees feel unfairly treated because of poor communication between themselves and the boss. For example, a machinist may feel that the company has wrongly withheld money from a paycheck when the reduction simply reflects an increase in Social Security taxes or health insurance premiums. Or, a nurse may feel angry over not being invited to a medical workshop when, in fact, it was postponed. In situations such as these, the manager can resolve the complaint by just communicating the facts. This, however, represents only the first step in the problem-solving process. Both the manager and the employee need to determine why communication broke down and what can be done to prevent this from happening again. Unless this second step is taken, the communication problem will probably resurface in the future.

On some occasions, employee complaints result from an honest mistake. Suppose that an employee complains when a promised pay raise does not show up in the check. Maybe it is not the manager's fault. The personnel department might have failed to complete the paperwork in time. If such mistakes occur, managers can defuse the situation by apologizing for any failure on their part and taking whatever corrective measures are necessary to insure that the errors are corrected and will not be repeated.

Unfortunately, not all complaints can be resolved by correcting errors and improving communications. When this happens the manager and the employee may have to agree to disagree. This somewhat radical approach recognizes that people disagree because of differing values, attitudes, and expectations and that this is completely legitimate. In fact, disagreement is a fact of organizational life and just because people disagree on an issue does not mean they cannot work together or that one party is necessarily wrong.

Another alternative and one often recommended or even required by some organizations is for the supervisor to suggest that a formal grievance be filed or the complaint be presented to the supervisor's immediate superior. This makes it clear to all that the supervisor's judgment is not final; it can be questioned, and there are other options available.

SUMMARY

In this chapter we have examined the concept of treating people fairly as a way of improving employee productivity and job satisfaction. This strategy is based on equity theory which suggests that employee feelings of inequity can lead to tension and if this is sufficiently high, employees may take action to reduce it. It suggests that people determine whether they are being treated fairly by comparing the ratio of their inputs and outcomes with that of another person (a comparison other). If the two ratios are perceived to be unequal, employees typically select an action from a group of four. They may reduce their own inputs, increase their outputs, reduce the comparison other's outcomes, and/or increase that person's inputs. Unfortunately most of these actions are harmful to organizations.

Organizational approaches related to equity can be divided into two categories: taking preventive maintenance and developing complaint resolution systems. The first involves developing fair policies and practices in the first place and also keeping lines of communication open between managers and employees. The latter entails developing systems for addressing any complaints which do arise. "Open door" policies and formal complaint systems such as ombudsmen are examples. Other organizations have found that while companywide systems or programs are helpful, individual managers also play an important role in resolving employee complaints.

In comparison with other strategies for improving employee productivity and morale, treating employees fairly is somewhat unique. Like positive reinforcement, it can be easily used in conjunction with any other strategies discussed in this book. Indeed, the general notion of equitable treatment is vital when using most, if not all, of the other strategies. For example, if disciplinary actions and procedures are to be fully effective, employees must perceive that they are being disciplined fairly. Thus, this approach has the flexibility to serve as an important adjunct to other strategies. Other approaches may be used independently, but the likelihood of success increases when employees are treated fairly.

Another attribute of the equity approach is that it is frequently, although not always, inexpensive to use. For example, if an employee feels unfairly treated as a result of a misunderstanding, the manager may need to do nothing more than communicate with the person in order to remedy the misunderstanding. The only cost involved is the manager's and the employee's time. Or, to take a second example, if an employee feels unfairly treated because of something the manager has inadvertently done (such as failing to pay for legitimate overtime) or someone else in the organization has done (e.g., another manager improperly asking the employee to perform a task), the required action can often be effected with minimal expense. There are situations, however, in which this strategy will entail considerable costs. If an employee feels unfairly treated because of truly intolerable working conditions, it may cost the organization a considerable amount to make the necessary changes. New buildings, facilities, and/or equipment may be expensive. Fortunately for most organizations, these latter situations are not too common.

A third attribute of the equity approach is that managers who use the strategy earn employee respect and are held in relatively high regard by their subordinates. All psychologically healthy employees want their boss to treat them fairly since equitable treatment reflects a respect for employees and a concern for their welfare and feelings. Hence, when managers deal fairly they are likely to be viewed favorably by their subordinates, and this may increase their ability to exercise influence and authority.

As a final point, it is important to remember that since "fairness" is subjective employee complaints are inevitable. Managers should not necessarily question their leadership style just because employees occasionally complain. By the same token, managers should recognize that they cannot always resolve every complaint they receive.

NOTES

1. A. Balfour, "Five Types of Non-Union Grievance Systems," *Personnel*, March–April 1984, pp. 67–76.

2. R. L. Miller, "Handling Employee Complaints," *Supervisory Management*, February 1978, pp. 38–43.

3. R. B. McAfee and W. Poffenberger, *Productivity Strategies: Enhancing Employee Job Performance* (Englewood Cliffs, N.J.: Prentice-Hall, 1982).

4. J. S. Adams, "Toward an Understanding of Inequity," *Journal of Abnormal and Social Psychology* 67 (1963), pp. 422–36.

5. P. S. Goodman and A. Friedman, "An Examination of Adam's Theory of Inequity," *Administrative Science Quarterly* 16 (1971), pp. 271–88. See also E. E. Lawler, "Equity Theory as a Predictor of Productivity and Work Quality." *Psychological Bulletin* 70 (1968), pp. 596–610; R. D. Pritchard, "Equity Theory: A Review and Critique," *Organizational Behavior and Human Performance* 4 (1969), pp. 176–211.

6. M. Wright, "Helping Employees Speak Out About Their Jobs and Workplace," *Personnel*, September 1986, pp. 56–60.

7. Ibid.

8. ibid.

9. E. Wakins, "The Business of Listening," *Today's Office*, February 1984, pp. 44–48.

10. R. G. Johnson, *The Appraisal Interview Guide* (New York: American Management Association, 1979).

11. J. L. Di Gaetani, "The Sperry Corporation and Listening: An Interview," *Business Horizons*, March–April 1982, pp. 34–39.

12. "An Interview with A. W. Clausen," *Harvard Business Review*, January–February 1980, pp. 104–14.

13. D. W. Ewing, "Due Process: Will Business Default?" *Harvard Business Review*, November–December 1982, pp. 114–22.

14. F. H. Dunn, "The View from the Ombudsman Chair," *New York Times*, May 2, 1976.

15. Ewing, "Due Process."

16. Ibid.

6

Setting Goals

Goals give focus and direction. They add challenge and motivation to human endeavor. They ensure that everyone works toward the same end.[1]

Time like money can be spent foolishly or invested wisely. It is not a question of lack of time, everyone gets exactly the same amount. The problem is how one uses or invests the time available.[2]

To effectively give instructions you have to reduce the "noise" of power and other distractions. Your goal is to create understanding between yourself and others.[3]

An interesting research experiment was conducted with forty-one typists from the word processing center of a major corporation. Typists were assigned to two different groups, one in which productivity goals were determined and assigned by the supervisor, and one in which goals were mutually set by the typists and their supervisors. Goals were established each week and the previous week's performance was used in setting goals for the next week. Performance was measured using an index of the weighted sum of the number of lines typed each week divided by the number of hours worked. The weights were based on the difficulty level of the material typed.

After ten weeks, both groups experienced significantly higher performance than was true before the experiment. Productivity increased by 18 percent in the participative group and by 15 percent in the assigned group. But why did their productivity improve? The typists were more productive because they had a clear understanding of what was expected of them.[4] Certainly their improvement was due to other factors as well, but having specific work goals was extremely important.

What this opening incident demonstrates is that clearly defined goals can often improve employee effectiveness and productivity. When people know what is expected they tend to get their work done within the specified time period and then move on to other activities. In addition, many organizations have found that an important side benefit of goal setting is that employee attitudes are often improved. For example, when Tenneco implemented a goal-setting program, management found that employee morale was improved, there was less job tension, and the work environment within the company was much more relaxed.[5]

Within the past few years a variety of laboratory and field studies have examined the effects of goal setting on mental and physical action. From these studies, we can draw two important conclusions. First, goal setting almost always has a positive effect on task performance. Second, goals affect task performance in at least four ways: by directing attention and action; mobilizing effort; prolonging effort over time; and motivating the individual to develop relevant strategies for goal attainment.[6]

In this chapter, we will examine several different ways in which goal setting can be used, including giving instructions, time management techniques, and Management by Objectives. Before we look at these devices, however, we need to consider several principles and concepts that provide a framework for goal setting.

PRINCIPLES AND CONCEPTS OF GOAL SETTING

Suppose that a manager wants to set goals for employees that will improve their job performance. How would he or she proceed? This is a basic issue that has been addressed by many researchers. Their findings constitute what might be considered a theory of goal setting. In this context, goal setting is defined as the process of developing, negotiating, and formalizing the targets or objectives that an employee is responsible for accomplishing.[7] Unlike other theories that are comprehensive in nature, this one is fragmented and consists of answers to four major questions (see Exhibit 6–1).

How Do Goals and Intentions Affect Performance?

In order to understand how goals affect performance, we need to remember that everyone has a wide range of values and attitudes. These represent emotional or affective responses to various situations. We look at the world around us and decide that something is good/bad, normal/abnormal, desirable/undesirable. On the basis of these judgments, we make decisions about how to behave or react. In other words, our values and attitudes lead to emotions and desires. These in turn result in the setting of specific intentions or goals, and ultimately we respond or perform some behavior in order to reach those goals.[8] Say, for example, that you

Exhibit 6-1
Theory of Goal Setting: Relevant Questions

- How do goals and intentions affect performance?
- Should goals be difficult or easy?
- Is it better to use general or specific goals?
- Does employee participation and knowledge of results affect performance?

conclude that your job performance needs to be improved. Your goal might be to increase your efforts and put more energy into the job. How would you do this? You might take a variety of actions, such as arriving on time instead of being ten minutes late, or reducing the number of errors that you make by a set percentage. In any event, you are consciously performing actual behaviors designed to achieve your intentions.

Should Goals Be Difficult or Easy?

The bulk of research supports the idea that individuals with difficult goals outperform those with easy goals.[9] In one study[10] subjects signed up for a creativity experiment and were randomly assigned either an easy, medium, or hard goal. The task required of them was to name, in one minute, as many objects as possible that could be described by a given adjective such as hot, cold, fast, or slow. There were fifteen trials using a different adjective each time. The group with the easy goal was asked to name four objects per minute. The medium goal was nine objects per minute. The hard goal was fourteen objects per minute. The results showed that even though the hard goal group did not always reach the goal, they still outperformed the other two groups. In addition, the medium goal group also did consistently better than the easy group. In the latter situation, people named their four objects and then stopped. They made no effort to continue since they had reached their goal.

Even though a positive relationship between goal level and performance usually exists, there are two important exceptions to this rule. One is that goal attainment must be clearly tied to rewards. If people do not understand the relationship between their performance and rewards, the goal may lose its motivating potential. Research has shown that people operating under a well-defined piece-rate system performed better when goals were difficult to reach. On the other hand, when a complex bonus incentive system was used, performance in the high goal condition was actually lower than in moderate or low goal conditions.[11] Apparently since the employees did not understand the system, they saw no reason to work harder.

The second exception is that people must believe that they are capable of reaching a goal.[12] Goals should cause people to exert themselves, but the outcomes must still be within their grasp. Unless employees expect that they can do what is necessary to achieve a goal, they will most likely become frustrated and their motivation to continue will not be high.

Is It Better to Use General or Specific Goals?

Most of the available literature supports the position that goals seem to regulate performance most predictably when they are expressed in specific, quantitative terms.[13] Telling employees to "do your best" or "try hard" is not enough. One must specify what "best" or "hard" means. This is not surprising. Increasing goal specificity on a task reduces role ambiguity and narrows the search for acceptable behaviors. The employee thus has a very clear idea of what is expected and can perform accordingly. People told to do their best do not really know what to do at all.

Two groups of subjects were required to perform a matching procedure on a complex task. Half were given specific, difficult goals to reach on each of the twelve-minute trials. The other group was told to "do your best." Interviews done following the experiment indicated that subjects in the specific goal group were actually trying to beat the standard set by the experimenter. As a result, even though the performance levels of both groups improved continuously over the twelve trials, the subjects with specific, difficult goals made more matches on all trials and increased their number of matches at a higher rate.[14]

A well-known study carried out at Weyerhauser Company also shows the practical significance of goal specificity.[15] Truck drivers at six company logging operations in Oklahoma were studied. Each operation consisted of six to ten people who performed one of the following tasks: felling trees; dragging the trees to a landing; loading the trees onto a truck; and driving the truck to the mill where it was weighed and unloaded. There were approximately six truck drivers assigned to each logging operation. A detailed analysis of each operation's performance revealed that trucks were frequently falling far short of their maximum legal net weight. In fact, most trucks were returning to the mill carrying 60 percent of the maximum load.

Measures of the net weight of all thirty-six logging trucks were collected for three consecutive months prior to goal setting. In order to be certain that fluctuations in weather and season would not bias the results, these premeasures were collected during the summer when logging conditions were optimal (i.e., July, August, and September). The results of the goal setting were monitored for nine consecutive months (i.e., October through June).

The specific goal of 94 percent was achieved after twelve weeks and represented a more than 50 percent improvement in performance over the "do your best" situation. Moreover, this increase held over time despite changes in season (fall, winter, and spring). While corporate policy prevented a detailed presentation of the effect, the researchers maintained that without the increase in efficiency due to goal setting, it would have cost the company $250,000 for the purchase of additional trucks in order to deliver the same quantity of logs to the mills. This figure does not even include the costs for additional fuel or the expense of recruiting and hiring additional drivers.

Does Employee Participation and Knowledge of Results Affect Performance?

Managers have often been told that employees will achieve higher goals if they are given a chance to participate in setting them and if they receive feedback on their goal achievement. Intuitively, this seems to be a safe assumption. In truth, however, the research is mixed.

Several studies have found a positive relationship between employee participation in setting goals and productivity. For example, research conducted with logging crews found that those who participated in setting goals set significantly higher ones and attained them more often than did employees whose goals were assigned by the supervisor.[16] The latter crews did no better than those who were just urged to do their best to improve productivity.

A company engaged in the design and manufacture of various types of van and truck bodies found that when engineers participated in goal setting, design errors were reduced and project completion dates were missed less often. Before the intervention, all projects were assigned to subordinates and due dates were established unilaterally by the manager. There was little, if any, input from the engineers. The subordinates frequently missed scheduled completion dates, and in their haste to finish past due projects many design errors occurred. Once participative goal setting had been implemented, the department manager met weekly with each of the three designers directly responsible for the design. During this meeting they would review the individual's project list and negotiate realistic due dates for which the subordinate would be held accountable. The study took place over a twenty-week period. Measurement commenced in week 5. By week 11 and for eight of the remaining weeks there were no missed completion dates. In addition, even though the number of design errors did rise sharply at first, by the twelfth week of the study, the error rate had decreased significantly and it remained at a much lower level than it had been before participative goal setting.[17]

One of the reasons participative goal setting may at times be superior to assigned goals is that it can lead to more difficult goals being set. When engineers and scientists involved in research and development for an international corporation were allowed to participate in goal setting, the results showed that there was, in fact, a positive linear relationship between participation and goal difficulty.[18] In other words, employee participation led to an upgrading of performance standards.

On the other hand, some studies have found negative results. For instance, in one experiment, subjects were assigned to either a participative goal condition or one of three assigned goal conditions. The findings of this study indicated that when goal difficulty was held constant, participation did not increase performance above that obtained with assigned goals.[19] It appears, therefore, that participation will not always lead to higher level goals and subsequent higher performance.

As far as knowledge of results (feedback) is concerned, research conducted in a farm machinery manufacturing plant found that this could be effective in improving performance.[20] In this case, the goal was to reduce the firm's accident rate, which at the time of intervention was three times that reported by the National Safety Council for similar organizations. The ten departments involved were divided into three groups based on their proximity to one another and the amount of interdependence between them. By the forty-fifth week of the study, and continuing for the next twelve weeks, three groups were receiving regular feedback on safety performance. A sixty-minute safety meeting was scheduled for the groups every week during regular working hours during which employees were told how their performance compared to that of the other groups. In addition, graphs were posted throughout the departments and at the end of each week average performance was recorded. The average total incidence rate for the three years prior to the study was 84.77 injuries. The yearly rate during the study was 55.14 injuries. The lost time rate also decreased from an average of 21.20 days to 9.88 days. Finally, the percentage of employees working in a completely safe manner went up from 62 percent to over 95 percent. In other words, safety rules were obeyed more often when employees received frequent feedback concerning their performance.

But will feedback by itself improve performance? Clearly the relationship between knowledge of results and performance is not a straightforward one. Most of the research suggests that knowledge of results is effective only if it is related to the accomplishment of specific goals.[21]

If the feedback involves nothing more than generalized praise, employees will not be able to make the linkage between it and particular goals. When this happens, even positive feedback may have no discernible effect on employees' behavior.

Summing Up Goal-Setting Principles

So where does the research on goal setting leave us? What are the useful implications from the perspective of day-to-day management? Even though much of the available research is less than totally conclusive, there are some things we can say with reasonable certainty.

1. Goals that are difficult but still acceptable to employees tend to have a positive effect on behavior. Remember, however, that rewards being offered need to be tied to goal accomplishment.
2. Specific, quantifiable goals are typically better than simply telling employees to "do your best." The evidence here is quite strong.
3. Employee participation in goal setting is useful if it results in more difficult goals being established. However, participation in and of itself does not directly result in higher productivity.
4. Feedback or knowledge of results is an important ingredient for successful goal setting provided that the employee can relate the feedback to specific on-the-job behaviors.
5. Goals can be an important positive force affecting behavior.

USING GOAL SETTING IN ORGANIZATIONS

Up to this point, we have been reviewing the basic principles of effective goal setting. When applied to work organizations, goal setting takes several forms. In the following sections we will examine three different approaches that involve goal setting, including giving employees instructions, using time management, and Management by Objectives.

Giving Instructions

Giving instructions is an important part of every manager's job, since even efficient workers need guidance. In addition, managers often cannot wait for people to behave appropriately. They must tell them what they are supposed to do in different situations. How much gets done frequently depends on the manager's effectiveness in giving instructions. When managers give instructions they are, in effect, providing employees with a set of goals. But how does one give instructions? In addition to following the advice suggested in items 1 through 4 above the manager will want to consider whom he or she is going to ask to carry out the instructions, when the best time to approach given employees is, and how to give them the directives. Exhibit 6-2 provides an overview of these three questions. Consider how they might be applied.[22]

Manager: This sales contract has to be typed immediately. I need it right away.

Typist: But I can't, I just can't. You're not the only person I work for, you know. Everyone around here thinks their stuff is so important. Well, I've had it—I just can't do it.

Exhibit 6–2
Considerations in Giving Instructions

Whom Do You Ask?

1. Determine who is most competent to perform a given task.

2. Ascertain who has sufficient time and resources to do the assigned task.

When Do You Approach Given Employees?

1. Approach the employees when they are most likely to be receptive to the instructions.

2. Take into account the employees' present work load.

3. Make predictions about potential roadblocks and make every effort to eliminate them before giving the instructions.

How Do You Give Instructions?

1. Be precise and clear in wording the instructions.

2. Make your presentation forceful but nonthreatening to the employee.

3. Always start with what the employee already knows. Do not make unfounded assumptions about prior knowledge.

4. Keep the instructions positive. Tell employees what to do rather than what not to do.

5. Give a "reason why" explanation and show the benefits to that employee.

6. Encourage questions and feedback whenever this seems reasonable.

7. Establish a target date for completion and set up a system to monitor results at several points along the way.

Source: R. B. McAfee and P. J. Champagne, *Organizational Behavior: A Manager's View* (St. Paul, Minn.: West Publishing Co., 1987), p. 215. Reprinted by permission.

Manager: Look, this means $15,000. Part of that money pays your salary! Get on this right now!

Typist: Okay, I'll do my best. But don't expect miracles. I do work for two other people, you know.

What do you think will happen in this situation? Would you expect the contract to be finished on time? More likely than not, the job will not get done and even if it is finished by the deadline, it may not be done right. Suppose, however, that the manager takes a somewhat different approach.

Manager: I'm really in a bind. This sales contract needs to be sent out today. It means $15,000 to the company. What's your workload like?

Typist: Well, I have several reports due and then there is that marketing prospectus you asked for. You said that was urgent.

Manager: Do you think you can work this in?

Typist: I can delay everything but one item our treasurer requested. You know how she can be.

Manager: I'll handle that problem if you can make sure that this gets typed. Can you do that?

Typist: Well, as long as no other emergencies develop, I believe I can get it done. If I have to, I can stay a bit late.

The second situation is much more likely to be productive. Even though the typist is overloaded, and probably not too receptive to additional work, chances are that the sales contract will be finished. What did the manager do differently?

One difference is that the manager described the predicament and the importance of getting the contract completed as soon as possible. The typist was asked for opinions and ideas, and an effort was made to remove roadblocks such as dealing with the treasurer. Also, the instructions were given in a firm but nonthreatening manner, making cooperation much more likely. Finally, the goal was challenging as well as being specific and clearly understandable. The manager's timing may not have been optimal, but then again, one does not always have the luxury of several weeks' advance notice.

When giving instructions, it is important to remember that listeners are influenced by both verbal and nonverbal communication.[23] The nonverbal items include behaviors such as eye contact, posture, gestures, and tone of voice.

One way of confirming that others really understand your instructions is to ask them to summarize in their own words what you have just said. When asked if they understand the instructions, some people will automatically say yes regardless of whether or not they understand. Getting feedback from them will lower the chance of misunderstanding.

Attentive listening is another way to increase the effectiveness of your instructions. If you listen carefully to others, you will not only know if your instructions are being understood but also you will learn more about the people you are instructing. You will find out how they feel about you as well as their opinions on a wide range of topics.[24]

The important point is that giving instructions well will increase the likelihood that goals will be accomplished. Remember that every manager must, at certain times, tell employees what they should be doing. The more adept you are at giving instructions, the better off everyone will be.

Time Management and Goal Setting

A second approach many managers use to establish goals is time management. More a set of techniques than a specific, unified concept, the idea that time can be used more effectively has become increasingly popular in recent years.

Time management is based on the assumption that time is an inelastic, finite resource. There are only twenty-four hours in a day and there is no way to stretch this out. Getting a job done requires that people prioritize tasks and develop clear timetables for reaching their goals.

Elements of Time Management

Any manager about to embark on a concerted effort at time management must address two key issues:[25] (1) What are the limits of my own as well as my employees' time and how can I provide both myself and them with more time to accomplish company goals? (2) How can I and my subordinates best use discretionary time? Fortunately, time management is a skill that can be learned and if the literature is short on theory, it provides many practical skill tips. All the practices discussed here can potentially help people to realize what their goals are and get things done.[26]

Time management proponents assert that both managers and their employees should set long-term (goals for the next six months to a year) and short-term goals (goals for this week). Once this has been done the various goals should be rated in order of importance as follows: *A* (must do), *B* (should do), and *C* (can be put off). A system using numbers (i.e., 1, 2, 3) would be just as good. Finally, one develops action steps that spell out how these goals are to be achieved. Take, for example, two outside sales representatives who decide as a top goal to improve their overall volume by 20 percent during the next six months. How will this be accomplished? They must establish new accounts and try to increase sales to present customers. Making five calls each week on potential new accounts might be one of the action steps taken.

Ultimately, all goals and action steps must be translated into daily activities. In this regard, time management advocates recommend the use of daily "to do" lists. People are encouraged to make a list regularly and at the same time every day. It can be done first thing in the morning or at the end of the day. (Exhibit 6–3 shows a typical worksheet.)

Exhibit 6–3
The "To Do" Form

ACTION PLANNING

	PRIORITY A–B–C	ACTIVITY DESCRIPTION	TIME REQUIRED
AM			
PM			

In the "To Do" section, one lists items that should be done today and also those that one wants to do in the near future. In this space everything that comes to mind is recorded. The items listed could include both large and small projects—those that are time-consuming, as well as items that take only a few minutes to perform. In order to avoid confusion one should try to be specific. For example, "phone calls" may be too general. Instead, if there are many calls, one might want to categorize or identify them by using the names of the people to be called.

When items are lengthy, they should be broken down into their component parts. Preparing a report could involve going to the library, talking with a particular employee, consulting an earlier report, checking some figures with the finance department, and finding out the deadline date. While it may be possible to complete the whole report in ninety minutes, including all the preliminary work, listing each step helps in planning and organizing the task. For example, if the key employee is hard to track down, he or she should be sought out first. Without the breakdown, you might wait until the project's end only to find that the person is gone for the next week.

The next step is to prioritize the listed items. The question to ask here is: "If nothing else gets done today, what is the one item that must be done?" When a salesperson looks at his or her list it may be clear what customer must be seen. On the other hand, the salesperson may see three items that need to be accomplished. Here is where the A-B-C priority system comes into play, for it helps one choose which of these three to tackle first. Without prioritizing, one may try to tackle all items at once and complete nothing by the end of the day. But suppose that at 11:00 A.M. a call comes in from the boss demanding that a project be completed by 5:00 P.M. What then? Clearly, the plan for the day has been blown sky high. When this happens, the day needs to be rescheduled quickly. The boss has provided a new A. This now becomes top priority and must be balanced along with the other goals on the list.

Time management advocates also suggest identifying high productivity hours and scheduling the most important tasks in these time slots. To identify high productivity hours, the following question is suggested: "When am I most mentally alert during the working day?" This helps people determine the period of the day in which they are able to concentrate with a clear mind. There may be one period (e.g., between 8:30 A.M. and 11:30 A.M.) or two or more periods (e.g., between 8:00 A.M. and 10:00 A.M., and between 2:00 P.M. and 4:00 P.M.).

Once the "To Do" list has been developed and prioritized, one must act on it. The A's come first, then the B's, and finally the C's. Drawing a line through the items that can be delegated to someone else or are completed is often recommended. It is rare for managers to accomplish all the C items.

What if the phone rings and you end up spending a half-hour on the telephone talking to an irate customer? When interruptions like this happen, the following question is suggested: "What is the best use of my time right now?" This question is designed to help reestablish priorities and get back to accomplishing the high priority goals.

In order for people to accomplish their "To Do" lists expeditiously, time management advocates have recommended an array of helpful hints designed to reduce wasted time. Many of these are listed in Exhibit 6–4. For example, they recommend that all the papers one receives (memos, letters, reports) be handled only once. They should be sorted into *A*, *B*, and *C* piles. Then each should be thrown away, filed, or responded to immediately in the shortest, simplest way (e.g., pick up the phone and call).

Time Management in Practice

The most important question is, of course, whether time management really works. According to a study done with the managers of a large health care facility, the answer to the question is yes.[27] In this situation, participants consisted of personnel in middle and senior administrative positions. They were divided into three groups based on length of tenure in their present position and the average number of employees supervised. Each group attended a time management workshop on four consecutive days per week during a two-week period. The ultimate purpose of this study was to determine whether or not managers could learn to manage time better. The results indicated that this was possible, thus validating the notion that time management training was worthwhile.

Management by Objectives

By far the most formal approach to goal setting is Management by Objectives (MBO). First introduced by Peter Drucker in the mid-1950s, MBO has become one of the most widely used management tools. It is reported that from 50 to 80 percent of U.S. businesses use some form of MBO.[28] MBO has also been applied in government organizations, school systems, and universities. What is MBO? How does it work?

In a sense everyone manages by objectives. One always has objectives, whether they are limited to the day's activities or extended to the end of the year, whether they are precise or vague, admitted or denied, communicated or withheld, observable or not. The difference between MBO and other approaches to goal setting is that the former is usually thought of as a program that the organization uses in an effort to address identifiable problems.[29]

While MBO is more easily described than defined, a review of the relevant literature suggests the following definition:[30]

Exhibit 6–4
Ways to Reduce Wasted Time

1. Record your ideas rather than trusting your memory.
2. Establish priorities for yourself either the night before or first thing in the morning.
3. Leave free time to take care of emergencies or unexpected interruptions.
4. Delegate whenever possible. Don't try to do everything yourself.
5. Deal with problems one at a time.
6. Do easy and routine projects during that part of the day when your energy level is at its lowest.
7. Make appointments and adhere to the schedule as much as possible.
8. Don't leave your office door open when you are really trying to concentrate.
9. If you want meetings to be short, meet with people away from your office and always remain standing.
10. Carry a small tape recorder or note pad to keep track of ideas when you are away from your desk.
11. Use waiting time on or off the job to catch up on your reading. Keep materials handy.
12. Establish a system which allows you to segregate papers on your desk. This will allow you to concentrate on one issue at a time and also prevent papers from becoming mixed up and lost.
13. Highlight the materials you read for later reference.
14. If you don't want others to disturb you close your office door and either transfer or have someone take your telephone calls.

MBO is a managerial process whereby organizational purposes are diagnosed and met by joining superiors and subordinates in the pursuit of mutually agreed upon goals and objectives, which are specific, measurable, time bound, and joined to an action plan; progress and goal attainment are measured and monitored in appraisal sessions which center on mutually determined objective standards of performance.

As Exhibit 6–5 demonstrates, MBO is both a process that entails a series of steps and a philosophy of management that emphasizes employee participation in goal setting. It requires that managers who use an authoritarian leadership style adopt a more participatory approach to employer-employee relations. Often, this is not an easy transition to make.

The MBO Process

In practice, MBO varies from one organization to another. In some firms it is a very formal, carefully defined management system that uses precise scheduling of performance reviews, formal evaluation techniques,

Exhibit 6–5
What Is MBO?

1. MBO is a Philosophy of Management

   - A philosophy which emphasizes accomplishments and results

   - A philosophy which is future- rather than past-oriented

   - A philosophy which encourages increased participation by employees

2. MBO is a Process Consisting of a Number of Steps

   - Develop specific long-range goals and organizational objectives

   - Develop objectives for various departments and units

   - Counsel employees to establish individual objectives for their jobs

   - Develop a plan for achieving the individual objectives

   - Implement the plan and take corrective action as necessary

   - Review progress toward both organizational and individual objectives

   - Appraise individual performance and provide employees with constructive feedback

   - Develop new or reconsidered objectives and continue the MBO process

and specific formats in which objectives and measures are subject to close scrutiny. MBO can also be considerably less formal. Still, no matter how it is structured, an effective MBO program usually consists of four essential elements.[31]

The first element involves goal setting. It begins with top management formulating long-term goals for the organization. Each unit or department then develops its own goals within the parameters of the total organizational goals. Finally, each employee develops individual job objectives in collaboration with his or her immediate superior. This overall approach helps assure that the various levels within the organization have a common direction. Take the case of a hospital that is seeking, as an overall goal, to reduce costs by 10 percent during the next twelve-month period, while maintaining the same level of productivity. Over this same period, the admitting department might attempt to reduce the standard time needed to process new patients from twenty-five to twenty minutes, and reduce complaints by 40 percent. Individuals working in admissions would then set their own goals within these parameters. For example, one clerk might set an objective of submitting all insurance forms to accounting by 12:00 noon for all patients admitted during the morning in order to reduce backlogs and complaints.

Advocates of MBO recommend that the objectives or goals be concise statements that give employees a clear sense of direction and purpose. Goals such as cutting costs, increasing quality, or improving customer relations are too general. They would have to be converted into more tangible outcomes that can be measured and evaluated. For example, one might say that departmental costs need to be cut by 10 percent, that customer relations can be improved by ensuring that all telephone requests are processed within thirty minutes from the time of the call, or that phase 1 of a new MIS (Management Information System) will be installed by June 15, according to specifications.

The second element is joint action planning. At this point, the means to the ends established in goal setting are jointly developed by superiors and their subordinates. In other words, the parties involved try to identify how the ends are to be achieved. This includes identifying the activities necessary to accomplish the objectives, establishing relationships between these various actions, assigning responsibility for each, and estimating both the time and other resources (facilities, equipment, money, human resources, etc.) that may be necessary. In effect, each of these activities is a separate step with its own special requirements. It is important to remember that the integrity of the action plan is maintained only when the plan is specific and realistic, when responsibility has been accepted, when accountability has been established, when there is commitment by all persons to the objectives, and when employees are given sufficient discretionary authority to operate on their own.

The third element, self-control of activities, means that individual employees—not the manager—will control their own behavior and the activities required to implement the action plan. This requires meaningful participation in both the goal-setting and action-planning processes, presumably resulting in a better understanding and a higher level of commitment to the objectives. Individuals are given the feedback and information they need to assess progress and to take corrective action on their own.

The final element, periodic performance review, means that the manager and subordinate evaluate the employee's performance in terms of established objectives. Problem areas are identified and obstacles removed so that additional levels of success and new objectives can be established. These reviews should be held as frequently as is practical during the goal period. They may be conducted on a one-to-one basis or in small groups.

The emphasis is not on finding fault or downgrading employees but rather on overcoming problems and roadblocks.

Examples of MBO in Organizations

Over the past twenty-five years, MBO has probably received more attention than any other single management technique, and since its inception it has been both praised and condemned. The arguments supporting the adoption of MBO as a managerial system include improved communication between superiors and subordinates, better planning and evaluation, and greater employee motivation.

While many organizations have implemented MBO programs, most have not done a careful evaluation of their effectiveness. In fact, as one author has pointed out, "most organizations have adopted MBO on faith as a result of questionable studies, or on the basis of unsubstantiated testimonials, many of them in the form of case studies."[32] The literature, however, does contain a few examples of companies that have attempted to evaluate MBO using objective outcome measures before and after the program's introduction. Briefly examining these can provide a better understanding of the MBO process.

The Purex Corporation. One of the most widely cited MBO programs was that of the Purex Corporation, a manufacturer of men's and women's clothing.[33] After successful use of MBO at one of its larger plants, Purex instituted it in the fifteen manufacturing plants of one of the largest divisions of the company. This was accomplished through a series of meetings conducted at each plant by members of the corporation's Management Analysis and Services Group.

The MBO program at Purex contained the following elements:

1. *Goal setting.* All managers were responsible for establishing tangible goals in all areas of responsibility. However, in order to ensure consistency from one group to another, these goals were subject to the review and approval of one's immediate superior.

2. *Self-control.* Various reports were used to compare actual performance against established goals. These reports were given directly to the individual concerned, as well as to higher levels of management, so that the supervisor could initiate corrective action when necessary.

3. *Periodic performance reviews.* The program also provided a mechanism for supervisors and subordinates to regularly review progress toward established goals.

4. *Program evaluation.* A variety of methods were used in an effort to evaluate the impact of the program. These included questionnaires, informal face-to-face guided interviews, historical analysis of production reports, computer control reports, and written performance reviews covering a period of approximately three years.

The company made the first real effort to assess the program's effectiveness eighteen months after its introduction. The findings were generally favorable and can be summarized as follows:

1. The overall level of goal accomplishment increased from one measurement period to the next. The net increases were calculated to be approximately 3.0 percent during the first year and an additional 2.7 percent during the next six months.
2. Before the program was instituted, average productivity for all plants was decreasing. After the introduction of the program, average productivity actually increased at a rate of approximately 0.3 percent per month.
3. Participants became increasingly aware of basic company goals.
4. The results of attitude surveys indicated improved morale and an increase in the level of motivation in most plants due to the periodic reviews.
5. Communication and mutual understanding between plant personnel and company headquarters improved.

The findings of a follow-up study at Purex one year later generally supported those of the original study. For example, the average level of goal attainment continued to improve. During the two-and-one-half years of the program, goal attainment increased by 12 percent.

According to the managers involved, the program had two major advantages. First, it improved management planning and control on the job and provided motivation to improve individual performance. Second, the program took managers away from the daily operations in the plant, thus forcing them to plan the use of resources and reducing the temptation to become totally preoccupied with day-to-day problems.

Despite the apparent success of the program, several problem areas emerged. More than a dozen managers reported that MBO was "used as a whip" and that it "treated people like statistics." An equal number felt that MBO had become a statistics game based upon unrealistic standards and unchallenging goals. There was also evidence of an overemphasis on the attainment of production goals and targets. Some managers complained that this was generally done at the expense of other goals, especially those related to quality. Finally, eight participants reported that the program failed to provide any tangible rewards for managers. In the words of one manager: "What does it mean to the individual when he successfully meets his goals? How does he personally benefit other than by a feeling of accomplishment and inner satisfaction?" In some instances, the program was even seen as a disincentive since it dramatically increased the amount of paperwork required of the managers. However, despite these concerns, top management at Purex judged the program to be quite successful.

Palos Corporation. A second example involved three of the six plants of the Palos Manufacturing Corporation, a firm that produces electrical products and machine parts for other industrial users.[34] The plants studied were designated as Palos Experimental Plant 1 (E_1), Experimental Plant 2 (E_2), and Comparison Plant 3 (C). At the beginning of the study the plants were quite similar in terms of size, span of control (number of subordinates per manager), educational level of employees, location, and the number of levels of management.

Before MBO was introduced in plants E_1 and E_2, the performance of first-line supervisors in both production and marketing was recorded. Then, the personnel managers in these two plants along with an outside consultant began the program. The entire management hierarchy of each plant attended a four-day training session, away from their worksites, focusing on the philosophy, process, and mechanics of MBO.

Did MBO lead to improved performance? Measures taken eighteen months into the program did indeed indicate improvements in the experimental plants. In plants E_1 and E_2, performance in the production departments improved in terms of quantity and quality. The comparison plant's quality rate actually decreased. Plant E_1 showed a reduction in absenteeism, but E_2 showed essentially no change.

The experience of the marketing departments using MBO was also favorable. Here, plants E_1 and E_2 improved substantially on three of the four performance measures. The comparison plant also showed improvement, but the results were nowhere near as impressive. In terms of direct selling cost, however, the results were essentially unchanged and only plant E_1 showed any positive change.

Despite some gaps in the data, it does seem that MBO had a positive effect in both the production and marketing departments. Thus, this study provides us with additional empirical evidence that MBO can improve employee performance and productivity.

A State Human Services Agency. Another example which demonstrates the potential for MBO in an office rather than plant setting involved a state human services agency charged with delivering vocational rehabilitation services.[35] The experimental group consisted of several offices in one region. The offices in the other two regions were combined to act as a control group. The MBO program was conducted in two phases, beginning with training and development. Seven two-and-one-half-hour sessions were conducted in order to provide supervisors with the background, philosophy, and specific steps for implementing MBO. The training stressed the writing of quantitative behavioral objectives and the use of systematic praise. All managerial personnel in the regional office were involved. A total of twelve managers completed the training.

The second phase consisted of in-depth individual counseling and interview sessions involving the researchers and each manager to establish objectives for the department and each employee. This phase culminated with the regional director and each supervisor negotiating specific objectives for the upcoming year. The supervisors were then told to work with each of their staff members (counselors) to develop quantitative, observable measures. A total of twenty-three professional counselors were involved. Measures of performance were taken for the experimental and control groups on a monthly basis for nine months before and eighteen months after the implementation of MBO.

The control group also consisted of twenty-three counselors and was matched as closely as possible with the experimental group in terms of work experience, educational background, and a variety of demographic factors. Both the control and experimental groups served the same types of populations and had similar responsibilities.

Four propositions were tested in the study. Two concerned the effect of MBO on quantity and quality of performance, while the others examined satisfaction with supervision and with the work itself. Quantity was measured by keeping track of the number of names of potential clients received by each counselor in a month, the number of persons passing the federal eligibility test that qualified them for benefits, the number of rehabilitation plans written by each counselor, and the number of clients who found employment for sixty continuous working days. The two quality measures were the number of errors that a counselor made with respect to the computerized case form used and the number of mistakes made on clients' billing codes for funds disbursement. Satisfaction measures were obtained through the Job Descriptive Index, a standard job satisfaction scaling device.

The results of this study indicated that MBO improved work quantity. Significant improvement for all four quantity-related items measured was found with the exception of rehabilitation. The combined measure (all four quantity items taken as a whole) showed a significant positive trend.

With respect to work quality, the results were also favorable. However, while there was a significant improvement in both error rates, this trend had already begun before MBO. As a result, there was some question as to whether the improvement following implementation was attributable to MBO or was just a continuation of the trend observed before the program was started. In retrospect, the reduction in the error rates may have been largely the result of the management's new emphasis on collecting and reporting error data. Since counselors knew that the information was being scrutinized, they may have been more careful.

The results of the satisfaction questionnaire were mixed. Satisfaction with the work itself did not increase following intervention. On the other hand, satisfaction with supervision significantly improved. Outcomes were generally positive and the program was viewed by the agency as worthwhile and successful.

MBO Pitfalls

These examples demonstrate that MBO can indeed be a productive management tool. But unfortunately, some organizations have made MBO a "paperwork mill," while others use it to "hammer" people when objectives are not met. A smart manager, however, applies MBO as a device to operate more productively.[36] To do this, though, requires that the manager deal with and attempt to overcome several common pitfalls.[37]

One of the most frequently cited criticisms of MBO is that it is time-consuming and involves too many burdensome procedures. Managers complain that a great deal of time must be spent in separate discussions with subordinates. Time is also needed to explain the program, set and communicate objectives, and review progress toward goals. Additional hours are required to complete all the necessary paperwork. Managers who already feel pressed frequently protest this increased demand.

Another problem arises from the presumed need to quantify all objectives. The truth, however, is that not all valuable results lend themselves to quantification. Still, the tendency in MBO is to use only those measures that can be quantified. Unfortunately, this could drive employees to engage in activities that are tangential or contrary to the true objective. In addition, quantifying the duties of many higher-level professional jobs may be difficult. How would you, for example, quantify the long-range goals of a scientist working on applied research?

A third typical pitfall is overemphasis on results (ends) at the expense of specifying how these objectives are to be attained (means). The problem here is that emphasizing results can encourage an "ends justify the means" mentality. Achievement-oriented managers and employees totally committed to achieving short-term results may threaten fundamental processes that in the long run may be much more important. Keep in mind that a sales representative may be able to meet quotas by overstocking customers in the short run at the price of damaging the long-term relationship.

Finally, excessive emphasis on individual results may be detrimental to the overall group effort. MBO focuses on objectives for individuals, but the key outcomes involve organizational results. Ideally, of course, there should be no inconsistency between the two. When supervisors work with employees to establish objectives, an effort should be made to coordinate the goals of all subordinates in that department or unit. But even this may not be sufficient since one's goals in MBO can be affected by the performance of others who are not under the control of that supervisor. Hence, individual goals may be accomplished at the expense of organizational goals.

If MBO is to be of value in the long run, these potential problem areas need to be understood and their effects minimized. The problems discussed here do not constitute a definitive list. Rather, they represent several typical issue areas.

SUMMARY

Goal setting is an important technique that managers can use to improve employee effectiveness and productivity.[38] When people have clearly defined goals they are more likely to get work done within a specified time period. As a side benefit, goal setting can often have a positive effect on employee morale.

The manager has much to gain personally from using goal setting. Use of this strategy serves to clarify the organizational goals toward which the manager must work. In addition, the delegation of functions, which is part of goal setting, reduces the manager's own responsibilities, and at the same time encourages employee independence.

If managers decide that they would like to use goal setting there are several principles that they need to keep in mind. These include the fact that individuals with difficult goals outperform those with easy ones, provided that goal attainment is clearly tied to rewards and that people perceive the goals to be reachable and reasonable. Also, goals seem to regulate performance most predictably when they are expressed in specific, quantitative terms. Employee participation in goal setting is useful if it leads to more difficult goals being set. Knowledge of results is effective if it can be linked to specific goals. The point, therefore, is to set difficult but still reasonable goals. Invite participation when this seems appropriate, and, assuming the goals are specific, give employees feedback.

When applied to work organizations, goal setting takes several forms. The first is giving instructions. This is a basic element of every manager's job in that even efficient workers need guidance. When managers give instructions, they are also providing employees with goals.

A second popular device is time management. This is based on the assumption that time is an inelastic, finite resource. Getting a job done requires that people prioritize work and develop clear timetables for reaching goals.

The elements of time management include setting both long- and short-range goals, prioritizing them, and developing action steps that spell out how these goals are to be achieved. Ultimately, these goals and action steps translate into daily activity or "to do" lists. These lists should be made every day and steps should be taken to minimize time-wasters.

By far the most formal approach to goal setting is Management by Objective (MBO). It involves a series of steps, plus an emphasis on employee participation in goal setting. It requires that managers who use an authoritarian leadership style adopt a more participatory approach to employer-employee relations. In practice, MBO varies from one organization to another. Yet no matter how it is structured, an effective program usually consists of four essential elements: goal setting, action planning, self-control, and periodic performance review.

Remember, however, that just because employees have established goals, this in no way guarantees that a particular behavior will take place. People typically have many goals and some of those may be in conflict with one another. As a result some goals may never be accomplished for lack of time or energy. While one task of a manager is to set or help employees set goals, another important responsibility is to help them prioritize their goals so that the most important ones are accomplished by the agreed-upon target dates.

NOTES

1. R. H. Magee, M. F. Magee, and M. M. Davies, "A Performance Planning Primer," *Training* 22 (1985), pp. 99–101.

2. R. W. Braid, "Effective Use of Time," *Supervisory Management*, July 1983, pp. 9–14.

3. D. K. Denton, "Giving Instructions: It's Not as Easy as It Seems," *Supervisory Management*, September 1983, pp. 33–35.

4. G. P. Latham and G. A. Yukl, "Effects of Assigned and Participative Goal Setting on Performance and Job Satisfaction," *Journal of Applied Psychology* 61 (1976), pp. 166–71.

5. J. M. Ivancevich, et al., "Goal Setting: The Tenneco Approach to Personal Development and Management Effectiveness," *Organizational Dynamics*, Winter 1978, pp. 58–80.

6. E. A. Locke, et al., "Goal Setting and Task Performance: 1969–1980," *Psychological Bulletin* 90, no. 1 (1981), pp. 125–52.

7. D. D. Umstot, T. Mitchell, and C. H. Bell, Jr., "Goal Setting and Job Enrichment: An Integrated Approach to Job Design," *Academy of Management Review* 3 (October 1978), p. 868.

8. W. C. Hammer, J. Ross, and B. Stow, "Motivation in Organization: The Need for a New Direction," in Dennis W. Organ, ed., *The Applied Psychology of Work Behavior* (Dallas: Business Publications, 1978).

9. Locke, et al., "Goal Setting and Task Performance."

10. H. Garland, "Goal Levels and Task Performance: A Compelling Replication of Some Compelling Results," *Journal of Applied Psychology* 67, no. 2 (1982), pp. 245–48.

11. J. C. Mower, R. Middlemist, and D. Luther, "Joint Effects of Assigned Goal Level and Incentive Structure on Task Performance: A Laboratory Study," *Journal of Applied Psychology* 66, no. 5 (1981), pp. 598–603.

12. M. Erez and F. H. Kanfer, "The Role of Goal Acceptance in Goal Setting and Task Performance," *Academy of Management Review* 8, no. 3 (1983), pp. 454–63.

13. E. A. Locke, "Toward a Theory of Task Motivation and Incentive," *Organizational Behavior and Performance*, May 1968, pp. 157–89.

14. E. A. Locke and J. F. Bryan, "Performance Goals as Determinants of Level

of Performance and Boredom," *Journal of Applied Psychology* 51 (1967), pp. 120–30.

15. G. P. Latham and J. J. Baldes, "The Practical Significance of Locke's Theory of Goal Setting," *Journal of Applied Psychology* 60, no. 1 (1975), pp. 122–24.

16. G. P. Latham and E. A. Locke, "Goal Setting—A Motivational Technique That Works," *Organizational Dynamics*, Autumn 1979, pp. 68–80.

17. M. K. McCuddy and M. H. Griggs, "Goal Setting and Feedback in a Professional Department: A Case Study," *Journal of Organizational Behavior Management* 6, no. 1 (Spring 1984), pp. 53–64.

18. G. P. Latham, "Does Participation in Setting Goals Boost Engineers' Performance?" *Chemical Engineering*, January 15, 1979, pp. 141–44.

19. G. P. Latham, T. P. Steele, and L. M. Saari, "The Effects of Participation and Goal Difficulty on Performance," *Personnel Psychology* 35 (1982), pp. 677–86.

20. R. A. Reber and J. A. Wallin, "The Effects of Training, Goal Setting, and Knowledge Results on Safe Behavior: A Component Analysis," *Academy of Management Journal* 27, no. 3 (1984), pp. 544–60.

21. J. L. Koch, "Effects of Goal Specificity and Performance Feedback to Work Groups on Peer Leadership, Performance and Attitudes," *Human Relations* 32, no. 10 (1979), pp. 819–40.

22. B. A. Potter, "Speaking with Authority: How to Give Directions," *Supervisory Management*, March 1980, pp. 171–81.

23. B. A. Potter, *Turning Around* (New York: AMACOM, 1980).

24. Denton, "Giving Instructions."

25. W. K. Schilit, "A Manager's Guide to Efficient Time Management," *Personnel Journal*, September 1983, pp. 736–42.

26. J. Davidson, *Effective Time Management* (New York: Human Sciences Press, 1978).

27. F. Hanel, G. Martin, and S. Koop, "Field Testing of a Self Instruction Time Management Manual with Managerial Staff in an Institutional Setting," *Journal of Organizational Behavior Management*, Fall/Winter 1982, pp. 27–36.

28. W. R. Fannin, "Making MBO Work: Matching Management Style to My Program," *Supervisory Management*, September 1981, pp. 20–27. See also R. G. Greenwood, "Management by Objectives as Developed by Peter Drucker, Assisted by Harold Smiddy," *Academy of Management Review* 6, no. 2 (1981), pp. 225–30.

29. C. M. Kelly, "Remedied MBO," *Business Horizons*, September–October 1983, pp. 62–67.

30. A. Raia, *Managing by Objectives* (Glenview, Ill.: Scott Foresman and Co., 1974).

31. Ibid. See also S. P. Robbins, *Management: Concepts and Practices* (Englewood Cliffs, N.J.: Prentice-Hall, 1984).

32. J. P. Muczk, "A Controlled Field Experiment Measuring the Impact of MBO on Performance Data," *Journal of Management Studies*, October 1978, pp. 318–29.

33. A. P. Raia, "Goal Setting and Self Control," *Journal of Management Studies*, February 1965, pp. 34–51.

34. J. M. Ivancevich, "Changes in Performance in Management by Objectives Program," *Administrative Science Quarterly* 19 (December 1974), pp. 563–74.

35. K. R. Thompson, F. Luthans, and W. D. Terpening, "The Effects of MBO on Performance and Satisfaction in a Public Sector Organization," *Journal of Management* 7, no. 1 (1982), pp. 53–68.

36. B. Richards, "Three Classes of Objectives and Plans Make MBO More Effective," *Personnel Journal*, December 1986, pp. 28–30.

37. Robbins, *Management*. See also R. W. Beatty and C. E. Schneier, *Personnel Administration: An Experiential/Skill Building Approach* (Reading, Mass.: Addison-Wesley Publishing Co., 1981).

38. Richards, "Three Classes of Objectives."

7

Redesigning Jobs

A problem is that often people have the knowledge but not the authority to apply it, and the people with the authority don't have the knowledge.[1]

I believe that humanization of work and efficiency can be compatible! I believe that in today's society they are inseparable.[2]

Job enrichment involves meaningful changes in job tasks by increasing opportunities for responsibility, personal achievement, feedback, growth, and advancement.[3]

Steep increases in profitability, productivity, customer satisfaction, and staff morale were reported by First National Bank of Chicago[4] in 1986 after employees, managers, and a consultant redesigned jobs in the bank unit responsible for issuing letters of credit. In April and May of 1985 employees in the letter-of-credit department were asked to complete a Job Diagnostic Survey. The results showed that up to 80 percent of the staff were dissatisfied with their jobs. The 20 percent who were satisfied were all professionals—managers and technicians. The rest were all in some stage of the assembly process. There was even one employee whose whole job was to feed tape into a Telex machine. Over a period of six months the 110-person staff of the letters-of-credit department redesigned their work, consolidating discrete tasks into complete jobs to be performed by broadly trained professionals. Traditional job specialties were abolished and a new, more responsible, and more highly paid job classification—"documentary products professional"—was created. Employees then underwent training that upgraded their skills and permitted them to perform the restructured work at salaries averaging 20 percent higher. "What we started with was a major fundamental problem—poor productivity and profitability," said Lawrence F. Buettner, the bank's vice president for documentary products. "We also felt we were not serving our customers.

Henry Ford was very correct to use an assembly line for building cars," Buettner said. "But paper just doesn't flow that way in a service business."

Job redesign has been a popular topic during the past few years in both the academic and practitioner literature, and as the First National Bank case shows, it remains a viable technique for improving employee productivity and effectiveness. While there is certainly more than one definition, in this chapter we will consider job redesign to be an effort to modify the content, methods, or relationships of jobs in order to satisfy the technological requirements of the firm and the organizational needs of the worker.[5] The important question for managers to address is how jobs can be redesigned so that both the goals of the firm and the personal needs of the employees are satisfied. In other words, how can one achieve a "fit" between people and jobs that promotes high productivity and, at the same time, offers a quality experience for those who do the work?[6]

In this chapter we will discuss the practice of job redesign, with special emphasis on job enrichment. We will consider the various forms of job redesign, the components of job enrichment, and the prerequisites for successful job redesign. Finally, we will examine several examples of firms that either are using or have used job redesign and enrichment.

FORMS OF JOB REDESIGN

There are a variety of methods for redesigning jobs. These range from work simplification to relatively complex job enrichment programs.

Work Simplification

Grounded in industrial engineering, work simplification involves combining or removing parts of a job, including the substitution of machines, to do work that is physically burdensome and/or repetitive. The objective is to make an employee more productive by eliminating duplication of effort, removing those tasks that are really not necessary, and generally minimizing the steps taken in performing a particular job. An example of this occurred at Cummins Engine Company where managers were able to reduce the fabrication cost of an item from $6.00 to $1.88 by just reorganizing work stations, paying close attention to detailed work movements, and minimizing the transfer of parts.[7]

Job Rotation

Job rotation involves physically moving an employee from one work station to another. The tasks retain their original design, but to provide variety the worker shifts among a limited set of tasks every few hours or from day-to-day. The rationale is that exposure to different people and positions will increase motivation and satisfaction. For example, in the microwax department of Shell's Stanlow refinery, operators were rotated from unit to unit. As a result, their competence improved and they were better qualified for promotion.[8]

Job rotation is appealing in that, at the very least, it provides a way to share unexciting jobs. However, this technique does not provide substantive changes in the content of jobs. Therefore, many organizations use it as part of a larger job redesign effort.

Job Enlargement

Job enlargement requires that managers expand the scope of a job by increasing the number of different tasks for which a worker is responsible. The idea here is to put more related tasks into a job offering the worker a greater part of the total process. Instead of moving from one work station to another as in job rotation, a number of tasks are grouped together, thus providing a longer work cycle and more variety. This is often referred to as "horizontal loading."[9] For example, an auto assembly line worker's job could be enlarged from installing just one tail light to installing both tail lights and the trunk lid. An auto mechanic might be allowed to align front ends, change brakes, and service transmissions in addition to changing oil. A clerk could be given responsibility for both typing and filing completed work.

Job Enrichment

Job enrichment is the redesign of a job so that it has more variety and requires a higher level of knowledge and skill. In addition, employees have greater responsibility, more autonomy, and increased control over the pace and scheduling of work. Job enrichment attempts to improve a job by making it more exciting and challenging.

Job enrichment includes the task variety encountered in job enlargement, but goes further. A set of tasks is grouped to form a job of sufficient complexity to require choices (discretion) about how to bring together the varied operations and get the job done. This is sometimes referred to as "vertical loading" in that the worker is allowed to set schedules, decide on work methods, check quality, and develop new solutions to problems. For instance, instead of simply feeding material into a machine, the worker with an enriched job might perform machine "set up," feed the machinery, inspect the output, accept or reject the output, and, if necessary, adjust or perhaps even repair the machine.[10]

ENRICHING THE WORKPLACE

How is a job enriched? Suppose that a firm decides that certain jobs need to be enriched. What specific actions should it take? To answer such questions we need to examine the basic building blocks or implementing concepts of job enrichment. As shown in Exhibit 7–1, these include changing the work content, the methods content, and the personal content of a job.[11]

Work Content

Work content comprises the tasks involved in performing jobs. These tasks can be enriched by adding more variety, providing closure, and expanding the level of knowledge and skill needed to do the work.

A manager can add variety to a job by combining tasks and giving employees a wider range of activities such as adding new or different machines or introducing new procedures and processes. Rather than attempting to break a job down into a sequence of smaller tasks, duties, and responsibilities, the manager would be pulling tasks together in order to create a larger work module. In other words, the job at this point is being enlarged so that each employee has responsibility for a variety of tasks. For example, at the Medfield, Massachusetts plant of Corning Glass Works, production jobs involved with the assembly of hotplates were redesigned by combining a number of previously separate tasks. Following the change, each hotplate was assembled from start to finish by one operator rather than going through several separate operations performed by different people. At Aetna Life and Casualty, insurance coders were given responsibility for all aspects of the coding process performed by their unit. Instead of performing only one or two elements of the coding process, they did all that was required to code a particular transaction.

Adding closure, or what is often referred to as forming natural units of work, can be accomplished in a variety of ways. Work can be grouped by geography (the area from which it originates), by using the alphabet, by organizational unit, or by the type of business. The idea here is to give employees continuing responsibility for an identifiable body of work, thus increasing their sense of ownership. Brief examples of the four possible groupings include assigning workers responsibility for specific field offices, compiling telephone directories by giving each preparer a segment of the alphabet, allowing clerks in a variety store to manage their own department as if it were a separately functioning retail unit, and assigning employees to specific product lines and giving them responsibility for everything from purchasing to scheduling and inventory control.

Increasing a job's work content also requires each employee to use more of his or her cognitive abilities. To make this possible, additional training to increase the employee's knowledge and skills may be needed.

Exhibit 7–1
Implementing Concepts of Job Enrichment

Work content	Adding variety
	Providing closure
	Expanding levels of knowledge and skill
Methods content	Modifying the work pace
	Permitting workers greater discretion
Personal content	Participation in planning, directing, and controlling activities
	Introduction of adequate feedback channels
	Establishing client relationships

Methods Content

The methods content of a job is also referred to in the literature as vertical loading. Two principal ways to change methods content are to allow employees to modify the work pace, and permitting workers themselves to decide how they will carry out assigned tasks. Thus, the employee is given responsibilities and controls that were formerly reserved for management. At Buick's factory number 8, workers were given the authority to adjust machine settings, reject faulty raw materials, and even stop the assembly line if a problem was evident. In other words, a worker can decide when to start and stop work, when to take breaks, and actually control the rate at which work is done. This gives the employee freedom to perform the work in the way he or she wishes and ultimately leads to increased feelings of personal responsibility and accountability for work outcomes.

Personal Content

The personal content of enriched work includes the opportunity to participate in the planning, directing, and controlling of activities being performed, the introduction of adequate feedback channels, and the establishment of client relationships.

Planning often entails responsibility for scheduling the sequence in which customer orders will be processed, assigning due dates for scheduled completion, and ordering needed materials. Directing may involve managing items as they progress through an individual's or a group's physical work area, establishing local priorities, and participating in making policy and administrative decisions affecting production. Controlling can be implemented by allowing employees to take corrective action as the product or service is created—for example, returning defective parts to the appropriate individual for correction and assuming responsibility for expediting work that is falling behind schedule.

Opening feedback channels helps individuals learn how they are performing on their jobs, and whether this performance is improving, deteriorating, or remaining at a constant level. Ideally, this information should come directly from the job. For example, a machinist at a lathe can feel the cut being made and can see whether or not the finished product meets required specifications. When jobs are designed this way, employees are continually aware of their performance quality and the task itself provides the feedback.

Finally, personal content can be enriched by establishing client relationships. The idea here is that the client, that is, the individual or firm using the product or service produced by the worker, is an important source of information. The person doing the job can gain a new perspective and valuable feedback by establishing direct relationships with clients. For example, a shipping clerk in a manufacturing plant might be given the responsibility for telephoning to personally check on the condition of a shipment when it arrives at its destination. By speaking directly with someone at the other end, personal contacts can be developed and the clerk may become more concerned that everything gets there on time and in one piece.

COMPANY APPLICATIONS

Since the concept of job redesign was first introduced, several hundred firms in the United States and elsewhere have implemented programs. Many of these have involved changes similar to the ones just discussed. Other companies have tried to enrich jobs by developing autonomous work teams that become responsible for specific production processes and take over many traditional managerial tasks including hiring, work scheduling, and so forth.

Some of the programs so widely cited in the late 1960s and early 1970s are no longer in operation. In some cases the experience with job redesign was not positive. Other firms, however, such as the Traveler's Insurance Company, successfully implemented programs and achieved good results but decided to discontinue the process anyway. In the case of Travelers, it was felt that while enrichment did work, the same results could be obtained from less expensive methods. In other firms, the programs simply did not live up to management's expectations.

Still, we would suggest that the problems many firms have experienced are the result of faulty implementation rather than any flaw in the basic concept. As the following examples illustrate, the technique does have widespread applicability. While it will not work everywhere, some firms have used it to good advantage.

The Volvo-Kalmar Plant

Faced with problems of absenteeism and turnover in the early 1970s, Volvo management established an entirely new production process at its Kalmar, Sweden, car assembly plant using the concept of autonomous work teams.[12] They still employ the methods established over ten years ago and management remains very positive about the program. The plant uses a combination of job rotation and enrichment.

At Kalmar, there are work teams composed of fifteen to twenty-five persons. The team members rotate jobs once or several times daily, depending on the tasks. Each team is responsible for the full assembly of a certain number of auto bodies within a set time. Work is distributed among team members who are mainly responsible for their own quality control. Since there are buffer stocks of parts positioned between the team areas, workers can schedule their own output, vary the rate of work, and create pauses when they need them.

While the body is being assembled in one part of the plant, the engine, gearbox, and front axles are put together in another area. The chassis and the fully assembled body meet on the lower floor and are "married." Then the car, situated on a special carrier, passes the working teams that fit the wheels and several other exterior items. Once this is done, the car is practically complete. All that remains is final adjustment and a delivery approval inspection. The assembly process terminates with the application of an underbody sealing compound and a protective coating over the surface finish.

As part of the redesign effort, several new production and assembly aids were introduced. For example, one design innovation allows the automobile body to be tilted 90 degrees sideways. This means that all assembly work on the underbody of the car can be carried out in convenient working positions.

The plant, of course, has not operated without problems. But management, working in cooperation with employees, has been able to implement a number of important changes. Quality controls were revised, new employees were assigned tutors to assist them in learning their jobs, new forms of communication were initiated, and a bonus program that amounts to 8 to 9 percent of base wage was established.

Recently, Volvo has conducted a comprehensive analysis of the Kalmar plant. Over the past ten years or so a number of improvements have been achieved. For example, the total time of direct labor per vehicle produced has gone down by over 40 percent. Quality faults have declined 39 percent since 1979. Between 1977 and 1983, the assembly time of a vehicle has been reduced by 40 percent. Financially speaking, the Kalmar plant has produced a favorable return on its invested capital. Assembly costs are lower than they are in any other of Volvo's passenger car assembly operations—in fact, over 25 percent less than at the Torsland works.

In addition, with the new technology and production arrangements used at Kalmar, the overwhelming majority of workers consider the organization of work to be good. The work methods are judged to be better than on conventional assembly lines. Finally, there is excellent job morale at the plant and employees have shown a growing interest in learning about the conditions governing production and operations as a whole. Annual turnover has decreased significantly. In short, job redesign at Kalmar has resulted in a technically, socially, and financially effective production plant.

General Foods—Topeka

Before the construction of a new plant in Topeka, Kansas, all Gaines pet food products were produced at a plant located in Kankakee, Illinois. When a new plant manager was appointed in 1966 the demand for Kankakee's products was creating a need for significant overtime, and production problems were considered serious. By 1968 it was clear that continued high demand was going to require additional plant capacity. As a result, efforts were undertaken to design a new plant that would maximize the use of behavioral science knowledge and would become a kind of laboratory or learning model for the corporation.[13]

The new plant had a number of unique features. For example, self-managed work teams assumed responsibility for large segments of the production process. The teams, composed of seven to fourteen members, were large enough to handle a set of interrelated tasks yet small enough to permit face-to-face decision making and coordination. Activities frequently performed by separate units were built into the operating team's responsibilities. Team members even screened job applicants for placement on their own team.

In lieu of a "supervisor," a "team leader" position was created with the responsibility of facilitating team development and decision making. Operators were provided data and decision guidelines that enabled them to make production decisions ordinarily made at higher supervisory levels.

As for plant rules, management refrained from specifying any in advance; rules evolved over time. Traditional status indicators were minimized. There was one entrance for everyone, one lunchroom, and one color scheme and decor used throughout the plant. Offices had glass walls, and, to facilitate worker involvement in quality control, small quality control labs were placed on several floors of the plant.

Another innovative feature at Topeka was its pay system. The plant had a single job classification and starting pay rate ($3.40 per hour in 1971) for all operators. Pay raises were linked to increases in a person's skill and experience. In other words, the pay system was designed to encourage employees to develop themselves. Also, there were no limits placed on the number of operators who could qualify for higher pay brackets. This encouraged employees to teach each other.

Early reports were quite positive. In addition to morale being very good, the hard statistics were also impressive. The plant started up and went three years and eight months without a lost time accident. Absenteeism between 1971 and 1974 was low, ranging from 0.8 to 1.4 percent. Turnover was only 10 percent a year.[14]

Yet the Topeka plant encountered a number of problems that illustrate some of the things a firm should be aware of when doing job redesign. For example, some team members and leaders have had problems with their expected roles. The problem was not so much that workers could not manage their own jobs but rather than some management personnel saw their positions being threatened because the work was performed almost too well. Also, the pay system, which allowed team members to vote on raises, caused many employees discomfort. As a result, the extent to which pay was clearly linked to desired behaviors varied widely from one team to another, and pay equity was a real issue. Third, the original idea of making all jobs in the plant interesting and challenging was not accomplished. Finally, the most serious problem concerned the turnover of management people. Between 1973 and 1976, four managers left the plant, creating problems of continuity and stability.[15]

In judging the Topeka experience, several major areas must be considered.[16] First, one can look at the extent to which the plant has maintained the improvements shown in its early years. According to recent reports, all the indicators are holding up well. Production is good and absenteeism and turnover are low. A second point is the extent to which the form of the original innovation has been sustained. From this perspective the results are mixed. In many ways the teams operate as they always have, but the plant now has a personnel manager and a quality control coordinator who have taken over some of the work originally done by the teams. A third consideration is the extent to which the plant has served as a prototype or model for other company plants. In fact, the Topeka plant has not become a prototype. Even so, General Foods describes the experiment as a success and top management has made no effort to replace the work teams with a more traditional system. Clearly the redesign works in this plant.

The Federal Government

The federal government conducted a work redesign experiment that is different from the two noted above in that it focused on clerical workers.

Also it represents one of the more rigorous studies and offers additional evidence of the wide-ranging applicability of work design techniques.[17]

The experiment involved clerical workers (mostly at the GS-3 level) in one unnamed federal bureau. The jobs consisted of sorting incoming mail, searching for lost or misplaced files, and filing. The site selected had a long history of morale problems and labor-management conflict. Before the program, attitudes toward all aspects of the work environment, as measured by standardized questionnaires, were quite negative.

Three experimental work units were identified and matched with three control units. In the experimental units, several important changes were made. For example, instead of working independently, employees in the mail posting department were divided into four six-person teams. Three of the teams worked on sorting and the others rotated through miscellaneous mailroom jobs. Rather than being given specific tasks, the teams were to decide for themselves how to divide the various operations. Daily productivity was recorded and posted.

Employees involved in searching for misplaced files were allowed to decide for themselves what needed to be done. If materials could not be found, they decided on the next step rather than referring it to their supervisor. Clerks kept their own records and allotted time to various tasks based on what needed to be done rather than what was assigned them. A team captain was selected to screen incoming work, complete unit time cards, dispatch outgoing work, and telephone other units regarding file problems.

Fixed production standards for persons doing filing were eliminated. Again, employees were allowed to switch back and forth between tasks as they saw fit rather than being told what to do each hour. Employees kept track of their own production records and these were posted in the office daily.

Pre- and postmeasures on attitudes and behaviors are shown in Exhibit 7–2. Productivity in the experimental units increased substantially while turnover, absenteeism, and complaints went down. Job attitudes, however, remained unchanged in both groups, demonstrating the point that there is not always a direct relationship between job satisfaction and performance.

Operating without Supervisors at Mountain Bell

For almost three years, one hundred unionized Mountain Bell telephone operators, working under the direction of one second-level manager, supervised virtually all aspects of daily operations at their workplace. Employees were directly responsible for training, service quality, productivity improvements, monitoring office practices and procedures, and maintaining attendance.[18]

Exhibit 7-2
Summary of Results of Job Enrichment Experiment

Measure	Experimental units	Control units
Productivity	+23%	+2%
Absenteeism	-5%	+7%
Turnover	-6%	+20%
Complaints and disciplinary actions	0	4
Attitudes	No change	No change

Source: E. A. Locke, D. Sirota, and A. D. Wolfson, "An Experimental Case Study of the Successes and Failures of Job Enrichment in a Government Agency," *Journal of Applied Psychology* 61 (1976). Copyright © 1976 by the American Psychological Association. Reprinted by permission of the authors.

Initially, the Hotel Billings Information System (HOBIS), which was jointly developed by Mountain Bell and the Communications Workers of America, basically resembled most other operator offices across the country. Operators, sitting in front of video display terminals, had to provide charges to hotels on customer-dialed long-distance calls, arrange refunds for customers who lost money in pay phones, and give credit on incorrectly dialed long-distance calls. The office handled roughly 11,500 calls each business day. A computer monitored the operators' actions and printed daily reports on speed, volume, and mix of calls by type (hotel or pay phone). One difference, however, was that at most traditional facilities of comparable size, eight to ten first-level supervisors and a second-level manager would be on duty; at HOBIS, a single manager presided over daily operations acting mainly as a resource person and mentor rather than as a traditional overseer.

The significance of this difference cannot be overstated. Strict work rules, heavy supervision, and narrow spans of control had been rooted in one hundred years of Bell System tradition. Operators worked while a supervisor walked back and forth behind them, recording their every movement. The supervisors in turn, were closely watched by their managers. Over the years, as technology changed, supervisors became even more responsible for employee performance. For example, the widespread use of computers and sophisticated monitoring systems in the 1970s both enabled management to evaluate the performance of each individual operator at fifteen-second intervals and facilitate the overall processing of thousands of calls. While the intent of such systems was to make operators more efficient, a by-product was to make the operators' job less interesting and more stressful.

Throughout the 1970s into the 1980s the atmosphere in Bell offices approached that of a traditional schoolroom. In many locations operators were required to get permission to use restrooms. To prevent operators from talking to one another, managers sometimes forbade them to sit next to their friends. Many of the formal work rules were carryovers from the days when the work force was entirely female. For example, a male operator in one office was not allowed to wear a baseball cap because the office rules stated that only bows or ribbons could adorn the heads of the operators. During this time, operators began to protest this atmosphere but felt powerless to change the system.

The HOBIS concept began to take shape in 1981 when the district manager of operator services in Phoenix attended a corporate policy seminar for mid- and upper-level managers during which innovative work systems were discussed. Back on the job he began testing the waters. He chatted with employees over coffee or in the hall, asking "what-if" questions about new work arrangements. He asked his first-level managers, "If we didn't have supervisors, could the operators perform your jobs?" The supervisors' answer was "probably" although some were not sure. The manager then asked the operators similar questions. They agreed overwhelmingly that they did not need direct supervision. He next tested the idea with his boss, who reluctantly agreed to allow the new work system to be set up in a facility being planned in Tempe, Arizona. Finally, the manager contacted the union. Although leaders liked the idea of a self-managed office, they knew that the prevailing management style was not conducive to such an experiment. Ultimately, the manager enlisted the support of the Communications Workers of America local president. By the fall of 1982, the key people who would be involved with the new office had been cultivated.

The next step was to choose a second-level manager for the office to handle administrative and personnel matters and also to choose six operators to serve on the office committee, which would be responsible for daily operations and staffing the office. Membership on this committee would rotate once the office was open. After the first six months, operators would serve six-month terms, with one member leaving and a new member joining each month.

Early on, the office committee met for five days of training with the company's quality-of-work life facilitator. For three and a half days, the office committee members worked on team building, improving communications, improving problem solving, and learning how to run meetings. The last day and a half was devoted to planning how the office would function. After the training was completed, the committee took responsibility for choosing one hundred operators to work under the new system.

The HOBIS office aggressively tried to improve customer service. For example, the office committee formed a customer contact task force to study the issues and make recommendations which included developing a customer contact seminar for all operators, giving recognition certificates to courteous hotel clerks, fostering more open communication and coop-eration among operators at work, and being more flexible with work rules in order to satisfy customers.

Although the training of operators was a management responsibility in the Bell System, HOBIS employees took complete charge of their initial training. With no supervisors in the office, the committee chose an opera-tor to coordinate the training program. That operator spent three days in a workshop and then returned to implement the training program.

There were, of course, problems with the new system. One of these in-volved a reluctance to make decisions likely to be unfavorable to the group as a whole. For example, Bell management charged the committee with developing productivity measurements. After ten weeks of hemming and hawing by the committee with no output in sight, management had to in-tervene and force the committee to take action.

But as HOBIS operators became more adept at problem solving, top management realized that nonmanagement personnel could perform many traditional management duties. Moreover, added responsibility gave variety to otherwise repetitive jobs, while allowing employees to or-ganize their own work left managers free to plan for the long term, and helped employees gain valuable expertise and knowledge.

Exact comparisons with traditional offices are hard to make, but the HOBIS experiment has clearly been a success. Absenteeism, grievances, and customer complaints fell to low levels, while productivity and em-ployee morale improved. Moreover, HOBIS achieved this performance during the time when AT&T was divesting its telephone operating compa-nies. In the transition, HOBIS was transferred from Mountain Bell to AT&T Communications. Despite these changes, most HOBIS employees reported feeling more satisfaction and less stress than they had felt in pre-vious jobs in traditional offices. As one operator put it, "I feel like my ideas count; I feel like I'm part of something."

In addition, the absence of supervisors meant that no one could listen in on operators' calls. The underlying assumption was that each employee could do satisfactory work. All measurements of call volume and cus-tomer satisfaction indicated that HOBIS met or exceeded the established requirements. In fact, some operators even requested that their peers lis-ten to help improve the quality of service. As for productivity, average AWT's (the amount of time an operator spends on each call—the Bell Sys-tem's traditional measurement of operator productivity) decreased 3.3 seconds in the first month.

Early in 1985 the decision was made to centralize the HOBIS operation and move it to Lakewood, Colorado. It initially appeared that the new of-fice would be structured in a more traditional manner. However, represen-tatives from the union convinced top management to follow the HOBIS model and implement the self-managed office concept.

Job Redesign at Shenandoah Life

In an effort to respond to changes in the life insurance business, primarily the shift from whole life policies to universal life products, Shenandoah Life developed and implemented self-managing teams.[19] The results of an internal analysis of universal life business revealed that the clerks responsible for processing the cases were arranged in highly specialized, assembly-line types of jobs in premium accounting, policy issue, policy holder services, general accounting, marketing services, policy records underwriting, receiving, and reinsurance. Before a policy was processed, it passed through thirty-two sets of hands, across nine sections and three departments. Even though this assembly-line system could be improved, management felt that the changes would not be sufficient to allow the company to serve the marketplace competitively. In any event, in March 1983 Shenandoah Life formed its first experimental self-managing team.

The team was composed of six nonexempt clerical employees. They were responsible, as a group, for processing all universal life business and health insurance generated in Virginia. Top management stipulated no individualized job assignments or accountabilities. The team's responsibilities included all tasks related to premium accounting, policy issue, and policy holder services. In addition, the team was responsible for constructing a model office for a computer system conversion project, and for building the model and systems to be used in developing future teams. The team members designed their own office layout as well as aspects of their salary system.

For example, the team implemented a pay-for-learning system. In this system a team member would be eligible to receive a defined pay increment after demonstrating competency at a particular task. The team, as a whole, determined which members were competent at particular skills and initiated salary increment requests. All team members were encouraged to develop the ability to process any piece of business from beginning to end without guidance or consultation. Team members were responsible for training one another.

Management expected the team to be as self-regulatory as possible. No supervisor was appointed, although the team did have several advisors with whom members could consult. These advisors included the second vice president for human resources, the personnel director, the manager of methods and procedures, and a methods and procedures analyst. The self-regulating activities performed by the team included deciding who would do what work, formulating a vacation schedule, final selection of new team members, designing the office layout, training one another or arranging for training, determining the basics of the salary system, and correcting members who were not contributing their fair share to the team's performance.

The team operated as an experiment for about one year. The problems that developed were relatively minor and easily resolved. In late September 1984, the remaining employees in the three functional areas of policy holder services, premium accounting, and policy issue were placed into teams serving specific geographic markets. The experimental team continued to service Virginia.

What has the self-managed approach contributed to the firm's productivity? According to the second vice president, the number of employees in the three functional units noted above has remained approximately the same while new business applications have increased 13 percent. Since September 1984, there has been a marked decline in the number of complaints about service and errors. Finally, job redesign has made the company more aware of the need to be flexible and has allowed it to operate more effectively in a rapidly changing business environment.

JOB REDESIGN AND THE MANAGER

All of the programs discussed here show that job redesign can potentially improve employee effectiveness and productivity. Suppose, however, that you find yourself in a situation in which it is impossible or impractical to apply all the principles and implement a large-scale program. After all, many managers, especially first-line supervisors, are not in a position to unilaterally plan and execute total job redesign programs. So what should one do? The answer is to implement those aspects of job redesign that are within one's authority and that seem likely to be successful. Take, for example, the issue of work scheduling, which is frequently the responsibility of a supervisor. With the possible exception of an assembly line, many work processes are open to discretionary scheduling. After all, the supervisor really only has to approve the schedule and see that it is workable. The people doing the job can often choose when to do what task, take breaks, and so on.

In other cases, supervisors can unofficially combine certain tasks and maybe even allow the informal group system to set up something closely akin to natural units of work. In addition, employees can be told to go ahead and check their own work, and certainly feedback channels can be opened without a formal decree by top management. Finally, workers might even be allowed to establish client relationships simply by using direct contact methods. When employees complete a task, they can talk directly to the person to whom they gave the work and get feedback.

Basically, then, the principles of job redesign can be applied even piecemeal. Certainly, support from the top of the firm's hierarchy is important in doing a formal program. But it is not vital on a smaller scale.

PREREQUISITES FOR SUCCESSFUL JOB REDESIGN

As the examples presented in this chapter show, job redesign programs can often deal with a variety of issues facing organizations. However, successful implementation requires that several potential problems be addressed before the project proceeds too far.

Involving Unions in Job Redesign

In general, labor unions in this country have not actively supported efforts to redesign jobs.[20] Several factors account for this. Many early union experiences with job redesign amounted to combining tasks so that workers would have only the perception that a "meaningful job" was being done. In other words, workers were often placed in a position where more work was expected for the same compensation. Unions saw this as exploitation and began to firmly resist any change in the content of jobs as a matter of continuing policy.

In order to overcome this problem, union leadership should be involved in all phases of job redesign, including planning. Management needs to point out that effective job redesign does not involve exploitation, but rather increases worker control over the conditions and structuring of jobs and thus gives employees more power in the organization.

Making Changes in the Work Itself

Even though many job redesign proponents argue otherwise, the fact is that the technology of production does have a significant impact on work roles. In some cases, the nature of the job may not lend itself to enrichment or redesign.[21] Unfortunately, the inability to change the work itself can be an insurmountable roadblock. There is no simple solution except to say that management needs to consider whether or not it is possible to meaningfully change jobs.

Using Monetary Rewards

Many firms have found that the question, "What's in it for me?" must be addressed right up front. Most employees do not want their jobs redesigned unless they can foresee that a tangible benefit will result from it. The issue of job redesign's effect on one's compensation is of particular importance to employees.

The key notion is not that the firm necessarily has to give people higher wages; it is more important that the employee's sense of equity (fairness) is not violated. There are several points to consider here. First, job redesign cannot compromise an ongoing incentive program such as a piece-rate or bonus plan. If people feel that they must work harder to achieve the same level of bonus, research has shown that they will reject the redesign effort.[22]

A second concern relates to the extent of job redesign. If the job is radically upgraded, employees may be entitled to more money. After all, their work presumably makes a greater contribution to the firm's productivity. On the other hand, changes in the job may not cause people to feel they deserve more. The point, then, is that every firm needs to look at its own situation and decide whether pay needs to be upgraded.

One possible solution is to allow employees to share in the annual cost savings and productivity gains resulting from job redesign. Offering monetary rewards can be a powerful tool to generate both interest and involvement.

Awareness of the Costs

While job redesign may result in long-term gains for the organization, it can be costly in the short run. The cost of implementing a program will vary from one situation to another, but in all instances, expenses are incurred.

Some of the typical design-related and performance-related cost items for a job enrichment program include wage increases, new or upgraded facilities, training, inventory, and so on. Even though not every cost will always occur, some of them will.[23] The question, of course, is whether subsequent performance gains outweigh the costs.

Generating Support from Top Management

Job redesign should be treated as an effort to introduce planned change in an organization. If a firm expects to be successful in the long run, there are certain steps that it should take. One of these is to involve all members of the organization in the process, particularly top management. Unless those in positions of power truly support the redesign effort, there will probably be a great deal of activity leading nowhere. The initial impetus may come from someone in a middle management position, but since job redesign typically involves people in several areas of the organization, support from higher management will be needed to coordinate the program. All too often top management takes a cautious wait-and-see attitude toward job redesign. They do not fully commit themselves. Unless the results are very dramatic, they may lose interest.[24]

Other Considerations

In addition to the requirements just mentioned, a variety of other factors could also contribute to the ultimate success or failure of a redesign effort. For example, when job redesign is introduced, it is often assumed that everyone wants an enriched job. Research, however, has shown that this is not always true. There is considerable evidence that even though some individuals respond favorably, other workers doing the same job would rather not have the work redesigned.

It is also important that management begins job redesign with realistic expectations about what it can or cannot accomplish. Finally, job redesign efforts will experience a life cycle. If the program continues over a period of years, problems will surface. Management must be willing to stick with it and see the difficulties as an opportunity to improve the original idea.

SUMMARY

Job redesign is neither a new nor particularly radical concept. Over the years, however, the focus has shifted and a variety of redesign concepts have found their way into industry. At one time job redesign and industrial engineering were often synonymous terms. In fact, increasing the workers' efficiency by using time and motion studies is still a viable approach to job redesign. Today, however, several other concepts and techniques fall under the general heading of job redesign including job rotation, job enlargement, and job enrichment. Variations of job enrichment include semi-autonomous teams and other self-managed team approaches. In this chapter we have examined various alternatives to job redesign, discussed implementing concepts, looked at several firms that are now using job redesign, and finally pointed out several of the prerequisites for successful implementation.

Does job redesign really make a difference in an organization's performance? The evidence strongly suggests that such programs can improve the quality of working life and ultimately contribute to the company's bottom line. According to a recent survey of Fortune 500 firms,[25] those that use innovative human resource practices and programs such as work redesign consistently outperformed less progressive firms in terms of sales, assets, return on equity, and return on total capital. The companies that were willing to invest in their human resources by providing innovative and alternative ways to work gained clear financial rewards.

Several additional benefits may accrue from well-conceived job redesign efforts.[26] First, increasing job variety allows the organization to develop a more widely skilled and flexible work force. It may be reasonably argued that, as a result, bottlenecks can be reduced and productivity increased. Second, the use of vertical loading can provide managers with more time to engage in planning and organizing for the future. In this regard, one study[27] concluded that job enrichment accustomed subordinates to responsibility, which better prepared them for promotion and thereby enabled supervisors to direct their time away from day-to-day problems and issues. Third, the cost of coordination may be lowered through a reduced need for supervisors and inspectors. However, these savings may be offset by increases in other costs such as training or additional equipment.

We would point out, however, that even though job redesign is often a useful strategy for improving employee satisfaction and productivity, it is not applicable for all jobs or situations. Some jobs do not easily lend themselves to meaningful job redesign and not all workers want their jobs enlarged or enriched. Many individuals would prefer to become proficient doing what someone else might consider a boring, routine task. They may not react well to job redesign.

Finally, job redesign is not a one-shot program. It is an ongoing effort. Whenever a job is changed, it will be new and interesting for a while. Over time, however, the newness wears off and employees may again become bored with the routine. At that point more changes may have to be made. You cannot assume that one job redesign effort will improve employee behavior indefinitely.

NOTES

1. M. Elden, "Torslanda: People Are Key Resource at Scandinavia's Largest Workplace," *ERGO*, November 1984, p. 6.

2. P. G. Gullenhammar, "Production Technology and QWL: Volvo's Lesson," *ERGO*, November 1984, p. 24.

3. F. Herzberg, "One More Time: How Do You Motivate Employees?" *Harvard Business Review* 52 (1974), pp. 70–80.

4. F. K. Plous, "Redesigning Work," *Personnel Administrator*, March 1987, p. 99.

5. E. Davis, "The Design of Jobs," *Industrial Relations*, October 1966, p. 21.

6. J. R. Hackman and G. R. Oldham, *Work Design* (Reading, Mass.: Addison Wesley Publishing Co., 1980).

7. E. J. Bryan, "Work Improvement and Job Enrichment, The Case of Cummins Engine Company," in L. E. Davis and A. B. Cherns, eds., *The Quality of Working Life*, vol. 2 (New York: Free Press, 1975).

8. R. W. Woodman and J. J. Sherwood, "A Comprehensive Look at Job Design," *Personnel Journal*, August 1977, pp. 384–90, 418.

9. P. P. Schoderbeck and W. E. Reif, *Job Enlargement: Key to Improved Performance* (Ann Arbor: University of Michigan Press, 1969).

10. C. Tausky, *Work Organizations* (Itasca, Ill.: F. E. Peacock Publishers, 1978).

11. A. Alber and M. Blumberg, "Team vs. Individual Approaches to Job Enrichment Programs," *Personnel*, January–February 1981, pp. 63–75.

12. T. Mcroczkowski and P. Champagne, "Job Redesign in Two Countries: A Comparison of the Topeka and Kalmar Experiences," *Industrial Management*, November–December 1984, pp. 17–22.

13. D. A. Whitsett and L. Yorks, "Looking Back at Topeka: General Foods and the Quality-of-Work Experiment," *California Management Review*, Summer 1983, pp. 93–109.

14. R. E. Walton, "Work Innovations at Topeka: After Six Years," *Journal of Applied Behavioral Science* 13, no. 3 (1977), pp. 422–33.

15. Ibid.

16. Whitsett and Yorks, "Looking Back at Topeka."

17. E. A. Locke, D. Sirotra, and A. D. Wolfson, "An Experimental Case Study of the Successes and Failures of Job Enrichment in a Government Agency," *Journal of Applied Psychology* 61 (1976), pp. 701–11.

18. T. O. Taylor, D. J. Friedman, and D. Couture, "Operating without Supervisors: An Experiment," *Organizational Dynamics*, Winter 1987, pp. 26–38.

19. J. B. Myers, "Making Organizations Adaptive to Change: Eliminating Bureaucracy at Shenandoah Life," *National Productivity Review*, Spring 1985, pp. 131–38.

20. R. B. McAfee and W. Poffenberger, *Productivity Strategies* (Englewood Cliffs, N.J.: Prentice-Hall, 1982).

21. Ibid.

22. P. J. Champagne, *Job Enrichment: A Case Study of Failure*, unpublished Ph.D. diss., University of Massachusetts, 1977.

23. A. F. Albert, "The Real Costs of Job Enrichment," *Business Horizons*, February 1979, pp. 60–72.

24. M. Beer, *Organization Change and Development* (Santa Monica, Calif.: Goodyear Publishing Co., 1980).

25. "The Changing American Workplace: Work Alternatives in the 80's," *An AMA Survey Report* (New York: Goodmeasure, 1985).

26. R. E. Kopelman, "Job Redesign and Productivity: A Review of the Evidence," *National Productivity Review*, Summer 1985, pp. 237–55.

27. W. P. Kraft and K. L. Williams, "Job Redesign Improves Productivity," *Personnel Journal*, July 1975, pp. 393–97.

8

Meeting the Unique Needs of Employees

> Listening to employees at any level in an organization convinces one rather quickly that people work for a variety of reasons.[1]

> All employees have needs but these needs are not all equally important. At any given time, some are more dominant than others and it is these needs that propel human activity. By understanding these needs, a manager can attempt to satisfy them; this in turn should lead to improved employee job satisfaction and performance.[2]

Since June 1984 the Minnesota Department of Energy and Economic Development in St. Paul has offered employees a wide choice in determining their work schedule.[3] Employees can choose to work eight-, nine-, or ten-hour days and take either a thirty- or sixty-minute lunch break, just so long as they work a total of forty hours per week. Employees also have a choice in determining when they arrive and depart from work. They can come as early as 6:30 A.M. and stay as late as 6:30 P.M. They are, however, required to work from 9:00 to 3:00 on the days they are there. (Those who work only four hours on a given day are excluded.)

Employees need not keep the same work schedule permanently. Indeed, one can ask that it be changed by submitting a written request to the supervisor at least fourteen days in advance. The supervisor then evaluates the request in terms of organizational needs and the schedules of other employees.

In evaluating the results of the program, Martha J. Watson, Personnel Director, stated, "Although we have not had the time, staff, or money to conduct a formal evaluation of our flexitime plan, we have not experienced any major problems since we implemented the policy." Among the benefits she cited are the ability to keep offices open to the public longer and the creation of more quiet time for employees. Employees can better cope with transportation and child care problems. They can more easily schedule medical and other appointments around work hours. Finally, managers report more satisfied, more cooperative, and more adaptable employees because of the plan.

In this case, we have a situation in which employees are given a choice in determining not only how many hours they work but when they work. We also see that this approach had payoffs for both the organization and the employees. Essentially, this organization has attempted to meet the unique needs of its employees by allowing them to choose a work schedule which best fits their own preferences.

In this chapter we want to examine the concept of motivating employees by identifying and attempting to meet their unique needs. We will begin by discussing the rationale behind this approach. We will then consider how organizations can and have implemented it through the use of flexible benefit systems, alternative work schedules, leaves of absence, and social programs. Finally, we will discuss how individual managers can address unique employee needs.

WHY SHOULD REWARDS BE TAILOR-MADE?

The rationale behind meeting the unique needs of employees rests on two closely related motivation theories: Maslow's hierarchy of needs and ERG theory. Each proposes that people are motivated to satisfy needs.

Maslow's Theory

One of the first behavioral scientists to make management aware of human needs and their effect on motivation was Abraham Maslow.[4] When developing his theory during the 1940s, he was interested in formulating a general theory of motivation, one not restricted to the workplace. Even so, his ideas have been widely applied to work situations. While he acknowledged that people really have a great many needs, he felt that all of them could be condensed within the following five categories:

1. *Physiological needs* are essential to survival. They include food, water, rest, and sex.
2. *Safety and security needs* include the need for protection against physical and psychological threats in the environment and confidence that physiological needs will be met in the future. Buying an insurance policy or seeking a secure job with a good pension plan are manifestations of security needs.
3. *Social needs*, sometimes called the need for affiliation, include a feeling of belonging, of acceptance by others, of social interaction, and of affection and support.
4. *Esteem needs* include self-respect, respect from others, and recognition.

5. *Self-actualization needs* include fulfillment of one's potential and growth as a person.

In essence, Maslow's approach to motivation can be summarized in terms of several major propositions. The first is that people are motivated by their needs, which can be arranged in a hierarchy as shown in Exhibit 8–1. In this context, a need is an internal stimulus that causes a person to act and has either a physiological or psychological basis. But as the hierarchy points out, some needs are more important or potent than others. If, for example, physiological needs are unsatisfied, the person will be dominated by them and all other needs recede into the background. Once sufficient food, rest, or water has been attained, higher safety and security needs emerge and dominate the individual. When, in turn, these are satisfied, the next level emerges and this process continues repeatedly as the person moves toward the top of the hierarchy.

One of the easiest ways to understand and remember Maslow's need hierarchy is to picture yourself on a deserted island having just survived an airplane crash. Which needs would be most important to you at that time? For most people, it would be physical survival or taking care of one's bodily needs, such as obtaining water and food. But once these were satisfied, what would then become important? The answer is probably a concern with safety and security. You would need to find shelter and clothing to protect yourself from the elements.

Both physiological and safety needs are related to the preservation of the physical self. But for many people this is not the only important concern. They also want to enhance their situation, and one of the major concerns people have beyond satisfying their survival needs is the desire for affiliation and companionship. This includes the need to be accepted by others, to be loved and understood. Maslow refers to these desires as "social needs." On an island you would eventually want to find others to converse with after your physiological and safety needs were fairly well satisfied.

But enhancing oneself goes far beyond the enjoyment companionship brings. Most people also have a need for recognition and admiration, even prestige. They want to feel that they make a difference, that their presence is important and appreciated by others. In other words, people also have needs that relate to their self-esteem. These include self-confidence and self-respect.

The ultimate need is what Maslow called "self-actualization," and it is perhaps the most difficult to conceptualize. Maslow defined it in terms of people seeking to become all they are capable of becoming. They want to realize their potential, to feel a sense of accomplishment, growth, and fulfillment. It includes the desire to feel competent in dealing with reality, to experience a sense of mental efficacy and mastery. What happens when

Exhibit 8–1
Maslow's Hierarchy of Needs

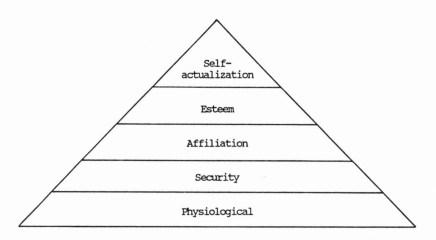

this need is fully satisfied? How does a supervisor motivate employees who have attained self-actualization? Maslow and other need theorists argue that this situation rarely, if ever, occurs. Few people reach a point of total self-actualization. They can always achieve greater competency and mastery in what they are doing.

A second major proposition is that satisfied needs do not motivate people; only unsatisfied needs do. The point here is that rewards may not have the desired or predicted effect on behavior because they are directed toward needs that have already been satisfied. A $5000 pay raise may have a significant effect on an employee whose base pay is $15,000. However, the same raise, offered to a top executive making six figures or more, will probably not have the same effect. Rewards that do not meet a person's needs are of little value.

Finally, Maslow proposed that when dominant needs go unsatisfied over a long period of time, a variety of dysfunctional behaviors may result. If employees are unable to satisfy their most important needs no matter how long they wait or how hard they try, they may either quit their job or engage in some form of coping behavior. Unfortunately, the latter alternative can have several negative side effects. For example, employees might act out their frustration by destroying company property or insubordination. Some may complain and bicker incessantly and, in so doing, have an adverse effect on co-workers. Others may develop severe mental problems or physical ailments such as headaches and ulcers. Eventually, however, there will be dysfunctional consequences for the organization.

Critics have frequently argued with the validity of the hierarchy of needs as presented by Maslow.[5] Can people's needs be divided into five categories and do individuals automatically move up the ladder as Maslow suggests? Do they even realize when a need has been satisfied? Regardless of whether one's needs are arranged in a hierarchy, all of us have needs that are dominant at a given time. Therefore, if we can find better ways to identify and then satisfy people's needs, odds are that we can affect their behavior.

ERG Theory

ERG theory, developed by Clayton Aldefer, also suggests that people's needs are arranged in a hierarchy.[6] However, Aldefer proposes only three categories:

1. *Existence.* This includes the need for food, clothing, shelter, safe working conditions, and economic security. These needs parallel Maslow's physiological and certain safety or security needs.
2. *Relatedness.* This involves the need for meaningful social and interpersonal relationships. These are equivalent to the needs at the middle of Maslow's hierarchy: some safety/security needs, social needs, and some esteem needs.
3. *Growth.* This includes the need for personal growth and being creative on the job. These needs are akin to Maslow's self-actualization needs and part of his need for esteem.

ERG theory is again based on three major propositions.[7] First, it proposes that the less each need level has been satisfied, the more it will be desired. For example, the longer a person's need for safe working conditions is not satisfied, the more than person will want a safe place. Second, the more lower-level needs are satisfied, the greater will be the employee's desire for higher-level need satisfaction. To illustrate, as a person satisfies existence needs, there will be an increase in the desire for social and interpersonal satisfactions (relatedness). Finally, when higher-level needs are frustrated, the individual will again seek lower-level need satisfaction. In other words, the theory suggests that a frustration-regression process occurs; if someone cannot satisfy growth needs, an attempt will be made to further satisfy relatedness needs. This proposition is probably the major factor that distinguishes this theory from Maslow's.

ORGANIZATIONAL APPLICATIONS

Even though both Maslow's need hierarchy and Aldefer's ERG theory were meant to be general theories of motivation, by inference each suggests that managers and organizations should be aware of the differences among individuals. What motivates one person may have little or no effect on someone else. In addition, since employees are motivated by various needs, some more compelling than others, organizations must provide people with an opportunity to satisfy those which are dominant. Stated differently, these theories suggest that organizational effectiveness is enhanced if employees are given freedom in choosing how to satisfy their own needs. In practice, organizations have done this in several different ways.

Flexible Benefits Systems

One method of tying needs to rewards is through the use of a flexible benefits system. This allows employees, within certain limits, to pick the benefit package they want and modify it according to their needs.

American Can Company is probably the best-known example of a company that allows employees to do this.[8] Their plan, covering nine thousand salaried employees, provides everyone with a core of standard benefits and then allows them to select additional ones on the basis of credits granted to each employee. Other benefits can also be purchased by employees who individually choose to set aside money through payroll deductions. Under this plan, employees have a choice of options regarding medical coverage, life insurance, disability income, vacation, and retirement and capital accounts.

In choosing medical options, employees can decide what percent of covered expenses will be paid by the plan as well as the size of the deductible. They can also select coverage for vision, hearing, routine health examinations, or dental care. In addition, disability insurance coverage can be extended beyond the core amount with the cost depending on the employee's age and salary.

Life insurance in amounts equal to four times an employee's annual salary can be chosen. This is in addition to the core, which provides insurance coverage equal to one's annual salary. Furthermore, employees can select survivor income benefits equal to either 20 percent or 40 percent of their base salaries. There are options covering accidental death or dismemberment and life insurance for spouses and dependent children.

The vacation option permits employees to purchase as many as five additional vacation days in any year. The cost of the option depends on the employee's pay level.

The retirement and capital accumulation options allow for additional retirement income beyond that provided in the company's regular pension plan. Money can also be allocated to American Can Company stock, to a diversified investment fund, or to a guaranteed interest fund.

Benefit options can be changed once a year. Each September, American Can sends employees a form showing their existing program and the number of credits to which they are entitled. They can then choose to keep the program or select new options. Changes go into effect January 1. Newly hired workers are given sixty days to select their benefits.

Both management and workers appear to favor the flexible approach. In fact, a company survey disclosed that 92 percent of those polled felt that the plan had substantially improved the company's benefits program.[9] The administrative costs, while significant, were less than expected. Basically, five employees administered the plan, although additional clerical help was needed toward the end of each year when benefit forms were being processed.

Comerica, a Detroit bank holding company, has developed a flexible benefits plan similar to the American Can approach.[10] Using credits based on the dollar value of different benefits, workers can buy or sell benefits as they choose provided they retain minimum health and life insurance. Employees receive an array of options including the right to buy life insurance for dependents, disability coverage, comprehensive medical coverage, and vacation days. Comerica reports that their program has been enthusiastically received by employees, with 94 percent electing to change some aspect of their benefits.

American Can and Comerica are only two of an increasing number of firms using flexible benefits plans. Companies such as Mellon Bank in Pittsburgh, Hewitt Associates, Sovran Financial Corporation, Little Company of Mary Hospital in Los Angeles, Johnson Controls, Inc., Northern States Power Company in Minneapolis, and North American Van Lines have also instituted such programs.[11]

The editors of *Employee Benefit Plan Review* reviewed eleven flexible benefits plans in 1986.[12] They found that there are as many differences among the plans as there are plans themselves. For example, they found that plans differed in terms of which employees are covered. Some plans covered salaried employees only. Others covered all regular full-time employees, and a few covered benefits for eligible part-time employees as well. Plans differed too in terms of how credits which employees can use to buy benefits are computed. At one firm (Security Pacific National Bank), credits are computed as a percent of the employee's salary, factored by age, length of service, and family status. At another (Bankers Trust Company) eligible employees receive a benefits allowance based on salary, age, and the cost of benefits provided under the previous plan. First Maryland Bancorp gave each employee $450 for 1985 and National Steel deposited $180 to start each employee's flexible benefits account.

While the plans differed, they also had several similarities. For example, all offered a choice of medical and related coverage and a core of life insurance and disability income coverages. Ten plans offered flexible spending amounts for dependent and health care expenses. Most plans allowed employees to pay for additional benefits with salary dollars prior to tax withholding.

Even though the plans discussed here revolve around traditional benefit items, the idea of allowing employees to choose rewards could be extended. Options such as office size and furnishings, length of lunch breaks, clothing allowances, automobiles, membership in various organizations, and even clerical help and other support services could be included.

One of the critical issues raised is whether flexible benefits programs actually result in higher employee productivity and job satisfaction. The research is not strong but the two programs noted above do provide evidence that employees prefer flexible benefits plans over traditional systems. However, whether these plans actually improve employee productivity is debatable. If flexible systems promote higher morale and this in turn leads to less absenteeism and turnover, productivity may increase because employees are more likely to be on the job.

Alternative Work Schedules

Many employees dislike working traditional hours and want to better balance work, family, and personal time. In this section, we will examine ways to meet this challenge by letting employees choose their work schedule. Even though employers provide various options, we will focus on three: flexitime, compressed work weeks, and job sharing and pairing.

Flexitime

This concept, which refers to flexible working hours, allows employees to decide, on a weekly or monthly basis, when they will begin and end their work day. While more than one hundred variations exist, the major ones include:

1. *Gliding schedule.* Within specified time periods, employees may vary their starting and departure times from day to day (e.g., 6:00–9:00 A.M. and 3:00–6:00 P.M.). Employees often need to be present during a core period such as from 10:00 A.M. to 2:00 P.M. and must work eight hours per day.
2. *Flexitour.* Employees preselect their daily starting and stopping time. They can change to a new work schedule at predetermined times (e.g., every month).
3. *Variable week.* Employees may vary the length of the work day so long as they are present for the core periods and work the required number of hours bi-weekly.

Flexitime has been used by many companies, both large and small, including Prudential Life Insurance, First National Bank of Boston, Canada Trust, Hewlett-Packard, Control Data Systems, Lufthansa, General Motors, and several Blue Cross/Blue Shield companies. A 1985 study conducted by the Bureau of Labor Statistics showed that 12.3 percent of the workers surveyed were operating under flexible schedules. A 1987 study conducted by the American Society of Personnel Administration and the Commerce Clearing House (ASPA/CCH) showed that 26 percent (117 out of 456) firms said that they were using flexible working hours.[13]

How effective has flexitime been? Most firms report favorable results, particularly in terms of employee attitudes. The ASPA/CCH survey mentioned above found that flexitime was perceived as favorably affecting employee activities with family and friends, employee morale, transportation to and from work, and employee access to services and events. Other studies also suggest that employees like flexitime, but the data on employee productivity is mixed. The ASPA/CCH survey found that firms believed flexitime to have a "slightly positive effect" on employee reliability and quantity and quality of work.

One review of the research examined the data from twenty firms.[14] It found that in ten cases, productivity improved from 2 to 12 percent, while in the other ten it decreased or remained unchanged. Another study which suggests when flexitime is likely to improve productivity involved computer programmers and data entry operators in two state government agencies.[15] The researchers found that flexitime resulted in no significant increase in productivity for data entry operators, each of whom had his or her own data input machines. However, a change to flexitime did improve the productivity of computer programmers who shared a computer system by 24 percent. In this situation, flexitime increased productivity because fewer employees were working at any one time and therefore each spent less time in queues making runs and getting output back. This suggests that flexitime may have a favorable effect on productivity when limited physical resources are being shared by a group.

It is important to note that flexitime does have several potential disadvantages. It can be difficult to tabulate each employee's work hours, maintain supervisory coverage during the entire work day, schedule meetings with employees, coordinate projects, and ensure that necessary but unscheduled work will get done. As a general rule, organizations that operate consecutive round-the-clock shifts face problems using flexitime.

Compressed Work Schedules

Since World War II, the standard work week in this country has generally been defined as five days. Today, however, a number of organizations such as the one described at the beginning of this chapter are compressing work weeks so that employees can work the equivalent of a full week in less than five full days. While the most common approach is the four-day, forty-hour work week, some organizations use twelve-hour work shifts with employees working alternately three- and four-day schedules. A few firms even use compressed work months. Some riverboat pilots, for example, work thirty days on and thirty days off.

Compressed work weeks offer a number of benefits. For example, employees should have increased leisure time and reduced travel expenses; set-up and clean-up costs should be lower; absenteeism should be reduced since employees have more time available to take care of personal matters and because the loss of a day's pay is more costly.

On the other hand, compressed work weeks may make communication among employees and between customer and employees more difficult. Firms may have more difficulty scheduling overtime because employees may not want to work it. Further, employee fatigue may result in lower performance quality or quantity. Finally, some employees may find that the longer work day interferes with their social life or nonwork responsibilities.

Several studies have examined the effectiveness of compressed work weeks in terms of several different criteria. One researcher, based on an analysis of prior studies, concluded that employee attitudes toward the compressed work week itself, the job, home, and personal life, and leisure/recreation opportunities were generally positive. Yet, the effect on employee job performance was mixed.[16]

Another study examined the relationship between a compressed work week and productivity and absenteeism in eight different organizations. Five reported an effect on productivity, the results ranging from a 4.5 percent decrease to a 3.1 percent increase. The median change was 0.0 percent. Of the five firms which reported absenteeism data, two found an improvement, one experienced an increase, and two said that absenteeism remained unchanged.[17]

In 1987, ASPA/CCH surveyed thirty-six companies using a four-day, forty-hour work week. Respondents were asked to assess their experience with this schedule. Most felt that it had a slightly positive effect on both quantity and quality of work. Employee reliability was favorably affected as was the quality of service delivered to clients. Firms also reported that the 4/40 schedule improved employee job satisfaction and the employees' ability to participate in outside activities. The only major disadvantage was that the 4/40 schedule seemed to increase supervisory stress levels.[18]

Job Sharing and Job Pairing

A third alternative, job sharing, involves two equally qualified part-time employees dividing the hours, responsibilities, and benefits of a full-time job by performing complementary tasks. Closely related is job pairing, which is basically identical except that each employee is accountable for everything that is done on the job, not just his or her own work. Both job sharing and job pairing are really a form of permanent part-time employment. However, unlike most part-time employees, people actually split a full-time job and are considered permanent employees. Benefits are often provided on a pro-rated basis and the skills and education of job sharers and pairers are equal to those of full-time workers.

Northeast Utilities in Hartford, Connecticut, offers its employees a job sharing program.[19] Here, tasks are divided into physical, mental, and interpersonal categories, and then distributed to the two job sharers in one of three ways. For partners with similar skills, the tasks are separated into those which are interchangeable; for persons with dissimilar skills, tasks are broken down so that partners have equal responsibility; for those having significantly different levels of skills and experience, tasks are divided such that partners have unequal responsibilities. To prevent misunderstandings, the company asks job sharers to sign an agreement which covers salary, benefits, work schedules, training, communication, accountability, reversibility of the job (to full-time status), and evaluation.

Job sharers at Northeast Utilities are paid commensurate with the job's established grade level. If employees work at least twenty hours per week, the company pays medical benefits, life insurance, and pension benefits on the same basis as full-time employees. Paid sick leave, employee education assistance, and vacation days are pro-rated according to hours worked.

Besides Northeast, many other organizations currently permit job sharing or pairing, including banks, libraries, museums, legal firms, and governmental organizations. Over one hundred college professors share jobs.[20] Many are husband-wife teams who share one salary and a single course load.

Job sharing and job pairing offer a firm several potential advantages. Productivity may be higher because employees have found a job that conforms to their special needs and because two people each working half a day may suffer less fatigue and boredom than one person working eight hours. Absenteeism and turnover may be lower for the same reasons. Allowing workers to share a job also increases the number of highly qualified applicants for a job. At the present time, many good individuals do not work because the job requires their full-time effort. Offering these individuals a part-time opportunity may encourage them to enter the work force and net the company an excellent employee. A further advantage of job sharing/pairing is that it helps to reduce work problems caused by vacations, lunch breaks, and absenteeism. When a full-time employee is away from work, the organization often needs a temporary replacement. With job sharing, this issue can be handled by having one person cover for the other.

Even though there may be advantages to job sharing/pairing, some potential problems have also been identified. Coordination between those sharing a job can create difficulties unless both parties make a conscientious effort to communicate effectively with each other. The same is true regarding coordination between the supervisors and the job sharers/pairers. Accountability can also be an issue. When two people share a job, it may be more difficult to determine responsibility for errors and mistakes. One solution is to hold both employees responsible for the entire job. Another potential disadvantage is the increased cost of benefits. While salaries and benefits such as life insurance and retirement can be pro-rated, statutory benefits such as FICA and unemployment insurance may be higher, depending on the total salary for the job.

How successful has job sharing and job pairing been overall? Even though the empirical research is again somewhat limited, one study in a mass-assembly department of a northeastern firm found that job sharing resulted in 7 percent higher output and a 12 percent lower scrap rate. A second study of fifty Massachusetts welfare case workers showed that each job sharer handled 80 percent of a full-time caseload.[21] In these situations people who worked only two or three days a week or only four hours a day apparently accomplished more per hour than their full-time counterparts.

In 1987, an ASPA/CCH survey found that eighteen firms (4 percent of those surveyed) were using job sharing, job pairing, or job splitting. Most were in the human services or manufacturing/processing industries. In the survey, firms were asked to evaluate their programs on six dimensions of organizational effectiveness. The results showed that three dimensions of performance were perceived to be positively influenced (quantity of work, quality of work, and employee reliability). In addition, job sharing had several favorable effects on the work force. Firms reported improved employee morale and motivation, employee acts of good organizational citizenship, organizational turnover, and loyalty to supervision and management. The only negative finding was increased insurance costs. Those costs associated with training, personnel or support services, and utilities were not affected.[22]

Leaves of Absence and Vacations

While alternative work schedules can help employees mesh work with their personal lives, there are times when the two are simply incompatible and the employee needs to be away from work for extended periods. When this happens leaves of absence and vacations can be of value.

Not all employees want to take vacations at the same time. One person may want to go skiing in the winter whereas another likes deer hunting in November. By the same token some employees will take their entire vacation at one time while others prefer to use a few days here and there.

Many organizations now have policies which permit employees considerable choice regarding their vacations. One large midwestern manufacturing company, for example, allows all employees four weeks vacation a year after ten years of service. But, workers exercise considerable latitude in choosing how the time is taken. They can use it all at once or distribute it over time, even half a day for forty days. Suppose that an employee does not want four weeks vacation. Under this plan they can work the time and get four weeks extra pay or they can even "bank" it for subsequent years.

Most large firms offer leaves of absence for medical reasons. But there are a variety of other leaves a firm might use. One large auto manufacturing company, for example, allows each employee three paid days personal leave per year. These can be used any time regardless of the reason, and supervisors are not permitted to ask employees why they want these "personal business days." A mental health organization gives its employees three paid "mental health days" per year which can be used whenever they simply do not feel like coming in to work.

In addition to short-term personal leaves, some organizations also grant more extended leaves of absence. For example, one large hospital grants employees, on a case-by-case basis, up to thirty nonpaid days per year. This can be extended up to eighteen months provided the employee can provide a satisfactory reason. Hospital administrators, of course, determine what constitutes a "satisfactory" reason.

Funeral leaves are also common. Frequently, employees can take up to three paid days to attend a close relative's funeral. A "close relative" is usually defined as a wife, husband, son, daughter, father, mother, brother, sister, or parent of spouse.

One large retail organization offers employees a marriage leave. Employees are paid for their wedding day and even if this falls on a Saturday or Sunday, they are paid and also allowed to take the preceding Friday off.

St. Vincent's Hospital and Medical Center has a unique time-off program whereby employees receive between 172.5 and 247.5 hours off annually, depending upon length of service and hourly or salaried status. Employees use these hours for sick time, vacation, personal time, and holidays as long as they attempt to schedule the time off in advance. Employees are required to use at least 120 hours per year and can carry over a maximum of 300 hours to the next year. Employees may cash in 75 hours each year as long as they maintain that number in their bank.[23]

Finally, some firms provide leaves of absence to engage in civic, educational, professional, or governmental activities, including politics. One large computer manufacturer gives its people an opportunity to take educational leave. Approval is based on how relevant the study program is to the company, the employee's academic and work record, and the appropriateness of the school to the employee's educational objectives.

Leaves of absence and vacation policies are so commonplace in industry that most managers and employees fail to recognize their highly individualized nature. Yet we know that certain people are sick more than others, that some want to engage in civic, educational, or professional activities, and that employees differ in terms of their vacation desires. In other words, these policies really are designed to meet unique needs, and beyond that, they typically have positive consequences for organizations. They help attract new employees and keep older ones. In addition, both can have a positive effect on productivity in the long run.

Social Programs

"Let's gather young power here/and light up like the hot light of the sun/ New land of green and sea/Growing splendidly in the world/This is Nippon Steel Kimitsu." This song is sung before each shift by managers and workers at Nippon Steel's Kimitsu mill in Japan. It follows a well-planned exercise session held near the company's modern steel plant.

Unlike the Kimitsu mill, workers in the United States do not sing songs praising their company. However, many organizations do hold periodic social activities for employees. In addition, approximately fifty thousand business firms have programs promoting exercise and physical fitness. So, too, some organizations have offered their employees numerous other options such as garden plots, organized flea markets, and musical programs. It is important to observe that all of these programs have one thing in common—employees have the choice of participating in them or not depending on their own needs and desires.

The Hyatt Hotel in Orlando, Florida has an extensive social program for its 650 employees.[24] It includes a roller skating party (Hyatt's Great Skate), an employee "Gong Show," a fifties party, a version of "The Price Is Right," and a take-off on television's "Family Feud" called "Department Feud." In addition, the hotel has an intrahotel bake-off and a hot dog-eating contest. Perhaps the two greatest productions of the year are the employees' annual awards banquet and the family picnic. The festive awards banquet honors all employees with two or more years of service. Special awards are also given to those who have shown superior service and one individual is singled out to receive an Employee of the Year commendation. This usually entitles that person to a one-week paid vacation to a designated city in the United States. The annual picnic provides a chance for all employees and their families to get together for a day and is usually attended by over 1200 people.

Companies such as Dofasco, Inc., a steel producer located in Hamilton, Ontario, have attempted to offer both social and recreational programs. This company has over fifty different activities from which employees can choose. These range from chess and model railroading clubs to shooting and hockey. Interestingly, the company itself makes no attempt to initiate new activities. Rather, they are added when a sufficient number of employees express an interest. Some six thousand employees and their families are active participants, paying a nominal fee for each activity in which they participate. In addition, the company also provides major financial support. In 1978, the firm opened a fifty-acre recreation park. This complex has softball and baseball diamonds, floodlit tennis courts, a golf driving range, a miniature golf course, an all-weather four hundred-meter track, and a combination soccer and touch football field. In addition, there is also a picnic grove and nature trails through a twenty-acre woodlot. Fifty more acres were subsequently acquired to provide a fitness center, an arena, a swimming pool, a rifle range, and meeting rooms for hobbies and crafts.

Among the more exotic things offered by companies are employee garden plots, flea markets, and musical programs. Dow Chemical Company, Control Data Corporation, and the Hughes Employee Association, Fullerton, California, are among those which allocate land for personal gardening. Generally, they provide the space, fertilizer, and water for the gardens while the employees are expected to plant their own seeds and tend their plots. The Dow garden program has more than 350 plots measuring 40′ by 40′ and participating workers are charged $8.00 per season.[25]

The General Mills Employee Club in Minneapolis, Minnesota, sponsored an employee flea market. The sale, which comprised ninety-five booths, was held in the corporate headquarters' twelve-acre parking lot and attracted more than three thousand people.

Allen Bradley Company in Milwaukee, Wisconsin sponsors an orchestra and chorus. The group performs periodically during lunch hour in the company's auditorium, gives concerts in the Milwaukee area, and occasionally goes on "tour" for two or three weeks.[26]

MANAGERIAL APPLICATIONS

Up to now we have been discussing ways in which organizations can satisfy employee needs by individualizing rewards and addressing specific needs. But suppose that an individual manager does not have the authority to implement a flexible benefits system or alternative work schedules. How can differing needs be satisfied? (See Exhibit 8–2.)

Determining Employee Needs

The first issue is to determine which employee needs are dominant. Careful observation or an attitude survey can often provide such information. On the other hand, if a manager has only a few employees or is concerned with just a single person, an interview may be more appropriate. The word *interview* often connotes a formal meeting between a boss and an employee. During an interview the manager asks the employee a series of questions. While some managers may want to follow this approach, a short informal meeting between a manager and an employee can often prove quite useful in determining employee needs. If they are alert, supervisors can often uncover information about an employee's unsatisfied needs when talking about ordinary job-related problems with the employee. It is not uncommon for employees, during job-related discussions, to make statements such as, "I'd really like to learn more about . . ." or "I don't like

Exhibit 8–2
Some Potential Ways of Satisfying Employee Needs

Need	Examples
1. Physiological	Cafeterias Vending machines Drinking fountains
2. Security	
Economic	Wages and salaries Fringe benefits Retirement benefits Medical benefits
Psychological	Provide job descriptions Give praise/awards Avoid abrupt changes Solve employee's problems
Physical	Working conditions Heating and ventilation Rest periods
3. Affiliation	Encourage social interaction Create team spirit Facilitate outside social activities Allow employees to schmooze Use periodic praise Allow participation
4. Esteem	Design challenging jobs Use praise and awards Delegate responsibilities Give training Encourage participation
5. Self-actualization	Give training Provide challenges Encourage creativity

to . . . ." While these statements may seem rather innocuous, they can tell a supervisor quite a bit about an employee's needs.

On occasion, a manager may want to ask an employee directly about what he or she wants from a job or feels about the present job. One may want to experiment with questions like, "What could I or the organization do to make your job more enjoyable?" or "What changes would you like to see made in your work situation?" Even questions like, "How could I or the company help you to improve your job performance?" or "What job would you like to be doing two years from now?" might prove fruitful under some conditions.

Negatively oriented questions such as "What don't you like about working for this organization?" should probably be avoided. Sometimes even satisfied employees respond by thinking up things they do not like.

Often employees may not accurately report their needs to a manager. For example, they may say that they want more pay when, in fact, they really want greater recognition or responsibilities. Remember that what employees say they want is often affected more by the need-satisfiers they believe they can get than by those they really want.

Many organizations provide workers with an opportunity to satisfy their physiological, safety, and social needs but not their esteem and self-actualization needs. When asked about their unsatisfied needs, workers in these organizations typically respond that they want more job security or pay. The rationale behind their answer is quite simple. They have learned over the years that the organization will not or cannot provide them with opportunities to satisfy their esteem and self-actualization needs. They feel they have no alternative but to try to get more of the rewards which the organization has provided in the past. The important point is that money and other relatively lower-level need-satisfiers often serve as substitute requests for higher-level need-satisfiers. Hence, when managers hear their employees asking for lower-level need-satisfiers, they should attempt to determine whether this is really what the employee wants or whether this demand represents a masked desire for higher-level need-satisfiers.

In summary, a manager can determine employee needs by using job satisfaction questionnaires, conducting a formal or informal interview regarding the employee's needs, or by being attentive to casual employee comments regarding likes and dislikes. Ideally, a manager would have—as a result of using one or more of these approaches—a general understanding of which needs of the employee are presently satisfied, which needs of the employee are presently unsatisfied, and which of the unsatisfied needs are most important to the employee.

Satisfying Employee Needs

Once employee needs have been identified, the next step is to try to satisfy them. Consider some of the things one might do, assuming that people have different types and levels of needs.[27] Since most employees have their basic physiological needs satisfied, we will move directly to security needs.

Security needs can be conceptualized in economic, psychological, and physical terms, and different incentives can satisfy each of these. Economic security needs can be met by adequate wages and salaries, fringe benefits, and retirement and medical benefits. Providing people with a clear list of specific duties and ways to achieve them, and using periodic praise and feedback may satisfy the psychological component. Beyond that, managers may want to help employees solve problems and avoid abrupt changes in policies and procedures. Finally, if physical security needs are dominant the answer may be improved working conditions, equipment, heating and ventilation, and rest periods.

Some employees are most concerned with belonging. They want to make friends, socialize, and be accepted by others. Designing jobs that allow social interaction, creating team spirit, allowing and encouraging informal groups, and providing outside social activities for employees can all be used. For example, one suggestion is to design groups so that employees can "schmooze"—to get together in groups of four or five, fool around, or use the telephone. Workers find informal ways to do this anyway, so why not recognize this fact and build it into the basic work structure? The net result may be positive. Many supervisors, when they see people engaging in nonwork behavior, automatically assume that they either do not have enough to do or are just goofing off. They attempt to stop the schmoozing and in the process may inhibit satisfaction of social needs.

People with high social needs may want more than just socializing with others. They may also desire acceptance by the manager and the company. Periodic praise, particularly in the form of a public award, is one option that can be used. Asking the employee to participate in a decision can also foster a sense of belonging.

Esteem needs involve the desire for recognition as well as a need for self-confidence. Designing more challenging jobs, using praise, giving recognition such as awards, involving people in decision making, delegating authority, offering promotions, and providing training and development that increase competency can all be used to satisfy esteem needs.

Finally, self-actualizing that involves personal growth and development can be promoted in several ways. Employees could be provided with training activities that not only increase competence but also give individuals a greater opportunity to make full use of their potential. In addition, providing challenging work and encouraging creativity might also allow many people to satisfy growth needs.

Some of these ideas may be easy and inexpensive to implement while others can be quite difficult and costly. In any event, there are ways in which managers may be able to satisfy individual needs in the workplace.

SUMMARY

This chapter focused on motivating employees by meeting their unique needs. It began by discussing Maslow's hierarchy of needs theory and ERG theory, which provide a rationale. Maslow maintains that employees are motivated to satisfy their unsatisfied needs and that needs can be arranged in a hierarchy of importance. Similarly, ERG theory holds that employee needs are hierarchical and that employees differ in terms of what motivates them.

Organizations can satisfy employees' unique needs in many ways. This chapter examined some of the major efforts including flexible benefits systems, alternative work schedules (flexitime, compressed work schedules, and job sharing/job pairing), leaves of absence and vacations, and social programs.

The chapter also considered what individual managers might do in order to address the unique needs of employees. We have suggested that one must determine employee needs and then find ways of satisfying them. Neither is simple to do but most managers can succeed if they try.

In closing, managers have much to gain personally from using this approach. First, workers should be more satisfied. It is easier and far more enjoyable to supervise satisfied employees than ones who are dissatisfied with their work situation. Unsatisfied workers may be less cooperative and friendly, and are more likely to be tardy or absent, to break company rules, and to quit.

Second, managers who use this strategy are generally viewed more favorably by employees. They are thought to be more considerate, supportive, and interested in their employees' welfare. This is true even if they are not totally successful in obtaining what employees want.

Finally, to the extent that managers can satisfy needs, employees are more likely to identify with the organization and be committed to its goals. When this happens, both the organization and the manager gain.

NOTES

1. L. L. Neider, "Cafeteria Incentive Plans: A New Way to Motivate," *Supervisory Management*, February 1983, pp. 31–35.

2. R. B. McAfee and P. J. Champagne, *Organizational Behavior: A Manager's View* (St. Paul, Minn.: West Publishing Co., 1987).

3. W. H. Wagel, "Flexible Work Schedules That Work for Everyone," *Personnel*, June 1987, pp. 5–10.

4. A. H. Maslow, "A Dynamic Theory of Human Motivation," *Psychological Review* 50 (1943), pp. 370–96.

5. M. A. Wabba and L. G. Birdwell, "Maslow Reconsidered: A Review of Research on the Need Hierarchy Theory," *Proceedings of the Academy of Management*, 1973, pp. 514–20.

6. C. P. Alderfer, *Existence, Relatedness, and Growth: Human Needs in Organizational Settings* (New York: Free Press, 1972).

7. C. P. Alderfer, "An Empirical Test of Need Theory of Human Needs," *Organizational Behavior and Human Performance*, April 1969, pp. 142–75.

8. G. Tavernier, "How America Can Manage Its Flexible Benefits Program," *Management Review* 69, no. 8 (1980), pp. 8–13.

9. B. S. Moskal, "More Flexibility in Benefit Plans," *Industry Week*, January 7, 1980, p. 110.

10. "Cafeteria Benefit Plans Let Employees Fill Their Plates, Then Pay with Tax-free Dollars," *The Wall Street Journal*, May 9, 1983, pp. 58–59.

11. "Roundup," *Personnel*, March–April 1983, pp. 47–49.

12. "Flexible Benefit Designs Take Many Approaches," *Employee Benefit Plan Review*, October 1986, pp. 61–66.

13. 1987 ASPA/CCH Survey, *Commerce Clearing House*, June 26, 1987, pp. 1–15.

14. R. E. Kopelman, "Alternative Work Schedules and Productivity: A Review of the Evidence," *National Productivity Review*, Spring 1986, pp. 150–65.

15. D. A. Ralston, W. P. Anthony, and D. J. Gustafson, "Employees May Love Flextime, but What Does It Do to the Organization's Productivity?" *Journal of Applied Psychology* 70, no. 2, pp. 272–79.

16. S. Ronen and S. B. Primps, "The Compressed Work Week as Organizational Change: Behavioral and Attitudinal Outcomes," *Academy of Management Review* 6, no. 1 (1981), pp. 61–74.

17. R. E. Kopelman, *National Productivity Review*, Spring 1986, pp. 150–65.

18. 1987 ASPA/CCH Survey.

19. "Impact," July 29, 1987, Prentice-Hall.

20. M. Frease and R. A. Zawachi, "Job Sharing: An Answer to Productivity Problems," *Personnel Administrator* 24, no. 10 (1979), pp. 35–39.

21. Ibid.

22. 1987 ASPA/CCH Survey.

23. "Flexible Benefit Designs."

24. K. Thomas, "Employee Morale Is Top Priority at Hyatt Orlando," *Recreation Management*, August 1981, pp. 22–24.

25. K. Thomas, "How Do Your Gardens Grow," *Recreation Management*, May–June 1981, pp. 24–26.

26. T. A. Hutton, "Involvement through Music," *Personnel Administrator*, January 1980, pp. 61–62.

27. A. Sondak, "The Importance of Knowing Your Employee's Needs," *Supervisory Management*, May 1980, pp. 13–18.

9

Building Effective Work Teams

The key elements in obtaining the necessary support and commitment primarily involve treating people so that they have a sense of personal recognition—that is, a recognition of their worth as individuals. These elements are trust, support, completion, acknowledgement, and communication and agreement. The degree to which they are fostered within a company will predict the success of any improvement effort. One technique that works well in developing them is having people work together as a team.[1]

In today's competitive world, the only edge you have is the way you organize people. Having them working together in well-developed teams will give you that edge.[2]

In some situations team building isn't an option; it's the only alternative.[3]

When Ohio Edison was installing air quality control equipment at its W. H. Sammis Plant it ran into several problems. The project was falling behind, causing the firm to face potential fines from the EPA and overruns of the target budget. In addition, employees were not cooperating. Meetings were filled with scapegoating, put-downs, and finger pointing. Decisions were being delayed and members were withholding vital information from each other.

In order to resolve the problems, the three groups involved in the project (project managers for Ohio Edison, the architect engineers and the general contractors) decided to hold team-building sessions. At the initial all-day meeting participants first discussed the reservations and skepticism they had about the meeting. The list generated by the participants included questions regarding whether participants would really get down to the nitty-gritty, whether hard feelings would result, and whether anything of value would come out of the session. The next agenda item dealt with participant expectations regarding the meeting and what could be done to make the session worthwhile. During the discussion, participants brought up a list of constructive and destructive attitudes and behaviors on the job including items such as embarrassing and belittling others, not listening, and refusing to accept responsibility. This phase was followed by a discussion of the problems to be resolved at the job site. What were the current problems and who needed to get involved in their solutions? Strategies were developed to solve the problems and follow-through personnel were assigned.

After this joint meeting, additional ones were held for others involved in the project. At one of these the project managers met with consultants to assess progress and set goals. In another, sixty first-line personnel involved in the project met in Waterford, West Virginia. At this meeting thirty-four issues believed to be responsible for delaying the project were identified. These items were alternately assigned to multiple company problem-solving groups. Still other meetings or training sessions were held which focused on improving communication skills, the dynamics of conflict and conflict resolution, and managing organizational interfaces.

What were the results of these team-building sessions and meetings? Team functioning and relationships improved significantly as exemplified by a "We can make it" and "on-line, on-schedule" spirit. All EPA deadline dates were met; no penalties were incurred; and the project was completed $30 million under budget.[4]

The productivity of any group is affected by its members' ability to work together effectively. They must cooperate so that each person's specialized skills and abilities are put to maximum use. Take, for example, professional sports where teams lose repeatedly even though the players are highly talented. Why? Not because they lack the appropriate skills and abilities. Often the answer is that the players do not work well together. They really do not operate as a "team."

In this chapter we want to examine how group functioning can be improved. Stated differently, we will discuss "team building" and consider both formal and informal approaches for developing effective work teams.

WHAT IS A TEAM?

Most of you are probably familiar with the concept of a team. We have all seen football, basketball, baseball, and soccer teams. However, when it comes to business organizations we sometimes forget that employees are really members of teams. For example, we do not call a group of secretaries or a finance committee a "team." Yet they are potentially every bit as much a team as are sporting groups.

What, then, is a team? This concept has been defined as a "group of people who must rely on cooperation and collaboration if each member is to achieve optimum success and goal achievement."[5] Another common definition is "a small group of people who are interdependent and must work together in order to fulfill their task. Such a group is at least by inference hierarchical; there is one leader who requires the efforts of the other group members in order to accomplish the job."[6] A third conceptualization defines a team as "an energetic group of people who are committed to achieving common objectives, who work well together and enjoy doing so, and who produce high quality results."[7] While each of the definitions is different, they all point out that a team consists of people who must collaborate with each other in order to accomplish goals. More specifically, a team has the following characteristics: (1) information is shared by all members of the group; (2) coordination takes place between the members; (3) specialized skills and abilities of the work group are known and used; (4) members cooperate and pitch in to help each other; and (5) a minimum duplication of effort occurs.[8]

INFORMAL APPROACHES FOR BUILDING EFFECTIVE WORK TEAMS

There are two primary ways organizations and managers can develop effective work teams. One is for the manager to use a variety of informal team-building activities on a day-to-day basis. The other option is for the firm to invest in more formal step-by-step team-building programs. In practice these two alternatives are not mutually exclusive; they are often used in conjunction with each other.

Imagine for a moment that you manage a group of eight architects or engineers. How would you develop them into an effective work team? What specific actions would you take?

Encouraging Employee Interaction

Perhaps the most elementary approach to team building is to locate group members close to one another so that they can easily see and communicate with each other. By being in close proximity, workers have quick access and can also observe each other's eye movements, hand gestures, postures, and other body language.

Once the lines of communication have been opened, managers can encourage employees to collaborate. For example, they could request that employees work together on specific projects rather than assign one person to do the entire task. In addition, a manager can encourage employees to talk with each other about job-related matters by asking whether there is any reason to bring everyone up to date on a project or to check with others in order to get their opinion. A manager may want to set an example by consulting with team members to get advice on specific plans, problems, or procedures. This can be done either individually or in small groups.

To further facilitate group interaction, a manager can attempt to bridge gaps between employees by making them aware of others who have similar interests or who possess useful expertise. The following statements illustrate this technique: "Terry is very adept at solving that type of problem"; "Ellen spent three years working for a bank so maybe she would be a good person to check with"; "I know Chris has worked with this machine. You may want to talk with her." Remember that the interaction need not be restricted to work-related activities. A manager can encourage people to get together after work as well as on the job. For example, a branch manager of a large bank often invited employees to join him for dinner when the bank closed on Friday.

Promoting Pride

Another way to foster teamwork is by promoting pride among group members. The underlying rationale here is that pride leads to teamwork, teamwork leads to group success, and group success leads to even more pride, teamwork, and success.[9]

Joe Paterno, the Penn State football coach, attributes a good deal of his team's success to group pride. He explains it this way:

You start with the idea that you build some pride. You make people feel that they're with a special company, a special institution, that's worth making sacrifices for. If you're the kind of guy that we call the "we and us" people that can work with the group, by being unselfish, benefits will accrue to you.[10]

There are no magic formulas for getting team members to take pride in their group. One device often used is to give special names to various groups such as the "Brainy Bunch," "Solution Seeds," and "Fact Finders." Other organizations stress the history of a group and point out its significant achievements or how difficult it is to join. In addition, some firms encourage managers to repeatedly tell employees how proud they are of them and that they too should take pride in their accomplishments.

Developing a Norm of Teamwork

A third strategy is to cultivate the belief that working together effectively is an expected standard of conduct.[11] Stated differently, a manager could foster a teamwork norm. One direct way to accomplish this is for the manager to make explicit statements about the desirability of teamwork such as: "I want to encourage all of you to work as a team, to develop a 'we' attitude as opposed to an 'I' attitude. I want you to keep sharing your ideas with each other, to keep up to date on what others are doing, and to fully use the skills and abilities of others." In addition, one could also encourage the informal group leaders to support a teamwork norm.

Rewarding Employees for Teamwork

Teamwork can also be encouraged by using rewards. A manager can praise employees for working together, passing along information, seeking advice, and cooperating with others. To illustrate, when one navy ship received a coveted award, the captain called the crew together and commended them for their teamwork and exceptional performance. As a follow-up reward, he announced that a special banquet would be held to celebrate the group's achievements.

In addition to praise, some researchers have suggested that paying employees on the basis of group achievement may help develop teamwork. They believe that since each person's pay is dependent on how well the group performs, collaboration will be encouraged. Think about the group incentive plans discussed in chapter 5. How could they be used? One might also follow the example of some Japanese firms, which always award bonuses to a work group as opposed to specific members, even if the achievements can be attributed mainly to one individual.[12] Rewarding everyone satisfies what the Japanese call "amaeru," a person's need to be accepted by others, or the need to depend on the benevolence of others. Those who have been rewarded even though they have contributed less feel obligated to equalize the imbalance by contributing more in the future. Besides, rewarding the group also encourages individuals to view others as supportive peers rather than competitors.

Closely related is the Japanese custom of developing mutual indebtedness among employees. Workers are encouraged to exchange favors, such as buying each other dinner. This web of mutual indebtedness developed outside work parallels the one that develops as the result of group rewards. Members once again feel indebted to one another and believe that if they do not repay the group, they will lose face.

Some Japanese firms also encourage teamwork by awarding bonuses as group prizes. A company bonus may involve a company-paid joint vacation given to several families. This helps develop a "group memory" since employees remember what "we" did together, and it symbolically bonds employees together, thereby encouraging them to cooperate and support each other at work.[13]

While team building requires cooperation within a group, other researches have noted that competition between groups can also be effective. To the extent that this is true, a manager may be able to foster teamwork by encouraging various groups to compete with each other and with others outside the company. One major risk, however, is that competition can lead to interdepartmental rivalries that are ultimately detrimental to the overall organization.

FORMAL APPROACHES FOR DEVELOPING EFFECTIVE WORK TEAMS

The informal day-to-day approaches just described are not the only techniques that can be used to develop teamwork. Other more formal approaches that involve step-by-step procedures, the help of consultants, and have application across the organization rather than in just one department are also available. These can be grouped into four categories: improving communication between team members; clarifying each member's role; improving interpersonal relationships between employees; and setting goals and improving the team's problem-solving abilities.

Improving Teamwork through Better Communication

If a group is to become a productive work team, it is essential that the members communicate effectively with each other. Indeed, one could argue that no teamwork is possible without clear communication.

Perhaps the most common approach for improving teamwork through communication is for supervisors to hold periodic meetings with groups of employees. These sessions often take the form of a "state of the nation" meeting whereby a work team's own supervisor or some other manager gives the employees information regarding anticipated changes, new policies and procedures, a description of company progress, and so on. The meeting might be held in an auditorium, a conference room, an office, or even in the work area.

One variation is for the management representative to ask for input on different issues from all group members. Questions such as the following can be raised:

1. What problems are you having on your job that the group might help you solve?
2. What is preventing you from doing your job more effectively?
3. Does anyone have any questions that need answering?
4. What should the work group be anticipating and addressing now?

Unfortunately, some managers fail to realize that meetings can potentially develop teamwork. Yet anytime team members are brought together and develop a better understanding of each other's work, obtain a grasp of what is going on, and see how the group's effort contributes to the overall organization's success, the potential exists for improving coordination and teamwork. Imagine how effective a sports team would be if its members never met to discuss game plans or analyze recent games. Indeed, many coaches require attendance at all meetings and even have team members live together in the same dormitory or hotel.

A second way to improve communication is demonstrated by one firm's effort to improve the functioning of its Corporate Services Group, consisting of fifteen division directors and their supervisor (vice president).[14] Through interviews, it was found that one major problem affecting teamwork was the lack of communication between the division directors and their superior. Employees expressed this in several ways including statements such as, "The vice president doesn't seem to want to know what I think," "I spend half of my time around here trying to answer those *!#@ memos the vice president sends me, and my staff spends half their time getting me enough information to answer them." A step-by-step procedure was established, which involved a three-hour discussion of actual memos sent between the vice president and the various division directors. In the course of these discussions, the group identified communication problems and attempted to develop viable solutions.

What were the results? The volume of memos written by the vice president decreased during the year following the discussions, and the quality of those sent improved. The division directors felt closer, in an emotional sense, to the vice president, and communication between all parties improved. Finally, the experiment raised the overall level of trust that existed between the vice president and the directors and also among the directors themselves. Teamwork and communication were improved by allowing group members to discuss, under controlled conditions, problems that were important, emotionally loaded, and integrally related to work.

Improving Teamwork through Role Clarification

Another teamwork improvement device involves clarifying each employee's role in the organization. Briefly stated, a role is the sum total of expectations that the individual and significant others have about how that person should perform a specific job. The employee's relationships with peers, superiors, customers, and others can result in a range of expectations about how a particular job should be performed. The employee must be able to integrate these expectations into a meaningful whole in order to perform effectively. Problems arise, however, when there is role ambiguity and the employee does not clearly understand what others expect, or when there is role conflict and the person receives contradictory expectations. When individuals do not fulfill others' expectations, the result is often disappointment plus the loss of credibility and trust. These reactions, in turn, lead to reduced coordination, cohesiveness, and teamwork. By the same token, when employees are uncertain about their job duties, the likely result will be confusion, anxiety, job dissatisfaction, and less teamwork. Research[15] has suggested seven situations that may lead to role conflict and role ambiguity:

1. The organization is new and employees do not know what is expected of them.
2. The company or unit has been reorganized and employees do not know how the new positions fit together.
3. Employees perform job duties that require little contact with one another. They attend few meetings and generally feel isolated. The job descriptions are old.
4. The unit is characterized by conflicts and disruptions. Employees feel their jobs overlap with others and that they should be told what others are doing but are not.
5. The boss engages in one-on-one management. Few meetings are held and groups rarely meet together to solve problems.
6. Employees are not sure whether others know what they are doing.
7. Crises arise because everyone thought someone else was responsible for handling a task so no one did it.

Organizations have tried a variety of techniques in an effort to reduce role ambiguity and role conflict. All involve having individuals present their own role definitions, generating a discussion, and then modifying the role based on the group's expectations.

Role Analysis Technique

One of the most interesting of these approaches is called the Role Analysis Technique (RAT).[16] First used at KP Engineering Corporation, a manufacturer of welding electrodes located near Bombay, India, RAT, in most cases, is a three-part process. The purpose of each employee's role is discussed, its mandatory and discretionary components are considered, and its linkages with other roles are highlighted.

The RAT process begins by having one employee (called the focal role individual) state his or her job in the organization. The specific duties of the job, its place in the organization, the need for it, and its function in achieving overall organizational goals are then examined.

Next, the employee lists on a chalkboard or flip chart his or her specific job duties. Other members discuss these and make additions and subtractions to the list. Ultimately, the group agrees on the employee's job responsibilities.

Once the focal employee's role is clear, the next step is to list the expectations which that individual has of the other group members. They in turn list what they expect, and through open discussion, reach an agreement regarding mutual expectations and obligations. The conclusions are written down and everyone receives a copy. This concludes the analysis of one individual's role. The process is then repeated until everyone has had their jobs analyzed. While this may sound time-consuming, keep in mind that the information gained from one job can be used in analyzing others.

One variation of the RAT has been used even when employees' jobs are highly visible and their current duties are well understood. This procedure was applied to a company's board of directors, its president, and the latter's support staff.[17] With the board listening, the president and the staff members were asked to answer the question, "If the board were operating in an optimally effective way, what would they be doing?" Their responses were then written on a chalkboard. After forty-five minutes or so, the list was modified based on the general consensus of the total group. The procedure was then repeated, but this time the president listened while staff and board members discussed the question, "If the president were operating in an optimally effective way, what would he be doing?" Again, responses were written on a chalkboard during the discussion. Finally, the president responded and they attempted to achieve a consensus.

In short, the RAT approach assumes that discussing mutual expectations and obligations can clear up misunderstandings and pave the way for improved coordination and cooperation. Employees no longer have to wonder why the other person is not doing what should be done. They all understand their job requirements.

Responsibility Charting

Another device is responsibility charting. Developed primarily for organizations undergoing rapid change, it focuses on allocating work responsibilities among employees. It has been used by several organizations including a large interior design company.

Responsibility charting starts with the construction of a grid that shows the types of decisions and classes of action a work group faces on one axis and the employees' names on the other. Each decision facing the work group is then discussed and responsibility for it is assigned to only one person. The letter R is placed on the grid to designate responsibility. Then each employee's role in the decision is determined from among the following choices:[18]

1. Approval required, or the right to veto (A-V). The decision must be reviewed by an employee who has the option of either approving it or vetoing it.
2. Support (S). Providing logistical support and resources for the decision.
3. Inform (I). Must be informed of decision only.
4. No assigned behavior ($-$). This person has no role in the decision.

This process is continued for each decision area. Once the grid is complete, everyone can determine at a glance each team member's responsibility on all those decisions that require interaction with others. All team members can then use this information whenever decisions need to be made.

Role Negotiation

A third device, role negotiation, is designed to be used when employees are unwilling to change their behavior because it would mean a loss of personal power or influence. This has been used with top management groups, project teams, and even between husbands and wives. It assumes that "most people prefer a fair negotiated settlement to a state of unresolved conflict and thus are willing to invest some time and make some concessions in order to achieve a solution."[19]

The essence of role negotiation is for employees to negotiate changes in job-related behavior. That is, employees ask each other to change their behavior so that they can do their job better.

In order to conduct negotiations between employees, each is asked to complete an Issue Diagnosis Form (Exhibit 9–1) covering the other team members. This form lists those behaviors that an employee would like to see another person (1) do more or do better; (2) do less or stop doing; or (3) keep on doing.

These lists are exchanged so that everyone has all that pertains to his or her work behavior. Then each member makes a personal master list itemizing the behavior that the others want done more or better, less or stopped, and continued unchanged (see Exhibit 9–2). These master lists are then posted for all to see. Each employee is allowed to ask for clarification, but no rebuttal or yes/no agreements are allowed.

At this point all group members should clearly understand what others want from them and negotiations can begin. The parties make contingent offers to one another such as, "If you do X, I will do Y." No one is allowed to ask for anything without giving up something in return. The negotiations end when all parties are satisfied that they will receive a reasonable return for whatever they are agreeing to give. Ultimately, all agreements are written down so that mutual expectations are clear.

Enhancing Team Effectiveness by Improving Interpersonal Relationships

Imagine an organization where employees did not like each other, where they did not trust each other, and where communication between people was limited and cautious. How effective do you think the work groups would be? As the incident that opened this chapter illustrates, poor interpersonal relationships between group members can adversely affect productivity. In this section we will examine several techniques organizations can use to improve these relationships.

Exhibit 9–1
Issue Diagnosis Form

Messages from Jim Farrell

to David Sills

1. If you were to do the following things **more** or **better**, it would help me to increase my own effectiveness:
   - Being more receptive to improvement suggestions from the process engineers.
   - Give help on cost control (see 2).
   - Fight harder with the G.M. to get our plans improved.

2. If you were to do the following things **less**, or were to **stop** doing them, it would help me to increase my own effectiveness:
   - Acting as judge and jury on cost control.
   - Checking up frequently on small details of the work.
   - Asking for so many detailed progress reports.

3. The following things which you have been doing to increase my own effectiveness, and I hope you will continue to do them.
   - Passing on full information in our weekly meetings.
   - Being available when I need to talk to you.

Source: R. Harrison, "When Power Conflicts Trigger Team Spirit," *European Business*, Spring 1972. Reprinted by permission of INSEAD (European Institute of Business Administration), Fontainebleau, France.

Helping and Hindering Charts

The use of "helping and hindering charts" requires every employee to prepare a listing of several ways in which others either help or hinder group's effectiveness. These lists are then combined by an outsider such as a consultant, resulting in a "helping and hindering chart" for each employee. These are posted and discussed, starting with the manager's chart. By going first, managers act as role models for others' behavior and also demonstrate a willingness to work together. To enhance the likelihood of success, all participants are asked to follow a set of rules governing how to give and receive feedback.

Helping and hindering charts can be an effective way to increase trust, communication, and interpersonal risk taking among participants.[20] The

Exhibit 9–2
Summary of Messages to James Farrell from Other Group Members

MORE OR BETTER:	LESS OR STOP:	CONTINUE AS NOW:
Give information on project Progress (completion date slippage) Bill, Tony, David.	Let people go on to other good job opportunities— Stop hanging on to your good engineers.— Tony, Bill.	Training Operators on preventive maintenance— Henry.
Send progress reports on Sortair project— Bill.	Missing weekly planning meetings frequently— Jack, Henry, David	Good suggestions In meetings— Tony, Henry.
Make engineers more readily available when help needed— Jack, Henry.	Changing time on Sortair to other accounts— David.	Asking the difficult and awkward questions— Tony, Jack.
		Good quality Project work— Bill, Henry, David, Jack

Source: R. Harrison, "When Power Conflicts Trigger Team Spirit," *European Business,* Spring 1972. Reprinted by permission of INSEAD (European Institute of Business Administration), Fontainebleau, France.

risks, however, should not be overlooked. Any time people discuss their relationships with one another there is a chance that anger and resentment will develop. Still, the presence of an outsider, using the charts to structure discussion, and setting communication rules can minimize risks.

Team Interaction Critique

Group interaction can also be improved by having team members, including the manager, meet to consider four major questions:[21]

How are we all doing as a team?
What should we keep doing?
What should we change?
What should we not do?

Before discussing these questions, each employee writes his or her answers on index cards. These cards are sorted and combined by another team member who reads the various answers to the group. The discussion that follows is then directed toward a better understanding of work-related behaviors. As a measure of control, personalities and personal habits are not the focus of the meetings. Of course, if they are affecting work they may need to be discussed.

Developing Teamwork through Goal Setting and Problem Solving

Clearly, ambiguous work roles and strained interpersonal relations can be roadblocks to team development. However, difficulties can also arise if a group is confronted with a variety of task-related problems and has no idea how or in what way to solve them.

Many organizations have attempted to teach work groups the steps they should follow in order to solve problems. A variety of approaches could be cited, but perhaps the most popular concept is the one many organizations use as a part of a Quality Circles program. This involves training employees to solve problems using a five-step procedure:

Step 1: Problem Identification. What is the problem or problems that the group must solve?

Step 2: Cause-and-Effect Analysis—The Fishbone Diagram. Once the problem(s) has been identified a cause-and-effect analysis can be used to pinpoint the cause into four major categories—methods, machines, human resources, and materials. Exhibit 9–3 shows an example of this technique as it applies to poor quality copies from a duplicating machine. Brainstorming, a group discussion process whereby employees are encouraged to "create a storm of ideas" without having these ideas initially judged, is often used in determining problem causes. Following the completion of the fishbone diagram the group picks the two or three causes it considers most important. These are singled out for further analysis.

Step 3: Action Planning. The causes singled out are now discussed and steps are determined for eliminating these obstacles.

Step 4: Taking Action. At this point the identified steps are carried out, in the hope that they will eliminate the problem.

Step 5: Periodic Review. At periodic intervals a review is made to assess whether the problem has been eliminated. If it has not, steps 2, 3, and 4 are repeated.

In addition to helping groups solve problems, goal setting has also been used as a team development technique. The philosophy behind this technique is that a group is more productive if all its members work toward the accomplishment of clearly understood organizational goals, which serve to unify group activity as well as to direct it. Goal setting has been used by work groups ranging from boards of directors to entry-level employees in

Exhibit 9–3
Cause-and-Effect Analysis (Fishbone Diagram)

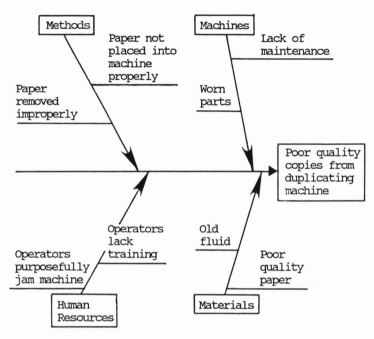

Source: R. B. McAfee and P. J. Champagne, *Organizational Behavior: A Manager's View* (St. Paul, Minn.: West Publishing Co., 1987), p. 283. Reprinted by permission.

order to establish objectives including sales targets, improving work quality, obtaining agreement on the organization's mission, setting goals for changing the organization's structure, and establishing individual job goals.

Two case studies show how group goal setting can be used. One of these involved the sales managers of a consumer products manufacturing firm.[22] Every three months these managers would set goals for the ensuing quarter and at subsequent meetings would evaluate the results and set new goals. The company reported an improvement in both group goal setting capabilities and group effectiveness. Sales improved 27 percent during the first year of the plan, and much of this increase was attributed to group goal setting. In the other situation, an automotive assembly plant used group goal setting with cross-functional teams of first-line supervisors representing all key areas within the plant including production, quality control, maintenance, and engineering. The teams met regularly to solve problems and set goals. During the first year productivity increased by 15 percent in some departments. The following year the reject rate was reduced from 14 to 7 percent. Communication between employees increased dramatically and coordination was also improved. The important point here is not that group goal setting always improves team effectiveness, for in some cases it has not. The studies demonstrate instead that group goal setting can and has been used in a variety of organizations in an attempt to improve teamwork.

Up to now we have been discussing goal setting and problem solving separately. Even though they can be viewed as distinct from one another, in practice the two are often intertwined. In other words, goal setting is used once problems have been identified during the problem-solving process, or goals are set and problem solving is used to eliminate obstacles.

TEAM DEVELOPMENT TECHNIQUES: GUIDELINES FOR USE

Consider the results of a team-building activity involving a public agency with about one hundred employees. The agency had apparently been plagued with conflicts between its employees.[23] The program designed to eliminate this involved bringing supervisors and their bosses together. After the sessions had been completed the participants were asked to evaluate them using two questionnaires. The results indicated that participants felt the meetings to be beneficial. But was the program a success? Yes and no. Yes, in the sense that the supervisors became more cohesive, trusting, and unified. No, in that the cohesiveness ultimately crippled the rest of the organization, which later had to be completely rebuilt.

During the meetings, supervisors realized that their employees had been playing them off against each other. They therefore decided to present a unified front by asking employees to confront only their immediate supervisor with complaints and by backing each other on disciplinary actions even when they felt that a mistake had been made.

Upon returning to the organization, the supervisors followed through on their plan. As a result, many employees reported that their supervisors were engaged in dishonest, arbitrary, and capricious behavior. Three weeks after the team development session ended, sixteen subordinates had filed grievances. Shortly thereafter, six had resigned and three more were terminated. Work by those remaining in the organization came to a standstill as tension reached an all-time high, far worse than it had been before the team-building sessions. It took two years of intensive work to resolve the problems caused by a seemingly successful team-building meeting.

The major lesson to be learned from this case is that team-builiding sessions are not always successful. They have the potential to backfire. Managers must pay careful attention to session goals, how they are organized, to the agreements reached by participants at the conclusion of the sessions, and to how the sessions are evaluated. Some guidelines for a successful program are suggested below.

Assessing Organizational Readiness for Team Building

Before beginning a team-building session, it is important to determine whether or not the firm is receptive. There are three parties to be considered: the unit supervisors, the subordinates, and top management.

With regard to the first group, one might ask the following: (1) Do the supervisors feel that team development is needed in their units? (2) Are the supervisors willing to participate in improving team effectiveness? If the answer to either question is no, team development is not likely to succeed. Team development requires that supervisors take a hard look at their own job performance, be willing to give and receive feedback, and be willing to make changes in their attitudes and behaviors. Beyond that, they may need to relinquish some power, influence, and control to their subordinates. In other words, the leader will be at risk and anxiety can result. Stop for a moment and ask yourself how you would feel about using each of the team development approaches we have described. Would you be reluctant to use them? In any event, if a supervisor feels threatened, team building is not recommended.

The two questions asked of supervisors can also be applied to subordinates. Do they feel a need for team building and are they willing to actively participate? Team building will be more effective when subordinates feel that their energies are well spent. It is not likely to be effective if only the manager, the personnel department, or a consultant wants to do it. Keep in mind that subordinates do most of the work during a team-building session; nobody else can do it for them.

Finally, there is the issue of top management's position on team building. Team development may not have a long-term effect if people in power do not support the changes decided upon during a session. Therefore, their strong support is often critical for success.

In addition to having the support of all parties, successful team building also requires sufficient time to hold the session, a satisfactory location, and a qualified person to conduct or monitor them. Sometimes managers and subordinates want to work more effectively but they are too busy to meet, or organizational demands make it impossible to do so. Remember that most team-building sessions require several days. Also, team building is not a one-time process; follow-up sessions are almost always needed. Additional sessions may also be necessary when jobs are substantially changed. Agreements made with one set of employees may not last when new people are hired and the entire process may need to be repeated. Thus the time demands may be too great for some organizations.

Team-building sessions also require a suitable location. As a general rule, groups need a site free from outside interruptions (e.g., telephone calls, people needing to go back to their offices). A retreat setting may be a good solution. It is also important that the room(s) used by comfortable and that participants are able to see and talk to each other. A chalkboard, easel, marking pens, and perhaps a screen and transparency projector are usually needed. If an organization does not have a room that meets these criteria, or is unable to rent a suitable facility, team-building may be difficult.

The final prerequisite for success is to have a competent person conduct and monitor the sessions. A good case could be made for having the work unit manager conduct these sessions, since he or she is ultimately responsible for making sure that employees function effectively. But if the manager feels reluctant or incapable, an outside consultant or someone else within the company could be used. The advantage is that this individual might be more detached and objective. The person would, however, be required to know the jobs well.

Implementing Team Building

Once the assessment issue has been settled the organization is in a position to begin implementation. This involves setting clear, reasonable goals and following a carefully developed procedure.

Setting Clear Goals

Goals should be clarified at the outset by the session leader and agreed to by the participants. This provides a framework for discussion and reduces the likelihood of being sidetracked by less important issues. The overriding goal in all sessions is to improve the team's effectiveness. Beyond that, each team-building technique (e.g., communication meeting, role clarification, interpersonal relationships, goal setting/problem solving) has its own unique goals. All these can be spelled out up front.

Following Definite Procedures

Once the goals are established and agreed to, the procedures and ground rules for the session need to be explained—and then followed. Earlier we described a number of different team-building techniques and outlined the recommended steps for using each. While no firm should follow them blindly, they do offer a tested methodology.

In addition, the session is more likely to be a success if the ground rules for discussion are explained. Some practitioners recommend that meetings will be most productive if these are written down and posted for all to see. The five most often recommended are:[24]

1. Each participant should be as candid and open as possible in a spirit of wanting to improve the team's functioning.
2. Participants who want to know how another thinks on an issue should ask that person directly. The response should also be direct even if it is to say, "I don't feel like responding right now."
3. If a participant feels the meeting is becoming unsatisfactory, this should be stated to the whole group.
4. Each participant should be given an opportunity to express an opinion on each issue.
5. Decisions made should be acceptable to all those affected by them.

Evaluating Team Building

At the conclusion of the team-building program it is important that a careful evaluation be conducted. This will increase the likelihood that future sessions will be successful. Questions about what happened during the program can be asked such as: What did the group do well? How could it have been more effective?

Equally important are questions relating to outcomes, that is, the decisions reached by the group and the commitments made by individual members. This involves a different set of questions and is often taken up during follow-up sessions or by the manager several months after the program's completion. Are the group members carrying out the tasks agreed upon during the team development session? Are they meeting their commitments with regard to changing their own behaviors?

Beyond these questions, an organization may want to address two additional global concerns. First, what effect has the team-building session had on the work unit itself? In other words, are the members more productive, and what effect, if any, has the program had on attitudes? In an extensive review of the available literature, it was found that only ten of the thirty cases studied really attempted to examine the effect on actual work performance (e.g., productivity, costs, absenteeism, turnover, or product quality). The remainder considered only participant attitudes.

The second global question is: What are the effects of a team-building session on other areas of the organization? As we saw in the case presented earlier, even though team development may improve the effectiveness of the unit involved, it can have a negative effect on the organization as a whole. Managers are the logical ones to raise this issue since they are usually in the best position to address it.

TEAM BUILDING: HOW SUCCESSFUL IS IT?

How effective are team-building techniques? Do they in fact improve communication between employees? Do they reduce role conflict and ambiguity? Do they improve interpersonal relationships, goal setting, and problem solving? And, ultimately, do they improve job performance and job satisfaction?

One in-house consultant reported that he developed over sixty-five teams ranging in size from seven to twenty-nine while working at Hewlett Packard Company. Four of these teams combined their efforts and reduced labor costs by over 15 percent; seven teams lowered their defect rate by an average of 66 percent over a six-month period; one team solved a vendor problem in three weeks and saved the company thousands of dollars per month; and twenty teams in one product line cut their scrap rate in half. The groups not only improved their productivity but employee response to the team concept was highly favorable.[25]

Two separate groups of researchers have attempted to address questions about the effectiveness of team building. One group analyzed thirty-six separate team-building studies and found that most of them showed positive results. However, they reported that because of inherent flaws in the studies and the measurements employed, no definitive conclusions could rightfully be drawn.[26] The second group of researchers reached essentially the same conclusion. They also found that methodological weaknesses in the available studies make it difficult to determine whether or not "teambuilding can be linked conclusively to improvement in performance of work groups. Indeed, at this point it is fairly safe to say that team development is often more likely to result in attitudinal changes than in changes in behavior."[27]

SUMMARY

This chapter has examined the problems and issues associated with developing effective work teams. While the concept can be defined in many different ways, a "team" is usually thought to have the following characteristics: (1) information is shared by all members of the group; (2) coordination takes place between the members; (3) specialized skills and abilities of the work group are known and used; (4) members cooperate and pitch in to help each other; and (5) a minimum of duplication of effort occurs.

A manager can develop an effective work team using informal, day-to-day approaches, and/or by following a more formal step-by-step technique. These two alternatives are not mutually exclusive; indeed, they can be implemented jointly.

While there are several informal approaches available to managers, four of the most common are encouraging employee interaction, promoting pride, developing a norm of teamwork, and rewarding employees for working as a team. Employee interactions can be encouraged by asking employees to work jointly on projects, suggesting that they talk with each other about work-related activities, and inviting employee interaction after work. Pride can be promoted by giving a special name to a group, reminding the group of its outstanding reputation, and by having managers tell employees how proud they feel. Promoting a norm of teamwork can also be accomplished by having a manager make explicit statements to employees regarding the desirability of teamwork, or encouraging the group's informal leader to support a teamwork norm. Finally, a manager can use rewards such as praising groups or basing financial rewards on team rather than individual achievements.

Formal approaches to team development typically involve step-by-step procedures and are often implemented organizationwide rather than in just one department. Four major approaches have been discussed in this chapter including holding communication meetings, clarifying roles, improving interpersonal relations, and setting goals and solving problems hindering teamwork. Each addresses different barriers to effective group functioning.

Not all team-building implementations have been successful. Indeed, one public agency found that attempts to improve group functioning actually backfired. In order to make this less likely, a manager or organization should first determine whether the organization is receptive to team building. How supportive are the unit supervisors, the employees, and top management? Is a competent moderator, sufficient time, and an appropriate location available for the sessions? Assuming these questions have been answered affirmatively, the team-building program can be implemented. This involves setting clear goals for the group, explaining the procedures to be followed, and following those procedures. Finally, at the conclusion of the team-building session, an evaluation is usually recommended.

The importance of teamwork cannot be overstated. Too often people work together without carefully analyzing their own functioning, without assessing their strengths and weaknesses, or considering how they could become more productive. As a result, needless conflict and alienation, as well as jealousies and feelings of frustration, frequently develop. The important point is that team building is an integral part of any manager's job and one that should not be overlooked.

NOTES

1. M. C. Allender, "Productivity Enhancement: A New Teamwork Approach," *National Productivity Review*, Spring 1984, pp. 181–89.

2. G. Dershimer, "Keeping Teams Turned On," *Management World*, March 1986, pp. 10–12.

3. B. W. Miller and R. C. Phillips, "Team Building on a Deadline," *Training and Development Journal*, March 1986, pp. 54–57.

4. Ibid.

5. W. G. Dyer, *Team Building Issues and Alternatives* (Reading, Mass.: Addison-Wesley Publishing Co., 1977).

6. D. Francis and D. Young, *Improving Work Groups: A Practice Manual for Team Building* (La Jolla, Calif.: University Associates, 1979), p. 8.

7. B. Newman, "Expediency as Benefactor: How Team Building Saves Time and Gets the Job Done," *Training and Development Journal*, February 1984, pp. 26–28.

8. F. X. Mahoney, "Team Development, Part 1: What Is TD? Why Use It?" *Personnel*, September–October 1981, pp. 13–24.

9. A. J. Dubrin, *Contemporary Applied Management*, 2d ed. (Plano, Tex.: Business Publications, 1985), p. 159.

10. H. Nuwer, "Team Builder," *Success*, October 1983, p. 24.

11. Dubrin, *Contemporary Applied Management*, p. 158.

12. J. P. Alston, "Awarding Bonuses the Japanese Way," *Business Horizons*, September–October 1982, pp. 46–50.

13. Ibid.

14. J. B. Harvey and C. R. Boettger, "Improved Communication Within a Managerial Workgroup," *Journal of Applied Behavioral Science* 7 (1971), pp. 164–74.

15. Dyer, *Team Building Issues and Alternatives*.

16. I. Dayal and J. M. Thomas, "Operation KPE: Developing a New Organization," *Journal of Applied Behavioral Analysis* 4, no. 4 (1968), pp. 473–506.

17. W. L. French and C. H. Bell, Jr., *Organizational Development*, 2d ed. (Englewood Cliffs, N.J.: Prentice-Hall, 1978).

18. R. Bechard and R. T. Harris, *Organizational Transactions: Managing Complex Change* (Reading, Mass.: Addison-Wesley Publishing Co., 1977), pp. 76–82.

19. R. Harrison, "When Power Conflicts Trigger Team Spirit," *European Business*, Spring 1972, pp. 57–65.

20. M. Beer, *Organizational Change and Development: A Systems View* (Santa Monica, Calif.: Goodyear Publishing Co., 1980).

21. F. X. Mahoney, "Team Development, Part 6: Variation of Procedure Meetings," *Personnel*, July–August 1982, pp. 64–69.

22. R. Likert and M. S. Fisher, "MGBO: Putting Some Team Spirit into MBO," *Personnel*, January–February 1977, pp. 40–47.

23. R. W. Boss and M. L. McConkie, "The Destructive Impact of a Positive Team-Building Intervention," *Group and Organizational Studies* 6, no. 1 (1981), pp. 45–56.

24. Dyer, *Team Building Issues and Alternatives*.

25. Allender, "Productivity Enhancement."

26. R. W. Woodman and J. J. Sherwood, "The Role of Team Development in Organizational Effectiveness: A Critical Review," *Psychological Bulletin* 88, no. 1 (1980), pp. 166–86.

27. K. P. DeMeuse and S. J. Liebowitz, "An Empirical Analysis of Team-building Research," *Group and Organizational Studies* 6, no. 3 (1981), pp. 357–78.

_____

10

Reducing Employee Stress

> There are discoverable limits to the amount of change that the human organism can absorb.... By endlessly accelerating change without first determining these limits, we may submit masses of [people] to demands they simply cannot tolerate.[1]

> Some aspects of the work environment may unexpectedly prove to be stressors; nonetheless, we ought to use foresight to guard in the best way we can against those stressors we can identify.[2]

> There are at least two compelling reasons for studying organizational stress. First, mismanaged stress can produce individual employee problems that have a negative impact on the organization as a whole. Second, when stress is correctly managed, it can lead to improved performance, worker satisfaction, and productivity.[3]

Officially the company insisted that it was just a coincidence. Yet less than a year after American Telephone and Telegraph announced the most sweeping reorganization in the Bell System's history, medical directors throughout the system were reporting higher levels of anxiety among employees coming in for routine physicals. The anxiety followed a shake-up that changed job titles, duties, and whole methods of working for about 250,000 employees, or about one-third of Bell's work force.

Most of the in-house doctors echoed the explanation given by the medical director of Pacific Telephone and Telegraph. "The Bell System is under stress because of external influences, but other industries are too," he said. "It's the life we live nowadays." Still, there was a pervasive uneasiness that the reorganization was tipping the scales from normal amounts of employee stress to truly deleterious anxiety reactions. As the assistant vice president of personnel relations for Bell Telephone of Pennsylvania put it:

"Even the smallest change creates quite a churn, and this [reorganization] is a significant change."[4]

When people face pressures caused by their job, such as those illustrated in the opening incident, they may experience stress. Indeed, stress and strain are universal experiences in the life of every organization and every executive, manager, and individual employee. Even though stress can be caused by a variety of factors other than one's job, the fact remains that in recent years, this has become a major topic among managers and other professionals concerned with enhancing employee productivity.

Stress is often discussed in terms of the negative effects it can have on individuals and organizations. In fact, most of the discussion of stress centers around two basic questions: (1) How can we minimize job-related stress?; (2) What can be done to relieve the symptoms of stress such as substance abuse, fatigue, and irritability? The point that can be missed if one concentrates too much on these questions is that stress is inevitable and indeed is essential to a person's growth, change, development, and performance. Like many other elements of a job, stress can have either beneficial or destructive consequences. The latter are not inevitable; they only result from the ineffective management of stress. The negative consequences can be avoided through proper application of diagnostic methods and preventive management interventions.[5]

In this chapter we will examine the nature of stress, its consequences, and how one diagnoses stress. In addition we will discuss a variety of methods used by organizations which can help individuals overcome the destructive aspects of stress and use stress as a positive force which may actually improve employee productivity.

THE NATURE OF STRESS

The word *stress* means an incredibly different array of things depending upon whom you ask. But simply stated, stress is the physiological or psychological response of strain individuals make to various forces and stimuli that surround them. The environmental conditions that are potential stress producers are called "stressors." The stress response occurs as a result of the individual's interaction with and reaction to the stressor.[6]

Both favorable and unfavorable events can lead to stress. Suppose that you have just received two very attractive job offers. This is certainly a favorable situation, but because you must make a choice there is stress involved. Which offer is the best, not just now but in the long run? What if the offer you believe to be better requires you to relocate your family? What problems, if any, will this cause? Alternatively, negative events such as losing your present job or facing an annual performance review knowing that the past year was not your best can also cause a good deal of stress.

CONSEQUENCES OF STRESS

The idea that stress can have negative physical and psychological effects on people is certainly not new. Research beginning in the late 1950s and early 1960s was pointing out the linkage between stress and a variety of physical ailments such as heart disease, ulcers, and arthritis. Employers at that time were also beginning to actively discuss problems associated with apathetic workers—people frustrated and dissatisfied with their lives and jobs. Managers were reporting sleeplessness, anxiety, and tension. In short, studies were showing the effect of stress on physical and mental well-being.[7]

Today we know a great deal more about the consequences of stress. Some of these are primary and direct while others, perhaps most, are indirect and result in less visible but equally important symptoms and responses from employees.[8]

Effects of Stress on Physical and Mental Health

Of all the possible consequences of stress, physical health effects are perhaps the most controversial and difficult to demonstrate. While it is certainly not our intention to review the medical literature here, suffice it to say that virtually no one denies that some linkages exist. Many current medical texts, in fact, attribute anywhere from 50 to 70 percent of illnesses to stress-related origins. Keep in mind, however, that the effects of stress on the body depend on its intensity, duration, and the coping skills of each individual.

For many years it has been commonly believed that bottled-up anger or prolonged strain will ultimately lead to some kind of physical or mental reaction. The two stress-related illnesses that have been studied extensively are mental illness and coronary artery disease. In the United States, there are some thirty thousand suicides and many cases of heart disease each year that are attributed to occupational and environmental stress.[9]

In addition to these primary stress-related disorders, research indicates that a whole spectrum of other physical problems may be directly or indirectly caused by stress. Among these disorders are peptic ulcers, respiratory diseases, allergies, diabetes, cancer, eczema, backaches, rheumatism, asthma, insomnia, and hypertension. Many of these physical reactions and problems can lead to decreased morale and lower productivity.

The importance of stress as a causative factor in all types of disease has led to the creation of several widely used rating scales for identifying stress levels and susceptibility to disease. One of the best known measures is the Social Readjustment Scale.[10] In this test, stress scores are attached to specific life events occurring over a one-year period. A score of 150 or less indicates a 35 percent chance that a person will have problems within the

Exhibit 10–1
Social Readjustment Scale

Below is a list of events that you may have experienced during the past year. In the left-hand column, please check off those events that did occur. In the right-hand column, please rate how stressful you perceived each event to have been, on a scale of 1 to 5. (Scale values: 1—not at all stressful; 2—slightly stressful; 3—moderately stressful; 4—somewhat stressful; 5—extremely stressful)

Personal
_____ Personal injury or illness (53)   _____
_____ Outstanding personal
achievement (28)   _____
_____ Revision of personal habits (24)   _____
_____ Change in recreation (19)   _____
_____ Change in church activities (19)   _____
_____ Change in sleeping habits (15)   _____
_____ Change in eating habits (15)   _____
_____ Vacation (13)   _____
_____ Christmas (12)   _____
Family
_____ Death of a spouse (100)   _____
_____ Divorce (73)   _____
_____ Marital separation (65)   _____
_____ Death of a close family member (63)   _____
_____ Marriage (50)   _____
_____ Marital reconciliation (45)   _____
_____ Change in health of a family
member (44)   _____
_____ Pregnancy (40)   _____
_____ Gain of a new family member (39)   _____
_____ Change in number of arguments with
spouse (35)   _____
_____ Son or daughter leaving home (29)   _____
_____ Trouble with in-laws (29)   _____
_____ Wife begins or stops work (26)   _____
_____ Change in number of family
get-togethers (15)   _____

Financial
_____ Change in financial state (38)   _____
_____ Mortgage over $10,000 (31)   _____
_____ Foreclosure of mortgage or loan (30)   _____
_____ Mortgage or loan of less
than $10,000 (17)   _____
Social
_____ Jail term (63)   _____
_____ Sexual difficulties (39)   _____
_____ Death of a close friend (37)   _____
_____ Begin or end school (26)   _____
_____ Change in living conditions (25)   _____
_____ Change in schools (20)   _____
_____ Change in residence (20)   _____
_____ Change in social activities (18)   _____
_____ Minor violations of the law (11)   _____
Work
_____ Fired at work (47)   _____
_____ Retirement (45)   _____
_____ Business readjustments (39)   _____
_____ Change to a different line of
work (36)   _____
_____ Change in responsibilities
at work (29)   _____
_____ Trouble with boss (23)   _____
_____ Changes in work hours or
conditions (20)   _____

Source: Adapted from T. H. Holmes and R. H. Rahe, "The Social Readjustment Rating Scale," *Journal of Psychosomatic Research*, 11 (1967), pp. 213–18. Copyright © 1967 by Pergamon Press. Reprinted by permission.

next two years; a score of 150–300 increases the chance of experiencing a disorder to 51 percent; and a score of over 300 represents an 80 percent chance of developing a serious problem within two years. The events and their associated scores are listed in Exhibit 10–1. It might be helpful if you stopped for a moment and took the test. In calculating your score, simply add up the numbers in the parentheses next to the items you checked.

In addition to physical manifestations, there is frequently a direct link between psychological disorders and stress.[11] The depression and frustration often experienced by those under stress may result in alcoholism (an estimated 15 to 20 percent of the adult population are problem drinkers), drug dependency (over 150 million tranquilizer prescriptions are written in this country annually), hospitalization (over 25 percent of the hospital beds are occupied by people with psychological problems), and, in extreme cases, suicide.

All these physical and psychological outcomes have a direct effect on organizations. Some of the costs associated with stress, such as absenteeism, turnover, and high accident rates, are relatively easy to measure while others, including frustration and job dissatisfaction, are more difficult to determine. Even though no one has exact figures, a variety of government, industry, and health groups conservatively estimate the costs of stress at roughly $75–90 billion annually.

Stress and Job Performance

Any stressor can lead to two alternative responses. Eustress is the adaptive, constructive, healthy response to a stressful situation. It leads to more effective performance on the job. On the other hand, distress is the maladaptive, detrimental, dysfunctional response that organizations would like to avoid.[12]

As this distinction suggests, stress does not always produce poorer performance. In fact, as Exhibit 10–2 shows, the relationship between stress and productivity typically follows an inverted-U-shaped curve. Too little stress often has negative organizational consequences as does too much stress. What the research demonstrates is that stress can be beneficial but only in moderation.[13]

The problem, however, is knowing how a given individual will react to various stressors. One person may be able to function quite well under conditions that would be considered dysfunctional for someone else. For example, some people work best under deadline pressure. Until the deadline is near, they do not feel sufficiently geared up to get the job done. For these individuals, the deadline creates a psychological stimulus that helps them to reach the peak of the stress curve. At the other end of the spectrum, however, are those who despise deadlines. Rather than being positive, the approaching deadline pushes them over the top of their productivity curve. They become disorganized, flustered, and nonproductive.

In addition, depending on the other things happening in a person's life, what may be normally nonstressful can become stressful. People who usually work well under a deadline may find it "the last straw" if they have been confronted with a whole variety of other problems both on the job and at home.[14]

Diagnosing Stress in Oneself and Others

Before managers can recognize stress in others, the first prerequisite is to see it in themselves. Unfortunately most of us have a rather low level of personal awareness. For example, could you answer these questions?[15]

1. What is your resting pulse rate?
2. What is your blood pressure at peak times during the day?

Exhibit 10–2
Relationship of Stress to Performance

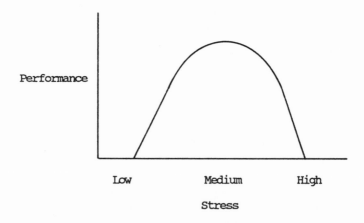

3. When is your energy level at its peak during the day?
4. What aspects of situations do you find most stressful?

Many managers would probably not be able to answer these questions and yet all are important in identifying when they are stressed. Signals that indicate high job stress include rapid pulse, pounding heart, increased perspiration, tensing of neck and back muscles, inability to sit still, tension headaches, insomnia, chronic fatigue, indigestion, and loss of appetite. The key here is to match these indicators with specific job situations or events. Once this is done, it becomes possible to reduce the stress by modifying the situations that create it.

Just as there are signals of stress overload, there are also indications that someone is operating at an optimal stress level. When a person is stimulated, feeling good, is mentally alert, and is calm in pressure-packed situations, he or she is probably experiencing the correct amount of stress. These positive indicators are just as important as the negative ones, and everyone needs to be cognizant of them.

For the typical middle manager or first-line supervisor, the key to successfully diagnosing stress among employees is to really know them as individuals. A stress-overloaded employee will usually exhibit a change in personality, work habits, or general behavior. Only by being familiar with customary behavior patterns can one identify important shifts, some of which may be very subtle. The following are some of the changes that may indicate stress problems:[16]

1. Working later more than usual or increased tardiness or absenteeism.

2. Difficulty making decisions.
3. An increase in the number of careless errors.
4. Missing deadlines or forgetting appointments.
5. Problems interacting and getting along with others.
6. Focusing on mistakes and personal failures.

Everyone displays some of the above behaviors from time to time. Only when a consistent pattern develops does a manager need to be concerned. If an employee's good habits become poor or sloppy, job performance becomes spotty or poor, or friendliness changes to irritability, the manager should begin to ask questions. More often than not, however, managers perpetuate the "conspiracy of silence." They just ignore the problem in the hope that it will go away.[17] To some extent this is understandable. Certainly, most managers do not have the time or training to be full-time counselors. Yet even so, they can refer people to others who have the necessary expertise. General Foods, for example, has instituted an Employee Guidance Program that allows managers to document impaired job performance and then refer the employee to a guidance program. Once there, trained professionals take over.[18] This particular program is specifically geared to alcohol and drug abuse problems, which is often one of the symptoms of stress.

MANAGING STRESS

Within any organizational setting there are a variety of actions that can be used to manage stress and minimize its dysfunctional consequences. These include efforts to use preventive maintenance techniques that preempt the harmful effects of stress and also devices that attempt to relieve stress symptoms that already exist.

Organizational Approaches to Stress Management

Many of the motivational strategies discussed throughout this book can be used organizationwide to manage stress. These include job redesign, flexible work schedules, team building, goal setting, and others. In a sense, all are concerned with improving the fit between the individual and the organization. In addition, they make the work situation more congenial and give employees a greater sense of purpose and direction. There are, however, many other techniques that a firm may use.

Designing Physical Settings

Despite our established mastery over many aspects of the physical environment, the work environment typically contains a number of potential stressors including light, noise, temperature, vibration and motion, and pollution. Most of the time these variables will become stressors when physical facilities are old or part of an operation such as manufacturing where heat, noise, and other physical stimuli are highly intense.[19] They can, however, cause stress even in a modern, well-designed office or plant.

There are several ways to deal with the stress created by environmental factors. One approach is to alter the environment by lowering noise levels, reducing glare, or manipulating room temperature. Another possibility is to protect people from stressors by providing ear plugs, tinted glass, or protective clothing.

In addition, managers may be able to minimize the effects of negative stressors by changing certain operating policies. Examples include providing more frequent breaks, waiving customary dress requirements, changing work schedules, or providing comfortable lounge areas.

Another aspect of the physical environment that could be related to stress is the actual physical layout of the work area. The arrangement of desks or work stations, how work flows from one area to another, and whether people work in large open areas or in relative isolation all serve to either facilitate or hinder work and consequently can be stressors.

Altering the Organization's Climate

The climate of an organization consists of the way people perceive their work environment. This involves everything from leadership styles to retirement policies, to increasing employee participation in decision making. The rationale for climate alterations is that a "good" climate contributes to satisfaction and positive perceptions of the organization. These in turn are presumed to be associated with reduced levels of stress.[20]

Consider one climate alteration that has received a good deal of attention: increased participation in decision making. In terms of stress, participative management is often effective because it allows employees increased control and discretion in meeting task demands. In other words, even though the nature of the tasks may not vary, the range of responses open to employees does change. As a result, they encounter less stress because they have more latitude in choosing how to respond to task demands.[21]

To illustrate, an authoritarian manager took over a medium-sized computer services department in the regional division of a large organization.[22] During his tenure, the morale and satisfaction with the department dropped markedly. Complaints from users in the division increased and efficiency declined somewhat, though not dramatically. Internal departmental conflicts increased and turnover rose. After fifteen months, the organization's midwestern headquarters sent a team of computer system professionals to visit the department. They recommended termination of the authoritarian manager and his assistant.

The department head who replaced this manager was much more participative in his managerial practices. His approach entailed daily production meetings with his section supervisors, during which active dialogue involving all participants took place. He encouraged his subordinates to take full charge of the lower-level decisions in the department, though he wanted to be fully informed about these decisions. During the seventh month of his tenure, the department manager, supervisors, and other employees participated in on-site training in participative management and communication, which further reinforced the manager's basic philosophy of participation in decision making.

After a year, the new manager's participative approach had produced a number of improvements in organizational effectiveness. A new report by the same professionals who had recommended termination of the first manager stated that the department was operating in an "excellent" fashion. Customer complaints were not totally eliminated, but they had declined. A more notable change was the attitude and climate within the department. While some conflicts did occur, they rarely approached the hostility level reached during the previous year. The most significant improvements were a decrease in operator and system monitor errors and unscheduled maintenance time. Slight increases in operating system effectiveness were also noted. In other words, the more participative style of the new manager relieved a good deal of individual frustration and stress while improving organizational effectiveness and productivity.

Clarifying Job Duties

Organizational stress can also be related to how precisely employees perceive their job duties. If their role is unclear and people have conflicting expectations or ill-defined responsibilities, a potential source of stress exists.[23]

As noted in the chapter on team building, one of the most common strategies for clarifying roles is the role analysis technique. This involves open discussion of role expectations by having employees address the following questions:

1. What do you think is expected of you on the job?
2. What do you expect from others?
3. What information do you need in order to function properly?
4. What areas, if any, do you think trouble others about the nature and scope of your job?

Answers to these questions may help enlighten employees about the job and thus aid in reducing ambiguity and conflict. In some cases, they may uncover needed changes in job descriptions, reporting relationships, or the way in which work is assigned.

Keep in mind, however, that clarifying and changing an employee's role can actually increase stress rather than reduce it. Some people may be comfortable in their present job and find proposed changes quite stressful. Once again, the manager should be aware of each employee's situation and act accordingly.

Stress Management Training

Employees can often benefit from training designed to improve stress awareness, and to aid them in deciding which personal stress management strategies are most appropriate. In addition, any training that helps people do their job more efficiently, reduces conflict, and improves communication can reduce stress. A medium-sized midwestern bank has used the concept of training for stress management. Its approach is to identify the primary sources of stress within the banking profession and to develop a set of strategies designed to deal with each identified stressor. Prior to the actual program, participants fill out a questionnaire that asks them to list the primary obstacles to successful job performance. The responses are then collated and grouped into a rank order by frequency. For example, customer demands/contacts was cited more than any other stressor and so was placed in group 1. "Watchdog approach from above" was cited the fewest number of times and was placed last in group 4. Each stressor and the related coping strategies are discussed in open bank seminars. Finally, several different stress management techniques are presented to the participants.[24]

It should be noted that the time, money, and effort a company commits to stress management training can lead to poor results if the programs are not properly designed and executed. On the other hand, a well-run program may yield a variety of benefits including improved productivity, lower absenteeism and turnover, reduced health insurance costs, and even increased morale and job satisfaction. Such training has the added benefit of showing people that the firm truly cares about their physical and psychological well-being.[25]

INDIVIDUAL APPROACHES TO STRESS MANAGEMENT

Even when a firm successfully addresses problems associated with physical settings, organizational climate, and job duties, some individual employees may still be faced with stressful demands. In this situation, managers may want to encourage people to take action on their own. Remember, however, that success here ultimately depends upon the employee's individual initiative. The organization may provide the facilities, an incentive to participate, or even attempt to order someone to participate, but in the final analysis the person must want to reduce stress.

Many individual approaches to stress management, such as prayer, are

Exhibit 10–3
Commonly Used Stress Management Techniques

-Leisure-time use

    Vacations

    Long weekends

    Mental health days

    Sabbaticals

-Relaxation training and meditation

-Biofeedback training

-Muscle monitoring

-Exercise/fitness programs

-Stress diary

highly idiosyncratic, and thus are not amenable to discussion here. What we will attempt to do is examine several of the more widely cited methods as shown in Exhibit 10–3.

Leisure Time Use

Time off is generally accepted as one of the important rewards firms offer. Yet relatively little attention has been paid to the wise and creative use of leisure time as a stress management tool. One cardiologist, for example, who deals exclusively with the stress-related aspects of heart disease, urges patients to make frequent use of three-day weekends as stress reducers. Even though there are no systematic studies, anecdotal evidence strongly suggests that a well-planned three-day weekend can be extremely refreshing, particularly during or following a period of extreme stress.

Counselors at many psychiatric facilities are allowed to take periodic "mental health" days. These are one-day absences that can be taken without advance request. A number of business organizations use the same concept. These are frequently called "personal days." Whenever the stress becomes too great, individuals can take a break from their work. There is growing evidence that people have a greater tolerance for adversity and decreased nervous system responsiveness following restful vacations. Thus, it seems appropriate that vacation planning should be considered part of any personal stress management plan.

In line with the concept of leisure time, sabbaticals have become an increasingly popular idea, especially for top executives. These may be structured through educational programs or social service leaves or they may be unstructured. University-based programs such as Harvard's Public Health Systems Management Course or the Sloan Programs at Massachusetts Institute of Technology are popular examples of the former type of sabbaticals. Unstructured sabbaticals can include activities such as independent research, domestic or foreign travel, or simply rejuvenation through sports and recreation. As with other leisure time approaches, the importance of sabbaticals has not been systematically studied. However, the evidence that is available suggests that they too can play a significant role in stress management.[26]

Relaxation Training and Meditation

Chinese Taoism, Zen Buddhism, Judaism, and various Christian leaders and sects have described means for achieving individual relaxation. Similar interest has also existed in the secular literature.

Looking at the range of techniques available, there are four elements that seem to be common to all:[27]

1. *A quiet environment.* Sound and other distractions may prevent proper relaxation. Any convenient, quiet place, including an office desk behind a closed door, is suitable.
2. *A mental device.* Silently repeating a sound, a word, or a phrase (a mantra); fixing one's gaze or one's "mind's eye" on an object; or focusing attention on the rhythm of breathing will help keep out distracting thoughts and other stimuli.
3. *A passive attitude.* Worrying about how well one is performing a relaxation technique is self-defeating. A passive attitude helps the individual ignore distracting thoughts and return to the mental device.
4. *A comfortable position.* The classic position is the cross-legged lotus position but a comfortable chair may be just as useful. Laying down is not recommended because of the tendency to fall asleep.

The most popular form of relaxation training is meditation. Research has shown that this approach can have a variety of positive outcomes such as reduced heart rate, lowered oxygen consumption, and decreased blood pressure. Studies have concluded that meditation can lower anxiety and have a positive effect on attitudes toward work. Companies that use this strategy and actually provide time during the work day to meditate include Connecticut General Life Insurance, Sunny Dale Farms, and New York Telephone. This last firm uses a program called Clinically Standardized Meditation (CSM) in order to manage stress. Eighteen months after CSM training began, meditators showed a marked decrease in depression, anxiety, hostility, and improvements in several physiological measures.

On the basis of its success, CSM training has been made available to all the firm's employees.

Biofeedback Training

Every time you take your pulse, monitor your breathing, or place a hand on your forehead to see if you have a fever—that is biofeedback. What makes this training different from everyday practice is the use of machines to monitor bodily processes and provide information about them. Conceptually, this training is based on three assumptions. First, neurophysiological functions can be monitored by electronic devices and fed back to the individual. Second, changes in physical states are accompanied by modifications in emotional states. Third, a state of relaxation is conducive to establishing voluntary control of various physiological functions.

The potential role of biofeedback as an individual stress management technique can be seen by looking at the kinds of bodily functions or processes that are to some degree under voluntary control. These include brain waves, heart rates, muscle tension, body temperature, stomach acidity, and blood pressure. Most of these processes are affected by stress. The benefit of biofeedback, then, is its ability to help induce a state of relaxation and restore bodily functions to a nonstressed level. One advantage of biofeedback over nonfeedback techniques is that the information provided gives individuals precise data about body functions. For example, by interpreting the feedback, individuals can know how high their blood pressure is at any given time. Through practice they can learn ways to lower it.

While much more research is needed concerning the potential benefits of biofeedback, there is sufficient data to conclude that it can be of value. The best results have come with specific stress-related problems, such as reducing migraine and tension headaches.

Some companies, like the Chicago headquarters of McDonald's Corporation, are providing biofeedback facilities. Here, executives take relaxation breaks using biofeedback devices to lower respiration and heart rates. Equitable Life Insurance Company has a biofeedback facility used by employees when they feel tense. The company has informally estimated that every $15 spent alleviates problems that would cost three times that much in lost productivity.[28]

Muscle Monitoring

Closely related to biofeedback is an approach called Muscle Monitoring. The underlying rationale is that we often get very tense—our muscles are tight, our jaw is set, or we may be clenching our teeth—without realizing it. The key is to become more aware of the body's reaction. One effective way of doing this is for the person to associate muscle responses with some recurring event on the job. One top female executive found that she had the tendency to stiffen her neck muscles whenever she became deeply involved in resolving a problem. By monitoring herself, she was able to change the habit and consequently prevent the headaches she had been experiencing.[29]

Exercise/Fitness Programs

Physical fitness experts have long argued that one of the easiest, most beneficial ways to bring about a favorable change in a person's lifestyle is to exercise. Many physicians believe that the single most important indicator of health is cardiovascular endurance and that is what regular exercise can develop, particularly activities such as jogging, bicycling, and swimming. The research indicates an overwhelming general consensus that proper exercise is a positive force in physical health that, in turn, may be related to improved behavior on the job. Available evidence would also support exercise as an effective stress management tool. Exercisers report feelings of reduced tension, heightened mental energy, and an improvement in feelings of self-worth.[30] If a firm is interested in developing a corporate physical fitness program, several basic actions are recommended (see Exhibit 10–4).

Many corporations offer extensive fitness programs aimed at both management and nonmanagement employees. In many cases, an employee fitness program is contained in a special room or area of the building, although companies may just have showers and locker rooms. Some firms are including elaborate fitness centers in the architectural plans before buildings are constructed, while other companies make arrangements with health clubs, YMCAs and schools, or provide a program which employees pursue on their own time.

Atlantic Richfield Company (ARCO). This firm, headquartered in Los Angeles, maintains ongoing physical fitness programs for both managers and employees. Currently, there are four ARCO locations across the country that have physical fitness centers, all owned and supervised by Fitness Centers of America. The contractor prescribes exercises aimed primarily at cardiovascular enhancement.

At ARCO's Los Angeles headquarters, the fitness center is open to upper- and middle-level management personnel, while the rest of the employees have access to a separate program administered by Fitness Centers. This restriction is necessary to avoid overcrowding in the exercise facilities.

The program, called CompuFit, is a self-administered plan which employees can do on their own time. The CompuFit plan is designed to enhance fitness levels without specialized facilities or gym equipment, by

Exhibit 10-4
Establishing an Exercise/Fitness Program

- Find out how employees feel about various programs.
- Provide the essential facilities and equipment either on-site or at a nearby location.
- If the firm cannot afford to construct facilities leasing is a viable option.
- Provide employees with complete medical evaluation before they begin a program.
- Offer employees an array of programs and provide the incentives which will induce them to participate. Don't assume that people will do it on their own.
- Make exercise/fitness a normal part of one's day. Allow employees to use the facilities at lunch time or even during business hours.
- Promote fitness through company newsletters, posters, and so on. Educate people about the company's position on physical and mental fitness.
- Provide a good example by having all top executives participate in the exercise programs.
- Encourage employees to limit their use of dangerous substances such as tobacco and alcohol.

using a variety of recreational activities selected by each participant. The program includes warm-up, muscle toning, cardiorespiratory conditioning, and cool-down exercises. Activity guidelines are based on each participant's physical condition and athletic interests.

Kimberly-Clark Corporation. Kimberly-Clark Corporation, headquartered in Neenah, Wisconsin, runs an extensive Health Management Program for its employees, their spouses, and retirees.[31] In 1977, the company built a $2.5-million Health Services Center, which consists of a multiphasic health-testing and exercise facility. The center, in addition to housing physical fitness and exercise accommodations, also contains medical screening facilities, health education classes, and an employee assistance program. The 32,000-square-foot exercise facility contains a swimming pool, indoor track (there is also an outdoor track), exercise equipment room, exercise area, saunas and whirlpool, showers, lockers, and laundry facilities.

Employees using the exercise facilities do so on their own time. But, since Kimberly-Clark has adopted a flex-time system, employees are able to exercise at various times during the day.

Tenneco, Inc. Tenneco maintains an elaborate health and fitness facility in its employee center in downtown Houston.[32] The facility, designed for the pursuit of individual fitness programs, is comprised of an all-purpose athletic room, a one-fifth-mile banked indoor track, separate men's and women's exercise rooms with Nautilus equipment, whirlpools, saunas, locker rooms, and showers.

When the center opened, James L. Ketelson, chairman and CEO of Tenneco, stated that productivity was a key consideration in developing the facility. "In that connection," he said, "this facility will help our business. There can be no question that healthy employees are more productive. So, by getting the best people and creating an environment in which they do their best work, the company will benefit."

A range of exercise classes is also offered to Tenneco employees, including aerobic fitness, walking, Nautilus, weightlifting, and racquetball. Other wellness programs include nutrition and weight control, stress management, CPR, and smoking clinics.

The Tenneco center is also equipped with an information system which provides employees immediate feedback following an exercise session on calories expended as well as a monthly activity report. When entering the Tenneco center, an employee inserts a metal card into a computer. When the person finishes a workout, the card is reinserted and a description of what has been done is punched into the computer. The machine then prepares a "fitness profile" that includes how many calories were burned off and how far the employee has to go on his or her specifically designed program. Every month the employee receives a printout of progress to date. If there is too little use of the center, workout privileges may be lifted.

The effects of exercise/fitness programs. A common misconception about exercise is that somehow it directly reduces stress. Actually it is a coping mechanism that can be used prior to or during a stressful situation. As such, it does not get rid of stress but rather reduces the physiological consequences of stressful situations in one or more of three ways.[33]

The first is that long-term aerobic exercise may decrease the level of physiological arousal that normally occurs during stressful situations. This response normally involves increased muscle tension, respiration, heart rate, dilation of the heart's blood vessels, and release of glucose by the liver. The physiological changes that develop with long-term aerobic exercise occur in the same systems that are activated during a stressful event. Therefore, more physically fit individuals will be better able to withstand the effects of stress.

Second, aerobic or anaerobic exercise allows the body to discharge the energy that builds up within an individual during stressful situations. Since most stressors do not involve a physical response (i.e., fighting, chairs being thrown, etc.), an individual under stress mobilizes his or her system for physical effort but does not expend the built-up energy. Exercise allows the person an outlet, thus reducing the potentially negative physiological and psychological effects.

Finally, either after or during a stressful experience, exercise may bring about a state of relaxation. This conclusion is based on a study which compared the effects tranquilizers and exercise had on anxiety. The researchers found that if an individual engaged in fifteen minutes of walking, at a heart rate of one hundred beats per minute there was a significant decrease in anxiety as measured by the electromyographic activity in the muscles. Tranquilizers did not have this same effect.[34] In other words, the person was more relaxed following exercise and presumably would be better able to cope with stressful events.

Beyond the fact that exercise allows people to better handle stress, there are a variety of economic gains that can be realized by the company. For example, research conducted at Tenneco shows a positive association between above-average job performance and regular exercise, and a negative association between poor job performance and irregular or no exercise. Further, the study indicates that exercise reduces health-care claims and costs. The average claim for nonexercising females at Tenneco was $1535.38, more than double the $639.07 average for those who exercise. For men, the average claim for nonexercisers was $1003.87, compared with the $561.60 for those who exercise. Be aware, however, that while certain costs may be reduced, if an employee is injured as a result of an exercise program the firm faces the risk of litigation, rising liability insurance premiums, and the costs associated with the employee's injury.

At Battelle's Columbus Laboratories a fitness program is estimated to be saving the company $150,000 annually in absenteeism costs. On average, employees who participate in the program are absent 2.8 fewer days per year than those who are not active.[35] Prudential Insurance recently completed a longitudinal study of 1389 employees in primarily sedentary, white-collar jobs who participated in a company physical fitness program during a five-year period. One year after entering the program, the major medical costs for the participants as a group dropped 45.7 percent. Their average number of disability days decreased by 20.1 percent, which translated into a 31.7 percent reduction in direct disability dollar costs. The per-participant cost of operating the program averaged $120.60 compared to average per-participant savings of $353.38.[36] Finally, a study of commercial real estate brokers showed that those who participated in a regular exercise program tended to generate greater sales commissions.[37]

In short, the available research does indicate that employees who participate in exercise/fitness programs can better deal with stress and performance on the job is higher. In addition, a variety of costs are reduced including health care claims and absenteeism. According to Stewart Beltz, president for the Association of Fitness in Business, "Every place that has [a program] is showing benefits. Some are tangible in the form of dollars, some are intangible in terms of morale and commitment to the organization."[38]

Keeping a Stress Diary

The rationale underlying the use of a stress diary is that the more a person understands a phenomenon, the better equipped that person will be to deal effectively with it. The diary is a record or personal log of the events that precipitate a negative stress response in that person. There are two phases involved in the use of a diary as a stress management device.[39]

In the recording phase the individual keeps a running record of the events that caused stress. Whenever a situation is encountered that causes significant discomfort, tension, or frustration, a description of that event is recorded including, as specifically as possible, what it was that caused the upset and what kinds of feelings (e.g., anger, frustration, anxiety) were experienced as a result. The events are recorded as objectively as possible, taking care to avoid evaluative or subjective statements. The length of time one keeps this record before entering the second phase varies, but generally three to four weeks is the recommended minimum.

In the analysis phase the accumulated events are examined in an attempt to identify common themes. For many people, the events in their lives that are sources of stress can be grouped into three or fewer categories. Knowledge of these categories can be used as the basis for reprogramming some behaviors. For example, you may discover that a common theme in many of the stressful events in your log is that stress was precipitated when people did not respond to you the way you felt they should. This knowledge, coupled with a decision not to take total responsibility for other people's reactions to you, may lead to a significant reduction in the degree of stress you experience in those situations.

SUMMARY

In this chapter we have discussed stress management as a productivity enhancement strategy. We have examined the nature of stress, its consequences in terms of physical and mental health, and its effect on work behavior. We have pointed out that too little stress can be as bad as too much and that the correct level of stress can actually improve performance.

Stress is an inevitable by-product of life and work. There is no way to eliminate it and rather than pursue this goal the idea is to learn how to effectively manage it. For any manager, the first step is to know how to personally recognize stress. Knowing when he or she is under stress and the physical or mental effects it causes allows the person to become more aware of others. Once managers are sensitized to the problems they are in a better position to differentiate between eustress (positive) and distress (negative) and they can work to enhance the former while minimizing the latter.

In this chapter we have also discussed a variety of organizational and individual methods for managing stress. In the first group, we have looked at methods such as designing physical settings to help eliminate stressors, changes or alterations which one can make in the organization climate, the need to help employees better clarify their roles in the firm, and finally, formalized stress awareness training programs. Frequently used individual approaches include more creative use of leisure time, relaxation and meditation techniques, muscle monitoring, exercise/wellness programs, and maintaining a stress diary. Do these various stress management techniques work? The bulk of the available evidence indicates that all of the devices discussed here can have a positive effect on employee productivity. In addition, effective use of stress management programs can result in a variety of other benefits to the firm including lower health insurance costs and better customer service.

When dealing with the issue of stress it is important to keep several points in mind. First, stress management is everyone's responsibility. It is not just top management's concern, nor should stress management be left entirely to specialists. All first-line managers and their employees need to become more aware of stress and its effects. Second, stress on the job may be due to a variety of problems people have away from work. Even though managers are not professional counselors, they should be able to recognize problems and refer people to others who are trained to help. Third, if a manager finds that stress is becoming a problem personally or for employees, he or she should examine the various stress reduction strategies and determine which might be used most effectively to promote organizational and individual growth, change, and performance.

NOTES

1. J. M. Ivancevich and M. T. Matteson, *Stress and Work: A Managerial Perspective* (Glenview, Ill.: Scott Foresman and Co., 1980).

2. Ibid.

3. J. C. Quick and J. P. Quick, *Organizational Stress and Preventive Management* (New York: McGraw-Hill, 1984).

4. "Coping with Anxiety at AT&T," *Business Week*, May 28, 1979, pp. 95–106.

5. Ivancevich and Matteson, *Stress and Work*.

6. Ibid.

7. *Work in America*. Report of a Special Task Force to the Secretary of Health, Education and Welfare (Cambridge, Mass.: MIT Press, 1973).

8. Ivancevich and Matteson, *Stress and Work*.

9. Quick and Quick, *Organizational Stress and Preventive Management*.

10. Instructor's Film Guide for *Managing Stress*, CRM McGraw-Hill Films, Del Mar, Calif., n.d.

11. M. T. Matteson and J. M. Ivancevich, "The How, What and Why of Stress Management Training," *Personnel Journal*, October 1982, pp. 768–74.

12. Quick and Quick, *Organizational Stress and Preventive Management*.

13. V. L. Huber, "Managing Stress for Increased Productivity," *Supervisory Management*, December 1981, pp. 2–13.

14. J. K. Ross and T. Halatin, "When Family Stress Affects Worker Productivity," *Supervisory Management*, July 1982, pp. 2–9.

15. Ivancevich and Matteson, *Stress and Work.*

16. Ibid.

17. J. A. Belahlov and P. O. Popp, "Employee Substance Abuse: Epidemic of the Eighties," *Business Horizons*, July–August 1983, pp. 29–34.

18. Ibid.

19. Ivancevich and Matteson, *Stress and Work.*

20. Ibid.

21. J. C. Quick and J. D. Quick, "Preventive Stress Management at the Organizational Level," *Personnel*, September–October 1984, pp. 24–34.

22. Ibid.

23. Ivancevich and Matteson, *Stress and Work.*

24. R. J. Mirabile, "Stress Management Training in the Banking Profession," *Training and Development Journal*, August 1983, pp. 40–43.

25. Ivancevich and Matteson, *Stress and Work.*

26. Quick and Quick, *Organizational Stress and Preventive Management.*

27. Ibid.

28. Ibid. See also Ivancevich and Matteson, *Stress and Work.*

29. Ivancevich and Matteson, *Stress and Work.*

30. G. Gatty, "How Fitness Works Out," *Nation's Business*, July 1985, pp. 18–24.

31. J. McKendrick, "Portraits of Fitness Programs," *Management World*, August 1982, pp. 19–20.

32. Ibid.

33. L. Falkenberg, "Employee Fitness Programs: Their Impact on the Employee and the Organization," *Academy of Management Review* 12, no. 3 (1987), pp. 511–22.

34. H. G. de Vries and G. M. Adams, "Electromyograph Comparisons of Single Doses of Exercise and Meprobamate as to Effects on Muscular Relaxation," *American Journal of Physical Medicine* 51 (1972), pp. 130–41.

35. McKendrick, "Portraits of Fitness Programs."

36. D. Feuer, "Wellness Programs: How Do They Shape Up?" *Training*, April 1985, pp. 25–34.

37. S. E. Edwards and L. R. Gettman, "The Effect of Employee Physical Fitness on Job Performance," *Personnel Administrator*, November 1980, pp. 41–44.

38. "Staying Well: What $5.50 of Prevention is Worth," *Virginian Pilot and the Ledger Star*, September 14, 1987.

39. Ivancevich and Matteson, *Stress and Work.*

11

Enhancing Employee Participation

Now we have a tremendous task ahead of us in retraining management to be more like consultants to their work force. This is because today's workers are different. They have more education, are more self-directed, and want to control their working conditions. This requires a more participatory or nondirective approach for the manager who wants to get results.[1]

Participation is an interactive, not a debriefing process. Managers continue to describe their efforts to become "more participative" by relating how they asked employees for their "input." Real participation requires one person to join with others in pooling information to reach some conclusions.[2]

The CEO has to set the tone for the whole organization. He has to say, "This is what I want to accomplish and I need your cooperation to help me do this." Some people have never managed that way, and it's hard to do.[3]

The A. E. Stanley Agriproducts Corporation began an experiment in "self-management" at its Lafayette, Indiana, plant several years ago. The plant employs salaried technicians using computer-controlled machinery to convert corn into high-fructose syrup. It operates 365 days a year. The employees work three twelve-hour days, take three days off, and then work three nights.

Employees are divided into sixteen teams of about fifteen persons each according to functions—production, maintenance, and quality control. Each team chooses two leaders from its ranks, one of them task-oriented, the other in charge of training, discussion, and records. The teams make their own work assignments within the plant's overall schedules, and have a voice in hiring, promotion, and discipline of team members.

It was three years before production at the plant began to justify the experiment. Since then, productivity has risen to extraordinary heights. Operating costs are below those of other plants, absenteeism and turnover are under one percent, downtime in a twenty-four-hour workday is less than one percent, and production runs at 115 percent of engineering specifications. According to James Sullivan, corporate human relations director, the idea was "to push the ideology of management down to the operators themselves. The work is challenging and the operators must make important decisions." He admits that "people and plants have moods, and some days are more energized than others." But he says giving people "so much voice in their own lives has paid off."[4]

A. E. Stanley is just one of many firms where managers in search of higher quality and productivity are increasingly finding ways to involve employees in setting company goals and in making decisions. This trend represents a major break with the past. According to the *National Productivity Review*, the movement away from hierarchical and authoritarian management structures to some form of participative management has all the characteristics of a firestorm.[5]

For most of this century managers have been trained to be autocratic —to direct, to control, to motivate, to plan.[6] Indeed, many managers look upon their job as the center of all decision making in their area of authority. They may even think that failing to make as many decisions as possible is shirking their basic duties. Yet, some managers have found that letting employees handle certain work-related decisions can lead to a variety of positive outcomes.

Participative management, if it is to have the long-term positive effects some contend it should have, needs to be viewed as more than an effort to make people happy, although improved employee morale may indeed be a by-product. The ultimate purpose of any program designed to promote worker participation should be to improve organizational effectiveness and employee productivity. In this chapter we will examine some of the issues surrounding the development and implementation of participative management. In addition, we will discuss several different participation programs including Quality Circles, self-managing teams, and labor-management committees.

DO EMPLOYEES WANT TO PARTICIPATE?

To what extent do firms use participative management techniques and how do employees feel about the process? In an effort to address such questions, a study of 363 people working for a number of different organizations (e.g., manufacturing firms, banks, retail stores, government agencies, schools and universities) located in a rural region of West Virginia and in urban Washington, D. C., asked these employees whether or not they participated in decisions on the job and if they believed that such an opportunity should be available.[7] The results indicated that the most widely used form of participation was that of self-pacing with 56 percent of the respondents reporting they were able to control their work pace. Other significant areas of participation were: the use of autonomous work teams, problem-solving committees composed of workers and managers, periodic supervisory consultation meetings, and management by objectives. The least used form of participation was worker selection of supervisors with only one percent reporting this.

The study also showed that many employees believed that they should have an opportunity to participate. Employee interest was particularly strong in the communication form of participation. Apparently employees believed that they had valuable knowledge to convey to managers. The area showing the least employee interest was participation in personnel actions. Although a majority favored input in selecting co-workers, there was considerable sentiment against participation in decisions affecting wages and promotions and particularly against the selection of supervisors.

So what conclusions can we draw? In general, these employees believed they should participate much more than they currently do. They felt that greater participation would be beneficial not only for them but also for the organization. In addition, the study suggests that not everyone wanted greater participation. Some were apparently quite content to leave decision making to others.

POTENTIAL BENEFITS/DISADVANTAGES OF PARTICIPATION

Based on the study described above it would appear that many employees want more participation. But, as a manager, should you encourage or allow this? What are the potential advantages versus drawbacks to employee participation?

Proponents argue that participation results in greater knowledge and expertise being brought to bear on a problem. If subordinates are highly knowledgeable about an issue, their input may improve the quality of the decision. Employees who participate may also feel they had an important role in making a decision and therefore will identify with it. They may feel it is "their decision" and that they are responsible for ensuring that it is effectively implemented. In addition, participation may result in greater job satisfaction because it satisfies needs for achievement, responsibility, recognition, and self-actualization. Finally, participation may be beneficial because it can increase cooperation and team spirit. By working together to solve problems, employees gain a better understanding of each other, recognize their common values and goals, and realize the benefits of coordination.

So much for the benefits of participation. What are the potential draw-backs? One of the arguments against participation is that it can undermine managerial prerogatives and control. Employee participation reduces man-agement's power to make decisions. Furthermore, if employees participate in some decisions, they may want a say in everything. There is also the issue of responsibility and credit. If a group makes a decision, who assumes re-sponsibility for failure or should be rewarded for success? Finally, employ-ees may have vested interests to protect and they may not always do what is best for the organization as a whole; they may do what is expedient and in line with their own short-range interests. Who, for example, would vote for a layoff even if this seemed warranted?

In sum, there are many potential benefits and drawbacks to employee participation. But they are just that—potential benefits/disadvantages. They do not necessarily surface in each case. The important point is that managers should not prejudge the value of employee participation; it is in-herently neither "good" nor "bad." The major issue then is not whether participative leadership should be used, but when and to what extent it is appropriate.

Determining the Appropriate Amount of Participation

In order to determine when employee participation is desirable, it is im-portant to remember that participative management is not a single unified idea. In fact, there is really a continuum of styles and approaches from which managers may choose, ranging from a totally autocratic to a com-pletely democratic approach. While there have been a variety of labels at-tached to these different levels of participation, one of the more common typologies is shown below:[8]

1. *Autocratic decision.* The leader makes the decision without asking for employ-ees' opinions. They have no influence. The decision may be announced and/or sold to employees.
2. *Consultation.* The leader asks subordinates for their opinions and, with this in-formation in mind, makes the decision.
3. *Joint decision.* The leader presents a problem, discusses it with subordinates, and together they make a decision. The leader has no more influence than any-one else over the alternative chosen.
4. *Delegation.* The leader delegates to subordinates the responsibility and author-ity for making decisions. The leader sets the limits or parameters but does not directly enter the process.

Given the different styles of participation, how does a manager choose the right approach? Vroom and Yetton suggest that there are seven diagnostic questions that managers can use to guide their selection of a style.[9] As the answers to these questions vary, so should the manager's style:

1. Does the problem possess a quality requirement?
2. Do I have sufficient information to make a high-quality decision?
3. Is the problem structured?
4. Is acceptance of the decision by subordinates important for effective implementation?
5. If I were to make the decision by myself, am I reasonably certain that it would be accepted by my subordinates?
6. Do subordinates share the organizational goals to be attained in solving this problem?
7. Is conflict among subordinates likely in preferred solutions?

INITIATING GREATER EMPLOYEE PARTICIPATION

Suppose that a manager has decided that some employee participation is desirable. How should he or she proceed? Some researchers have suggested the following guidelines:[10]

1. Start with small decisions. Ask employees to participate in small decisions first and then work up to larger concerns.
2. Start with local issues. Initially, most employees are most interested in solving issues directly related to their work unit. Letting employees actually choose the issues may further improve chances for success.
3. Neither promise nor expect too much. A manager can't expect that a group will be highly effective right from the start. Decision making is a skill and it must be learned.
4. Provide training in participation/decision making. Any group can make decisions but training always improves the process. This can involve a discussion of the steps in decision making, cause-effect analysis, and so on.
5. Make sure the group has a leader. In most situations the manager will want to play the role of discussion leader. Eventually, however, someone else may be able to assume these responsibilities. A leader prevents dominant personalities from having a disproportionate influence, solicits opinions from reticent participants, redirects unfocused discussion back to the problem at hand, and guides the process of screening alternatives and selecting the solution.
6. Provide rewards and feedback. Rewards are critical to the success of any group just as they are critical to individuals. Praising exemplary behavior and giving credit where it is due will encourage the group to become more effective problem-solvers/decision-makers.

APPLICATIONS OF PARTICIPATIVE MANAGEMENT

A common theme underlying all attempts to promote greater employee participation is "ownership." As the term is used here, it refers not just to stock ownership but also to a conscious effort on the part of top management to place greater decision-making responsibility and behavior control in employees' hands. This process of developing a sense of ownership can take a variety of forms, ranging from relatively informal efforts to more complex, formal programs such as Quality Circles, self-managing teams, and labor-management committees.

An example of a firm using an informal approach is the Dana Corporation, an axle manufacturer based in Toledo, Ohio.[11] Once described by its own chairman as having "the rottenest product line ever granted by God to a Fortune 500 company," throughout the 1970s it ranked number two in return on total capital among the entire Fortune 500, and though battered along with the rest of the automotive and trucking industry during the 1980s, it has made a strong comeback. Ren McPherson, Dana's former chairman, used one simple guiding principle in turning the company around: "Turn the company back over to the people who do the work."

The key was the radical decentralization of the personnel, legal, purchasing, and financial departments. For instance, per McPherson:

Centralized purchasing always looks good on paper and virtually never works as planned in reality. Yes, we've got some areas where in theory we need to purchase centrally in order to get a volume based price break. But look, I want my ninety store managers [his term for factory managers] to sign up for their quarterly objectives and I don't want them to come in ninety days later and say, "Ren, I would have made it, but the guy in purchasing didn't get my steel on time and I had to short my two top customers. Maybe next quarter . . . ." I won't accept that. See, I've got the ultimate weapon. I've got ninety very bright factory managers. If seven of them know they need to get together to buy a certain steel shape and get a price break, well, they'll get together. They don't need a corporate daddy to tell them when or how to do it.

Another example of a similar effort is Quad/Graphics.[12] "We don't believe that responsibility should be that defined," CEO Quadracci explains. "We think it should be assumed and shared. Nothing should ever be somebody else's responsibility. Anybody who sees that something needs to be done ought to assume responsibility for doing it. Our people shouldn't need me or anybody else to tell them what to do." In fact, Quadracci often refuses to tell his employees what to do. For example, when the shipping department needed greater back-haul revenue to finance expansion of the trucking fleet, Quadracci handed each of his drivers the key to one of the company's trucks. From now on he told them, they were owner operators-partners in a new division called DuPlainville (Quad/Graphics headquarters) Transport, Inc.—and it was their responsibility to make the rigs profitable on return trips. When the truckers asked what they should take on the back-hauls, Quadracci shrugged, "How should I know? I don't know anything about driving an 18-wheeler. I'm not going to carry your loads."

Other organizations using a variety of relatively simple yet innovative efforts to promote participation through ownership include Tupperware, IBM, Seattle First (Seafirst) Bank, and even the Post Office.[13] If, however, a firm wants to take a more structured approach, several options are available.

Quality Circles

In the past few years there has been an enormous volume of literature written about Quality Circles and whether or not they will become a permanent, self-sustaining part of the management process or just a fad remains to be seen. They have been a central aspect of Japanese management for over thirty years, but firms in this country have shown a real interest only since the late 1970s.

A Quality Circle (QC) is a small group of workers who voluntarily meet on a regular basis to solve work-related problems in their shared area of responsibility.[14] Circles typically range in size from four to fifteen members, with eight being considered optimal. They are organized in various work units and are led by a supervisor or senior worker. Participants are taught elementary techniques of problem solving including basic statistical methods. Originally, groups concentrated on solving job-related quality problems that were expected to lead to cost reduction and increased productivity. Now, however, circles focus on a wide range of problems such as improving working conditions and the self-development of workers. The latter includes developing leadership skills in first-line supervisors and workers, improving morale and motivation, stimulating teamwork within work groups, and recognizing worker achievements.

Mechanics of Quality Circles

In session, a Quality Circle would typically follow the process shown in Exhibit 11-1. The initial meeting would be an orientation to problem-solving devices such as brainstorming, cause-and-effect analysis, and documentation techniques. The first step is to use brainstorming in order to set the ground rules. During these sessions members are encouraged to respect the opinion of others and not criticize the ideas presented. The suggestions are recorded and members vote on each so as to develop a rank order. Everyone is free to vote, by a show of hands, as many times as they wish. Ultimately, the name, ground rules, and so on are established by the group. As members become more familiar with brainstorming, they begin using it to rank the problems that will be worked on by the group. An

Exhibit 11–1
The Quality Circle Process

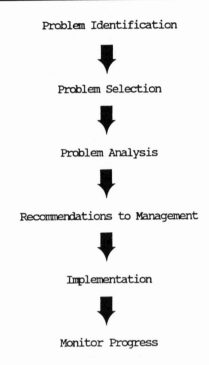

Problem Identification

Problem Selection

Problem Analysis

Recommendations to Management

Implementation

Monitor Progress

important point to note is that each group concentrates on problems within its area of responsibility and seldom ventures outside this sphere.[16]

Subsequent meetings consist of further brainstorming and cause-and-effect analysis. Members select a problem and, using statistical techniques, analyze and then determine probable causes of it. The group can consult with both internal or external sources to help develop and clarify the issues. Once a consensus has been reached, the problem and solutions are formally presented by the group for management's consideration. The members typically forward their suggestions with a cost-benefit analysis. Managers often ask questions and usually inform the circle when to expect a decision regarding their proposal.

Supervisors play a crucial role in the activities of the circle. They usually receive training in the mechanics of Quality Circles, group dynamics, communication, leadership, and coaching, in addition to specialized training in problem analysis and problem solving.[17] Supervisors, typically called "leaders," plan the activities of the circles, run the weekly meetings, help the circle members get needed data, and help members finalize their solutions and prepare for management presentations.[18] This "management presentation" allows circle members to receive feedback and recognition for their efforts.

Quality Circles in the United States

Since Honeywell and Lockheed introduced Quality Circles in this country, more and more corporations have implemented programs. Among more than five hundred companies, Bethlehem Steel, Westinghouse, Ford, Hughes Aircraft, General Electric, Boeing, Marietta, R.C.A., Control Data, and General Motors already have programs in place, while a number of others are seriously considering installing circles as a way of promoting greater productivity, quality, and morale.[19]

It should be noted that not every Quality Circle program has been successful. Take a moment and look at the guidelines shown in Exhibit 11–2. All of these issues need to be addressed before the firm commits itself to a QC program.

Honeywell Corporation. Honeywell Corporation learned of the Quality Circles results at Lockheed and decided to experiment with the concept.[20] To date, the results have been impressive. Twelve groups meeting over a period of nine months implemented solutions to more than one hundred production problems. Altogether, they documented $86,430 in savings with a 36 percent reduction in assembly costs. There were also undocumented improvements in worker attitudes and the working climate. A circle in an electronic unit saved the company more than $35,000 per year by suggesting a different wiring procedure. At one Honeywell plant, twenty-six groups reduced assembly time, saving $624,724. Finally, assembly operation circles reduced direct labor hours by 46 percent as well as showed improvements in communication with a series of proposals involving tooling, materials, and test procedures. These are but a few of the many examples of positive changes made by Quality Circles at Honeywell. Perhaps more important, the implementations have been enthusiastically supported by individuals at all levels of the company. The reactions of front-line workers can best be summarized by one employee who stated, "This is the best thing the company has done in fifteen years."

Portsmouth (VA) Naval Shipyard. In 1979–1980, a pilot program of eight circles was introduced at the Portsmouth Naval Shipyard.[21] Since its inception, thirty-two more circles have been established and twenty-eight more are being planned. Groups with such names as "The Brainy Bunch," "Solution Seeds," and "Magic Gorillas" have presented major proposals resulting in annual savings to the yard of more than $909,927. For every dollar invested, the shipyard has saved $3.22.

One group addressed a complex problem involving back ordering materials. This process was frequently forgotten until it was urgently needed. At that point, work delays would set in as employees waited for the materials they needed. The proposed solution was to earmark crucial materials and

Exhibit 11–2
Guidelines for Quality Circles

- The members of a circle should be performing compatible jobs and tasks.

- All members of a circle should be active participants.

- Circle leaders need to be well trained in the use of problem-solving methodologies.

- Circle participation should be voluntary. Nobody should be coerced into participating.

- The focus of a circle should be on improving the group's performance. This requires that teamwork be a basic part of the firm's culture.

- The circle should concentrate on problems that are within its domain.

- Success requires the initial enthusiasm and continuing strong support from top management.

- The firm should be willing to let circles mature over time. In other words, consider the long-term gains and not just short-term costs.

- Before a program is undertaken determine the organization's state of readiness and whether the necessary resources will be available.

institute a follow-up procedure. This same circle then began studying another major problem—how to streamline massive amounts of paperwork.

The benefits, however, have gone far beyond the tangible. Even problem solutions that have directly saved little or no money have boosted morale. For example, one circle comprised of technicians in the nuclear support branch tackled the problem of bookcase doors that frequently jammed. Their solution was simply to remove the doors. While this may seem trivial, the time previously spent complaining and fussing could be devoted to more productive tasks.

Henry Ford Hospital. Henry Ford Hospital, a private not-for-profit regional health care system located in Detroit, Michigan, began to investigate the application of Quality Circles in the spring of 1980. At this time, no other hospital had implemented a QC program.[22]

In January 1981 employee recruitment meetings were held in six departments which had volunteered to pilot Quality Circles. Interest was very high with some departments actually having to limit QC membership in order to maintain departmental operations. Circle meetings, initiated in February 1981 were held during work hours, on a weekly or biweekly basis. The criteria established for determining and selecting a problem were as follows:

—must be related to member's work
—affects quality
—affects patient satisfaction
—helps reduce costs
—improves the work environment
—can be completed within three to six months

In terms of tangible gains the results from several departments were impressive. For example, Dietetics (Dining Services) identified staffing and employee work assignments during weekend coverage as a major problem. Their solution was to redesign work assignments and job descriptions for food service assistants. The result was a payroll savings of $7000 per year. The Greenfield Facility (General Stores Warehouse) felt that a serious issue was the lack of supplies available in the warehouse for distribution. They chose to test alternative reshelving methods which resulted in approximately a 12 percent productivity increase. For Environmental Housekeeping Services, also known as the "Tidy Bunch," a primary concern was curtailing the waste and loss of disposable plastic bags. They developed alternative work procedures which allowed them to reduce bag usage and develop security measures to prevent loss. The potential savings from these actions was estimated at $15,600.

In addition to these gains a number of other benefits were realized as well. These included a perceived increase in employee morale and motivation, increased cost containment awareness, greater cooperation and support from nonQC members, and development of team cohesiveness. In short, the QC program has provided the hospital with a vehicle that more fully utilizes the creative potential of employees throughout the organization.

Self-Managing Teams

Today, many executives with effective Quality Circles have seen improvements that result from really promoting the participation of so-called "ordinary" employees. How can this program be extended and strengthened? How can it be institutionalized and more fully integrated into the organization.?[23]

Self-managed work teams may be the answer to questions such as these. Operating under a variety of labels including self-managing work groups, autonomous work groups, and sometimes simply teams, this concept has as its basic theme the attempt to vest a high degree of decision-making responsibility and behavior in the work group itself.

A self-managing team usually elects an internal leader, who continues as a full-time team member. Often, management appoints an external leader, not a "foreman" or "supervisor," but a "coordinator," "facilitator," or "consultant."[24]

Teams frequently undertake responsibilities that go far beyond the traditional "bottom-rung" jobs. Some of these include: (1) preparing an annual budget; (2) taking on timekeeping responsibilities; (3) recording quality control statistics; (4) compiling in-process inventory statistics; (5) making within-group job assignments; (6) solving technical problems; (7) training fellow team members; (8) adjusting production schedules; (9) redesigning and modifying production processes; (10) setting team goals; (11) resolving internal conflicts; and (12) assessing internal performance. Obviously, adopting this approach requires that managers have a high degree of confidence in employees. Also, for long-term success, teams must live up to management's expectations.

After a review of the literature and visits to various companies, the manufacturing executives of Fairchild Republic Co. (FRC) decided to initiate a pilot program involving team and other participative management concepts. FRC is Fairchild Industries' largest division, with more than six thousand employees at its facility in Farmingdale, New York. FRC manufactures military aircraft, commercial aircraft subassemblies, and related subcontracted parts.[25]

The pilot program involved a small sample of union workers and their supervisors. Approximately 10 work groups or shops were involved, for a total of 150 workers from an approximate plantwide manufacturing total of 3000. The program was concentrated in shops which built complete subassemblies that were passed on for eventual attachment to military airframes and aircraft. The general manager of the subassembly area was assigned the task of coordinating the program.

The basis of the program was straightforward. Teams composed of supervisors and employees in a particular unit met twice a week both at the start of and at the end of a shift (on company time) for approximately fifteen to thirty minutes. During morning meetings supervisors outlined daily and weekly schedules and priorities were determined. Employees reviewed and discussed problems they foresaw. At the shift's conclusion, the teams met again for a work quality and quantity review session. Employees discussed accomplishments and difficulties they had encountered, and voiced their recommendations for improvement or change.

The problems and issues brought up in the team meetings were reviewed by a steering committee composed of union and management representatives. This group considered the recommendations and assigned teams to investigate problems and implement solutions including some that went beyond the immediate work group.

The program's goal was to create teamwork by having natural work groups review their goals and plans plus identify problems. Beyond the fact that this process helped workers to better understand and identify with company actions, it also allowed hourly workers to make constructive comments and suggestions, flag problems, and simply ask questions. Not only did this demonstrate that the company's interest in the workers extended beyond the production count for the day, but it also allowed the work units to identify themselves as viable teams. While the firm has provided no hard data, the general feeling of those involved was that employee solutions in terms of solving productivity problems had substantial value.

Organizations typically introduce self-managing teams in the hope of gaining productivity, improving quality, reducing overhead, and reducing conflict. From an employee's viewpoint, a team can provide opportunities to exercise more control over many aspects of daily work life. Are they successful? While the evidence is quite limited, some practitioners contend that self-managing teams can provide firms with a 20 to 40 percent productivity improvement. Savings come about because employees require less direct supervision (therefore, there is less overhead), and scrap, lost time, and poor-quality products are often significantly reduced.

Many other potential benefits of the team approach are more indirect and subtle. For example, teams may be more adaptable and flexible, responding smoothly to changing conditions. The evidence indicates that they are frequently more effective in adapting to new processes and equipment. According to one manager, "They'll make it work!" Also, employees who work in teams generally have relatively high job satisfaction and morale, and this positive atmosphere even reaches higher level managers. As one plant superintendent said, "It's a lot more fun coming to work."

According to an informal estimate, over two hundred plants in the United States have started using the self-managing team concept. Why has the diffusion been so limited? One explanation is that managers, especially middle managers, feel threatened by the teams because they believe that their power and influence will be reduced. Perhaps an even more important reason is that start-up costs can be significant, and typically a wait of eighteen to twenty-four months is required before the results become apparent. Furthermore, union support for self-managing teams has not been uniform. Although the United Auto Workers have actively supported and proposed implementation, other unions have seen the concept as a potential threat to their power.[26]

Labor-Management Committees

The third example of a formal effort to promote greater employee participation is for a firm to develop joint labor-management committees. World War II saw the flowering of this concept. During that period, some five thousand committees in plants employing more than seven million workers registered with the War Production Board. At the end of the war, however, the urgency of working together drained off, and most committees were abandoned.

In recent years there has been a renewed interest. According to Wayne Horovitz, former director of the Federal Mediation and Conciliation Services (FMCS), there are a thousand or more in-plant committees operating today.[27] While they are widely spread throughout the country, the greatest concentration is in the East and Midwest. These committees are found primarily in unioned industrial firms. However, there is no real reason why they may not be used successfully in a nonunion, white-collar environment as well.

Starting the Committee

Labor-management committees typically involve eight to twelve members, half designated by management and half employee representatives. In a unionized firm these committees will be established by collective bargaining agreements and will not, in that environment, deal with negotiable issues like wages and benefits. In any case, they are advisory bodies that focus attention on matters of mutual interest to managers and employees. Labor-management committees have been used in public sector organizations as well as private firms. They have been credited with reducing turnover, absenteeism, and grievances as well as improving operational efficiency and product quality in firms as large as General Motors and as small as the Valspar paint plant in East Moline, Illinois (forty-five employees).[28]

While either labor or management can take the first step in establishing a labor-management committee, in most cases the initiative comes from management. In other instances, a third party may suggest the formation of a joint committee. For example, mediators from the FMCS sometimes propose a permanent joint committee as part of a strike settlement. Occasionally, a local elected official may initiate the idea. When Jamestown, New York, was suffering from labor strife and out-migration of industry, the mayor initiated a network of labor-management committees at the regional, company, and plant levels. These committees have been credited with eventually reversing the economic decline of this community. Regardless of who actually initiates the idea, it is recommended that it be done in a way that encourages both labor and management to feel a sense of shared responsibility for the outcome.[29]

There is also a need to express the objectives of the committee in terms that take into account the interests and concerns of both sides—that is, the objectives should include raising operational efficiency, productivity, or product quality as well as enhancing working conditions and job satisfaction for employees. Similarly, assurances should be given that workers will not lose their jobs or be demoted as a result of the labor-management committee's actions.

Early successes build credibility for the idea of cooperation between labor and management. Hence some suggest that the committee should first take on simple issues that are likely to provide tangible, visible, and noncontroversial results.

Tarrytown Plant of General Motors

In the late 1960s and early 1970s, this General Motors auto assembly plant suffered from much absenteeism and labor turnover. Operating costs were high, and frustration and mistrust characterized the relationship between management and labor. At times, as many as two thousand labor grievances were pending. Union officials battled constantly with management. Workers were mad at everyone. Production, efficiency, and quality were so low that many people feared General Motors would shut the plant down.[30]

In an effort to turn things around, in the model changeover for 1973, the truck assembly line was moved to another plant, and plans were made to transfer the soft trim and hard trim departments into the building that had formerly housed the truck assembly line. In a meeting of managers and supervisors with plant engineers, the unprecedented decision was made to ask workers on the line to help plan the new work area. Charts and diagrams of the facilities, conveyors, benches, and material storage areas were drawn up for the workers. Lists were made of the work stations and the personnel to staff them. Although initially wary, the union, worried about the loss of eight hundred jobs on the truck assembly line and urged on by some of the younger workers, decided to go along. Soon, several other departments began to encourage input by hourly employees with marked success. For example, body-shop employees met in a series of "rap sessions" to find solutions to welding problems. Within several months, the number of welding discrepancies was reduced from 35 percent to 1.5 percent.

Encouraged by these early successes, UAW Local 664 and the management of Tarrytown agreed to launch a formal program using labor-management committees. In April 1974, a professional consultant was brought in to involve supervisors and workers in joint training programs for problem solving. This pilot program involved thirty-four hourly employees in the glass area of the soft trim department, who agreed to meet on Saturdays and after work, to be trained in participative techniques and to work together in problem solving. Then in November 1974, General

Motors shut down Tarrytown's second shift and laid off half the work force—two thousand workers. The new pilot project was temporarily discontinued. When it resumed operation, only twelve employees remained in the program.

When the program was evaluated at the end of 1975, the participants agreed that they had been able to significantly improve the work environment. On the other hand, it was felt that many persons had not participated because the team meetings took place after hours. The decision was made therefore to expand the program and provide training during regular work hours. Almost six hundred workers became involved, but this too was short-lived due to the start-up of the second shift in September/October 1976 and the attendant confusion of again reorganizing the plant.

Early in 1977, Tarrytown made the big commitment to committees. The effort was to be implemented on a plantwide basis involving approximately three thousand workers and supervisors. Following the selection of trainers, the program was officially launched on September 13, 1977. Each week, twenty-five different workers from each shift reported to the training rooms on Tuesdays, Wednesdays, and Thursdays for nine hours a day. During these sessions, workers learned about three things: (1) the concept of labor-management committees; (2) the plant and the functions of both management and unions; (3) the nature of problem-solving training sessions. By December 1978, more than three thousand workers had taken part.

The results from Tarrytown have been impressive. According to the union, it went from one of the poorest plants in terms of product quality to one of the best in the division (eighteen plants). Absenteeism fell from 7.25 percent to between 2 and 3 percent. In December 1978, at the end of the training session, there were only thirty-two grievances on the docket. Overall, efficiency was up and costs were down.

Niagara of Wisconsin

This mill was originally established in 1898 by Kimberly-Clark in a small town in rural, northern Wisconsin.[31] The product then, as now, was coated publication paper. The mill has traditionally been the only large employer in the area. For the first seventy years, labor unrest was almost nonexistent and not one strike took place. But as the 1960s wore on, labor-management relations began to deteriorate. The union became more militant and management started to treat workers as adversaries. In September 1970, the union went on strike. This lasted until February 1971 and created a great deal of bitterness.

The reasons for the strike were complex. However, in the late 1960s profits at the mill began to slip badly. As a result, the home office put a great deal of pressure on local management to improve the situation. When things did not dramatically improve following the strike, Kimberly-

Clark decided to sell. In the event no suitable buyer could be found, plans were to shut the plant down. The official explanation for the sale was that the market for coated publication paper was simply not strong enough to justify continued operation. In addition, the facility was old and the state was demanding that a new pollution control system be installed at considerable expense. These, however, may not have been the only reasons. According to Peter Russ, the personnel director, the bitter five-month strike may have been the real issue.

In 1972, the plant was sold to Pentair, a Minnesota-based corporation which operated paper mills in several locations. The workers were naturally pleased that the Niagara mill would remain in operation since, for most, closing would have meant serious trouble. Few possessed highly marketable skills; there were no other employers in town. Besides, Niagara was home and always had been. Most were ready to make almost any concession to the new management.

As a condition of the sale, Pentair negotiated an agreement with the local town to reduce the assessment on the property, and was able to forestall implementing the state's pollution control directives. (Eventually, a water treatment facility was built, however.) In addition, Pentair negotiated a new labor agreement. This included a three-year freeze on wages; roll-back of vacations and holidays (from an average of five weeks to no vacation in 1972); elimination of the pension plan and sick leave; and a substantial reduction in the 1970–1971 work force (22 or 23 percent for hourly and 30 percent for salary employees), to be accomplished mainly through attrition. Pentair did make one major concession: it established a profit-sharing plan and agreed to take a look at the contract just as soon as conditions improved.

Local management and union representatives decided that either they would work together to keep the mill viable or face the loss of jobs. As a result, a new "we" feeling took the place of the old adversary attitudes. Pentair did its best to reinforce this new spirit of cooperation by providing positive feedback as profitability improved. (Kimberly-Clark had never provided local management with detailed information on profits.) In addition, it showed its gratitude in December 1972 by sending a $10 check to each employee as an unexpected bonus. The amount was small but the significance and impact were great. Pentair also committed itself to continuing monthly production bonus plans. For many workers this amounted to $60 to $70 per month. In June 1973, six months after beginning the production bonus, a small pension plan was established. All of this convinced people that Pentair intended to stay and would be able to provide stable employment. Recent labor agreements have brought workers' pay and benefits back up to industry levels. For example, the profit-sharing plan in 1978 and 1979 effectively added $1 per hour to each worker's pay. Average checks of $2296 were given out.

Late in 1975, local management convinced the bargaining committee to attend a conference on "Labor Management and Productivity—Cooperative Approaches." This resulted in the establishment of a union-management committee with secondary-level supervisors and four union representatives. For two years, the committee met once a month to deal with a variety of issues (e.g., how to better schedule maintenance work, whether or not to permit payroll deductions to other than the local bank and credit union—matters concerning anything except wages and benefits). The impact of labor-management cooperation has been dramatic. Customer service and product quality have improved. As a result of the program, production rose to 450 tons per day as opposed to 360 tons per day in the early 1960s.

Conditions Favoring Success

What factors have led to successful implementation of the labor-management committee concept? First of all, a successful committee communicates its deliberations and actions to all interested parties. As the National Center for Productivity recommends, "communications should be a two-way street, with reactions and concerns of the workforce and management feeding back to committee members so that future meetings will include topics of concern to both parties."[32]

Second, successful committees recognize the importance of employee attitudes. The comments of one official of the International Brotherhood of Boiler-Makers to a group meeting makes the point:[33]

From management's standpoint, are you willing to go back to your respective places, open up a door in a conference room, go in that conference room with labor's representatives, leave your authoritative hat at the door, and talk eyeball to eyeball and gut to gut across that table? Let them lay it out to you without feeling hostile, without . . . reprisal?

On the union side, are you willing to go in there and make suggestions to improve the quality of work and reduce the inefficiency of that plant that you and your people are walking around in, that plant you see every day? Are you willing to take the initiative in this crisis situation that this American economy finds itself?

A third characteristic of successful committees is that they have support from the top on both sides—the CEO, division chief, or plant manager on the one hand, and the union's international vice-president, local president, or business agent on the other. Without this endorsement, the credibility of the effort is in doubt from the outset, and the committee's chances of achieving any important innovations are greatly reduced.

A fourth characteristic concerns the union hierarchy. If the leadership is internally divided or does not have the trust of the rank and file, conditions are unfavorable for an effective labor-management committee.

Much the same is true if the union is not treated as an equal partner by management. In such situations, union leaders may be forced to take rigid attitudes to protect their personal positions. For political reasons, they will reject any initiatives that involve cooperating with management. On the other hand, when the union is strong and viable, chances of success are improved.

Finally, management must be perceived as being both technically and organizationally competent. If workers sense that management does not know what it is doing, they are unlikely to engage in a labor-management committee as a serious joint undertaking. Managers must demonstrate that they understand competitive market conditions and the relevant technology, and that they have basic administrative skills.

SUMMARY

Increasing numbers of corporations are introducing participative management programs in an attempt to increase productivity, reduce cost, and achieve a variety of social benefits in the workplace. In this chapter several such programs have been examined including Quality Circles, self-managing teams, and labor-management committees. In addition, a number of other motivational programs discussed earlier in this book involve increased employee involvement. These include job enrichment, gain sharing, flexible benefits, and cost reduction plans such as the Scanlon Plan. In all cases employees throughout the organization become more directly involved in the decision-making processes of the firm. In some organizations the programs may be quite formal, but in others, efforts to increase employee participation can be relatively informal.

The chapter has also looked at some of the important issues that managers need to consider in order to enhance the success of a participation program including the question of how employees feel about participation, differing management styles, and the advantages and disadvantages of participative management. Before a decision is made to proceed with a formal program, managers need to analyze the options and determine which approach has the greatest chance for success. Remember that no one approach will guarantee a firm's success, and that there is every reason to believe that a poorly conceived strategy could actually lead to a decline in employee productivity. Still, the evidence presented here suggests that many employees do want to participate and develop a sense of ownership. Good participative management implementations have the potential to result in enhanced employee motivation and productivity.

Based on their experience with employee involvement, executives in several large corporations have developed four basic principles that others might use when implementing participative management.[34] First, employee involvement is not an end in itself. There is no evidence that participative management produces superior organizational performance if the company's overall management style is autocratic. Unless the entire management team can be induced to adopt a less directive leadership style, the costs of implementation may well outweigh the benefits. Second, employee involvement should be tied to specific performance objectives. Unless the organization's overall performance really improves, senior executives may question the value of the program. Third, the program should be introduced gradually. It may take one or two years just to bring all levels of management into the process. Proceeding too rapidly may expose the organization to a number of risks that could lead to the program's failure. Fourth, the program should not be publicized in the early stages. Making a program highly visible at the outset provides a focus for informal activities that can undermine the program's overall objectives. In addition, by announcing the program formally, supervisory and work-force expectations may be created that cannot be met in the short term.

NOTES

1. *Nation's Business*, "Who's in Charge Here?" May 1985, p. 64.

2. R. Hinckley, Jr., "A Closer Look at Participation," *Organizational Dynamics*, Winter 1985, p. 57.

3. *Nation's Business*.

4. Ibid.

5. Ibid.

6. Ibid.

7. W. E. Halel and B. S. Brown, "Participative Management: Myth and Reality," *California Management Review* 4, no. 3 (1981), pp. 20–32.

8. G. A. Yukl, *Leadership in Organizations* (Englewood Cliffs, N.J.: Prentice-Hall, 1981).

9. V. Vroom and P. Yetton, *Leadership and Decision Making* (Pittsburgh, Pa.: University of Pittsburgh Press, 1973).

10. R. M. Kanter, "Dilemmas of Managing Participation," *Organizational Dynamics* 11 (1982), pp. 5–27. See also N.R.F. Maier, *Problem Solving and Creativity in Individuals and Groups* (Belmont, Calif.: Brooks-Cole Publishing Co., 1970).

11. T. Peters and N. Austin, *A Passion for Excellence* (New York: Random House, 1985).

12. Ibid.

13. Ibid.

14. E. Yager, "Quality Circles: A Tool for the 80's," *Training and Development Journal*, August 1980, pp. 60–62.

15. A. D. Jabobs, "Productivity Improvement—Beyond Quality Circles or How I.E.'s Can Work Smarter Not Harder," *Industrial Management*, January–February 1982, pp. 3–5.

16. D. Dewer, *Leader's Manual and Instructional Guide* (Red Bluffs, Calif.: Quality Circles Institute, 1980).

17. S. Zahra, "An Exploratory Empirical Assessment of Quality Circles," unpublished Ph.D. diss., University of Mississippi, 1982.

18. Dewer, *Leader's Manual and Instructional Guide.*

19. J. E. Burns, "Honeywell Quality Circle Boom—Part of Growing American Trend," *Industrial Management,* May/June 1982, pp. 12–14.

20. "Honeywell Imports Quality Circles as Long Term Management Strategy," *Training/HRD,* August 1980, pp. 12–14.

21. L. Hogberg, "Idea of Quality Top Japan Import," *The Virginian Pilot-Ledger Star,* April 27, 1981.

22. J. I. Dutkewych and K. Buback, "Quality Circles in Health Care: The Henry Ford Hospital Experience."

23. H. P. Sims and J. W. Dean, Jr., "Beyond Quality Circles: Self Managing Teams," *Personnel,* January 1985, pp. 25–32.

24. Ibid.

25. J. W. Ferrara, "Fairchild's QWL Program Improves Performance," *Personnel Administrator,* July 1983, pp. 64–67.

26. Sims and Dean, "Beyond Quality Circles."

27. W. L. Horovitz, "Labor-Management Committees: Their Impacts on Productivity," in Jerome M. Rosow, ed., *Productivity: Prospects for Growth* (New York: D. Van Nostrand Co., 1981).

28. P. J. Champagne and M. L. Chadwin, "Joint Committees Boost Labor-Management Performance and Facilitate Change," *Advanced Management Journal* 48, no. 3 (Summer 1983), pp. 19–27.

29. Ibid.

30. R. H. Guest, "Quality-of-Work Life—Learning from Tarrytown," *Harvard Business Review,* July–August 1979, pp. 76–87.

31. P. J. Champagne, "Using Labor-Management Committees to Improve Productivity," *Human Resources Management,* Summer 1982, pp. 67–73.

32. Champagne and Chadwin, "Joint Committees."

33. Ibid.

34. P. R. Richardson, "Courting Greater Employee Involvement through Participative Management," *Sloan Management Review,* Winter 1985, pp. 33–44.

Index

About the Authors

PAUL J. CHAMPAGNE and R. BRUCE McAFEE are Associate Professors of Management at Old Dominion University, Norfolk, Virginia. They have written more than 50 articles that have appeared in journals such as *Personnel, Management Solutions, Human Resource Management*, and *Personnel Administrator*. Recently, they collaborated on a textbook entitled *Organizational Behavior: A Manager's View*. In addition to their writing, they are involved in management consulting and offer training programs and workshops on topics such as enhancing employee productivity, performance appraisal, managing problem employees, and communication.